Keeping the Peace

Keeping the Peace
Conflict Resolution and Peaceful Societies Around the World

Edited by Graham Kemp and Douglas P. Fry

ROUTLEDGE
NEW YORK AND LONDON

Published in 2004 by
Routledge
29 West 35th Street
New York, NY 10001
www.routledge-ny.com

Published in Great Britain by
Routledge
11 New Fetter Lane
London EC4P 4EE
www.routledge.co.uk

10   9   8   7   6   5   4   3   2

Library of Congress Cataloging-in-Publication Data

    Keeping the peace : conflict resolution and peaceful societies around the world / edited
by Graham Kemp and Douglas P. Fry.
      p.   cm.—(War and society ; v. 8)
    ISBN 0-415-94761-8 (hardback : alk. paper)—ISBN 0-415-94762-6
(pbk. : alk. paper)
    1. Peace–Social aspects.   2. Conflict management–Social aspects. I. Kemp, Graham,
1954– II. Fry, Douglas P., 1953– III. Series: War and society (Routledge (Firm)) ; v. 8.

JZ5538.K438   2003
327.1'72–dc21   2003008813

To Leslie and Dorothy Kemp
and
Sirpa Fry

Contents

Foreword

ELISE BOULDING

This is a much-needed book at a time of acute discomfort about a century of failed efforts to outlaw war. It can not be done, say the so-called realists—humans are basically aggressive and will inevitably turn to war. But humans are basically peaceful, say the utopians—look at the forest peoples, the people of preurban times. It's the old nature-nurture debate. But human diversity did not arise with civilization. As the studies in this book show, no two humans are alike, and even the smallest society has to deal with conflicts arising from that diversity. Every society has to cope with its hotheads.

The most important point made by bringing together a collection of studies of societies known as generally peaceful, from different parts of the globe, is that peaceful societies have many differences to deal with and have found many ways to deal with those differences that effectively hold violence in check. Some, like the Norwegians, were in fact formerly warrior societies that developed cultural technologies for dealing with violence. The United Nations General Assembly's declaration of the years 2001 to 2010 as a *Decade for Education for a Culture of Peace and Nonviolence* suggests the possibility that the ingredients of a peace culture exist in every society, ingredients which need to be identified and intentionally nurtured.

The concept of identifying cultural technologies for dealing with difference peacefully so they can be more widely developed and practiced is a very thought-provoking one and receives strong support in this book. The large number of ongoing violent conflicts between ethnic and cultural groups on every continent during the opening years of the twenty-first century, including rising levels of violence in Western countries, is compelling evidence of the need to identify such technologies. And yes, *every* society has such technologies (see Boulding 2000), but they are often hidden away out of the public eye, forgotten, and in need of rediscovery. This book needs a companion volume, *Hidden Technologies for Peaceful Conflict Resolution in Violent Societies.* Along these lines, the movement to discover traditional ways of peacemaking in troubled societies has recently generated some interesting publications (for example, Malan 1998; Ross 1996; also see European Platform for Conflict Prevention and Transformation 1999).

In the present volume, the contributors describe social practices that recur in all the societies considered: (1) *mediation,* the practice of a community gathering to hear all sides, usually with elders providing leadership; (2) *avoidance,* the practice of giving others their needed space (don't crowd me!); (3) *self-restraint,* no self-promotion (don't be a show-off!). The positive value put on peaceableness itself, on the absence of violence, and on social control reflects a strong common recognition of interdependence. The people in these societies know they need each other. (There is also widespread awareness of the danger of alcohol as a factor leading to the loss of control.) But there is great cultural diversity from society to society in how these values are expressed, ranging from the talkative, rather disputatious Rotumans in the South Pacific to the gentle, child-loving Zapotec in Mexico, with the cautious Semai of Malaysia in between.

The emphasis on diversity in styles of peaceableness from society to society is very valuable in countering both the realist and the utopian views of "what humans are really like." Practices in child rearing are a key factor in the development of adult behavior patterns, and different approaches to training children in self-control are well described in some, but not all the chapters. It would be good to know more.

For insight into dealing with the growing violence in Western societies, the chapter on Norway is of particular interest. The focus here is on the Norse people, the warrior Vikings who became the peaceable Norwegians and who gained their independence from Sweden in 1905 without military action. (The Sami people, formerly called Lapps, of the far north of Norway are also a peaceful people but with a very different culture.) Norwegians have difficulty in dealing with diversity—they value "sameness." But they also have a two-hundred-year-old practice of compulsory mediation of interpersonal conflict outside the court system, which continues to this day and is much emphasized in local communities and schools. All children are taught the skills of mediation.

The growing number of international nongovernmental organizations (NGOs) that are currently trying to facilitate conflict resolution and reconciliation processes in bitterly violent conflict settings would do well to study this book carefully. It will encourage them to look for hidden or abandoned traditional peacemaking technologies of the peoples they are working with, technologies that can be built upon in a new-old process of social learning. The more these peacemaking technologies are discovered, rediscovered, and further developed, the better humankind's prospects are for a more peaceful twenty-first century.

Preface

The collaborative spark of creativity resulting in this book occurred in Valencia, Spain, during the meeting of the International Society for Research on Aggression in July 2000. For some years, Graham, as a peace scholar, had realized that peaceful societies might hold important lessons regarding the creation and maintenance of peace. Doug, as an anthropologist, had recently become interested in the diversity of conflict management techniques used in different societies, including those with very low levels of violence. Riding in a taxi through the busy streets of Valencia, we developed the plan to invite anthropologists with first-hand fieldwork experience in peaceful societies—those with nonviolent values and very low levels of aggression—to write directly on conflict management. A few details changed along the way, but the heart of the book has remained the same.

In essence, then, the book seeks to understand the means through which some societies, more peaceful than our own, maintain their peacefulness. The key word is *maintain*—as an ongoing, active process—because these societies are not peaceful simply due to the absence of conflict. Alan Howard, writing about Rotuma, explains that disputes are endemic, but "what is remarkable is that they so rarely escalate to violent encounters." And Alice Schlegel refers to the Hopi as "contentious but not violent." The same could be said of many of the societies discussed in this work.

Some of the societies—for example, the Mardu, Paliyan, and Semai—have no known history of warfare or feuding. Others—such as the, Hopi, Zapotec, and Norwegians—have engaged in intergroup violence in the past. The distant ancestors of the La Paz and other Zapotec people, for instance, established an empire—with the military organization that implies—before the time of Christ. But today the La Paz Zapotec value and in large part enact a nonviolent social life. Some peaceful peoples have faced and continue to face threats of violence and other forms of encroachment from the outside world. In a few cases, as among the Semai, nonviolence seems to have been an effective survival strategy in responding to such threats as slave raiding.

Peaceful societies are not utopias. They consist of real people facing the same kinds of problems that confront people everywhere: domestic disagreements and other interpersonal disputes; internal political, economic, and social conflicts; and threats of violence and exploitation from outside the society. Yet they have created peaceful cultures, identifying means by which humans can manage their conflicts without resorting to violent behavior. They have identified forms of socialization that promote peaceful interaction, developed beliefs that favor nonviolence over aggression, and fostered attitudes and perceptions about violence that prevent its establishment as a social norm.

A study of peaceful societies and how they manage conflict nonviolently, as represented in this collection, offers ideas from which we all could learn. Naturally, each society has its own particular history, belief system, institutions, and form of social organization, as well as its own physical, economic, and social environment. Not all ideas from peaceful societies will translate directly to other social settings, but in this volume, the reader will soon see that certain conflict management themes recur across cultures. A sampling of such themes include, for example, child-rearing practices that promote nonviolent approaches to conflict, a concept of justice that focuses on restoring relationships and overall group harmony rather than on determining who's right and who's wrong, cultural beliefs that strongly devalue violence, and—an unexpected recurring theme—the avoidance of alcohol consumption. Within such patterns may lie some lessons also applicable to other social settings.

Humans have survived and developed over the millennia as a species capable of great cooperation, learning from each other through the exchange of knowledge, ideas, attitudes, and values. Might people in societies plagued by violence and threatened by warfare learn something about creating and maintaining peace from those societies that have been highly successful at these endeavors? It is worth remembering that some peaceful societies have known violence and warfare in the past yet have managed to develop more peaceful social existences. Does this not represent a chance for us all? A cherished hope is, as expressed in the UNESCO constitution, that "since wars begin in the minds of men, it is in the minds of men that the defences of peace must be constructed"; or, as the Seville Statement on Violence in

1986 put it more succinctly, "The same species who invented war is capable of inventing peace."

We are grateful to our families and friends for sharing in the development of the book, helping out, and being supportive in many ways. Special thanks go to Maurice Yolles of the Lentz Foundation, Moyna Kemp, Corinne Kemp, Rowena Kemp, Sirpa Fry, C. Brooks Fry, and Hanna Korpela. Bruce Bonta also kindly offered useful suggestions. We greatly appreciate War and Society series editor Stephen P. Reyna's encouragement and enthusiastic support of the project from the very beginning. Heartfelt thanks are owed to our first editor at Routledge, Julene Knox, for her strong support of the project, useful suggestions, and competent guidance on any number of issues. We also thank Ilene Kalish, Donna Capato, Celia Tedd, and especially Salwa C. Jabado for their helpfulness and efficiency throughout the editing and production process. Mary-Neal Meador did a splendid job copyediting the book. Finally, we are most grateful to our contributors for meeting the deadlines, responding to our numerous queries, consistently expressing enthusiasm for the project, and especially for providing their well-written and thought-provoking contributions.

Graham Kemp and Douglas P. Fry
October 2002

Introductory Note

The first two chapters in this book are written by scholars in the field of Peace Science. In the first chapter, Graham Kemp examines what the concept "peaceful societies" means and does not mean. In the next chapter, Ximena Davies-Vengoechea critically explores the meaning of "peace." These two chapters are intended to raise conceptual issues and pave the way for the subsequent cultural case studies of peaceful societies written by anthropologists who have conducted fieldwork among some of the world's most peaceful peoples. Each societal case study explores the creation and perpetuation of peace, and each examines the nature and operation of nonviolent conflict management processes. The book's concluding chapter highlights commonalities in the ways people in these peaceful societies manage conflict without violence and then considers the question: What lessons do peaceful societies hold for the rest of us?

I
The Concept of Peaceful Societies

GRAHAM KEMP

In this chapter, Graham Kemp examines the *peaceful society* concept and suggests a context for thinking about the cultural case studies in the book. Kemp points out that too often peaceful societies have simply become pawns in sterile debates, such as whether violence can be attributed more to nature than nurture or whether the human condition is more Hobbesian than Rousseauan, or vice versa. However, to view peaceful societies in this way is to overlook the most important issue: What can peaceful societies teach us about creating and maintaining peace? Kemp suggests that peace is not a state, but a dynamic process, and that peaceful societies have developed effective *cultural technologies* for peace. That is, they have developed mores, values, beliefs, and institutions that very effectively minimize violence and actively promote peace.

—DPF

In 1976 David Fabbro presented a paper on peaceful societies to the Programme of Peace and Conflict Research at Lancaster University in the U.K. He later refined this work, and it was published in the *Journal of Peace Research* in 1978. His paper identified seven peaceful societies from the anthropological literature—five of which he termed *traditional* and two *created*. His aim was to produce an article "concerned with the study of peace . . . via the study of a number of peaceful societies" (Fabbro 1976:40). Fabbro was working within an academic climate of the Programme that placed an emphasis on peace creation. This perspective saw peace as something more than the absence of violence and viewed a study of peace, not violence, as the credible way for Peace Science to move forward (Fabbro 1976:36). It saw a distinction between *security*—the absence of violence—and *peace,* which in the words of the Quaker George Fox (1975: emphasis added) is about living in that "life and power which takes away the *occasion* for all wars." This issue is explored further by Davies-Vengoechea (this volume). For Fabbro, though, the hope was that through studying peaceful societies, we might find a better path to peace for our own societies (Fabbro 1976:36). He saw his paper as a tentative start, to stimulate debate; but as the editor of the *Journal of Peace Research,* Nils Peter Gleditsch, commented a decade later, the topic was simply not taken up. Not until 1996 did another paper (Bonta 1996) on this subject appear in that journal, and that remains it. In 1980 Fabbro left the Programme and did no further work on peaceful societies.

In 1982 I joined the Programme, now renamed the Richardson Institute of Peace Studies. The Reader at the time, Dr. Paul Smoker, asked me to look further into Fabbro's work. What I discovered was a difference between what Fabbro had intended in his work and what many people assumed his work was about. This misunderstanding may explain the lack of response Fabbro's article achieved. In proposing this volume, the editors again found the same false assumption being applied to our aim. To understand what is meant here by peaceful societies, we need to begin by examining the nature of this erroneous assumption.

The assumption is that in talking about *peaceful societies,* we are trying to prove something. For some, the value of locating and identifying peaceful societies has been to help resolve the long-held debate on the nature or nurture origins of human aggression and violence. This was not Fabbro's aim, nor is it the central aim of this work. We need to counter this pervasive erroneous assumption, for it blinds many to the real value of the concept of peaceful societies.

One problem with the nature-nurture debate is that it is not really a scientific one, but the product of a major European political question over the past few centuries—a question that involves the political rights of man, or more specifically, the political rights of *all* human beings. The debate stems from the works of political philosophy, such as those of Hobbes (1651) and Rousseau (1755), from the seventeenth and eighteenth centuries.

On one side, there was a belief that human violence and evil stem from human nature, and that it is the forces of civilization (nurture) that bring good and peace to the world. This was the traditional view, which essentially maintained the rights of the existing ruling classes, who perceived themselves as civilized. Thus, they possessed the right to remain the sole arbiters of power, law and order, and government. Such beliefs also provided Europeans with a justification for ruling over other cultures as the bringers of civilization to more "primitive" peoples of the world. As a result, humanity was perceived as being essentially of two classes, those properly nurtured (civilized) and those not—the uncivilized or primitive, whose natures ruled them too much, making their lives "poor, nasty, brutish, and short" (Hobbes 1651). The contrary conception, developed in the eighteenth century (Rousseau 1755), was that by nature humanity was good; it was civilization that created evil in the human condition. Thus the breakdown of the established order would free humanity to fully experience the nobility of its nature. In political terms, this perspective supported the right of nonruling classes to rebel, to challenge existing authority, to allow their voices to be heard, and to eventually be trusted to be part of their own government. Such ideas played a role in the growth of democracy and self-determination. Understandably, for people in European societies, there was much political investment in the possible truth of one side or the other. They thus looked to science to help settle the issue. In particular, Europeans were beginning to explore the world. The resulting new sciences such as anthropology and archaeology could not but be motivated to take part in the quest. The aim was to find a true primitive society, that is, one close to nature. This would tell what human nature was truly like.

There is, of course, nothing wrong with a political agenda stimulating scientific study, but there is a problem if it then blinds that science in its work. Despite, for example, the sophistication of native societies of the New World, Europeans were too quick to see them as primitive because they did not bear the same cultural trappings and technology of European societies. The sophistication of the Native American societies can be illustrated by noting that the Iroquois' Great Law of Haudenosaunee underpinned the United States Constitution, the League of Nations, and the United Nations (see, for example, Johansen 1982; Martin 1997; also see a reply to the French by a Micmac leader in 1676 on who is truly civilized in McLuhan 1973:48–49). Having been identified as primitive, their peaceful actions were soon held forth as proof of the existence of the noble savage; at the same time, their warlike attributes proved that, without the trappings of civilization and order, humanity's nature was no better than that of a brutal savage. This contrary analysis of the same societies revealed the strength of the political agendas over actual scientific observation (Boland 1995).

This political issue remains with us; people are still divided over how far to trust individuals or society (Furnham and Henderson 1983). The Right of our political society blames the individual and seeks greater controls and deterrence, while the Left sees fault in society and its process of socialization and thus seeks radical reform. Scientific studies on the issue of nature or nurture often reflect the current political strength of one side or the other (Eckhardt 1972; Bookin-Weiner and Horowitz 1983).

So far I have stressed the political nature and origins of the nature-nurture debate. Is there not a scientific basis for viewing behavior as based on nature or nurture? The answer is no. The puzzling fact is that the nature-nurture idea continues to prevail against all evidence to the contrary. For more than half a century, ethology (behavioral biology) has abandoned the idea of nature *or* nurture. Instead it sees behavior as a complex combination of inherited biological propensities and environmental interaction (Eibl-Eibesfeldt 1975; Lorenz 1965; Tinbergen 1973a, 1973b; Ehrlich 2000).

> The contrast of the "innate" and the "learned" as mutually exclusive elements is undoubtedly a fallacy.... It is perfectly possible that a particular motor sequence may owe to phylogenetic processes all the information underlying its adaptedness and yet be wholly dependent on individual learning for the "decoding" of this information. (Lorenz 1965:79)

One can refer to the example of sight. Without the inherited biological components and a neurological ability to interpret what we see, we could not see. Yet without interaction after birth with the environment, we would not see. For humans it is not just the physical stimuli of light and color; much of what we see around us has meaning and consequences from social interactions as well as from the physical environment. Sight is a far more complex behavior than any genetically determined *or* nurtured acquisition (see Purves, Lotto, and Nundy 2002).

The development of behavior is recognized to be even more complex—so complex that at times it is hard to tease out biological propensities and their limitations from the final developed behavior. For example, work on violent human behavior reveals that biological propensities that we might not expect can contribute to terrible human violence (Eibl-Eibesfeldt 1971). An analysis of war propaganda would suggest that it is far more an appeal to an inherited propensity toward self-sacrifice—to a group, family, and comrades, that is, our love of those we value—that creates a stronger means of seducing humans to go to war and murder thousands, even millions of human beings than any biological propensity for killing (Eibl-Eibesfeldt 1971; Kemp 1988). For example, Spartan society, in developing more effective military units, discovered that if you take adolescent boys from their families, and make their military unit their "family," then their group loyalty makes them fight and kill for longer on the battlefield. For those who have decried warfare as a human invention, the battle of Thermopylae was a black day for humanity.

In addition, when ethologists studied conflict behavior, they found biological propensities in social mammals, including humans, which programmed strong inhibitions against violent outcomes in intraspecies conflict (Schuster 1978). For humans this does not mean that they are either nonviolent or violent by nature, more that behaviorally they have to work with or around that program. For example, the inhibitions towards violence are at their strongest when communication is direct and face-to-face. This has proved problematic for the military. The military has to train its soldiers to overcome those inhibitions, or to work around them, for instance, by using long distance weapons such as bombs, missiles, and artillery, which keep opposing humans from communicating (Eibl-Eibesfeldt 1971; Kemp 1987).

Moving beyond nature-nurture gives us a far more complex view of how we should see other societies. It suggests that each society can be seen as a working entity, able to culturally adapt human biological propensities to meet differing social and physical environmental needs. In this we can speak of *cultural technology*—the "software" of human survival. Anthropology can thus open up for consideration the richness of human ways of organizing society, a spectrum that includes peacefulness as well as the institution of war. This is not the case with the nature-nurture debate, which essentially undermined much of anthropology's work, by seeing human societies in terms of providing proof for a European political issue. Examining societies as sources of new ideas, knowledge, and wisdom was too often put aside.

To take an example, in 1968 Napoleon Chagnon published the first edition of a book on Yanomami society under the title *Yanomamö: The Fierce People*. Later, Chagnon (1992) was indignant about criticism that his analysis of the Yanomami was simply about countering the nurture argument; this is not what he meant by labeling them the "fierce people." Instead, he wanted readers to see his work as an understanding of Yanomami society. Yet whatever the intention, Chagnon (1992:xiii) opened a more recent work with these words: "The Yanomamö are the last major primitive tribe left in the Amazon Basin and the last such people anywhere on earth." Chagnon's emphasis on the Yanomami as primitive once again relegated them to the role of pawns in the nature-nurture debate. In his 1990 lecture on the rainforest, HRH Prince Charles, in referring to the Yanomami's valued understanding of the rainforest environment, stressed, "For us to call them "primitive" is both perverse and patronising." In publishing this lecture, Survival International featured those words prominently. They also emphasized in their literature on the Yanomami that "The Yanomami are neither saints nor savages. They *are* people" (Survival International 1990:10). Here lies an essential truth, that no matter where or what a human society may be or call itself, its members belong to the same species the world over. We are all neither saints nor savages, but people. Thus the Yanomami are not intrinsically different from anyone else in the world, nor are the Semai or any of the societies considered in this volume. This volume is not about peaceful people, but peaceful societies. We are looking at societies who have successfully adopted peacefulness. It is what they can teach the rest of us about peacefulness that is important.

Before we can continue, there are two concepts we need to understand. First, peaceful societies need not be peaceful in the absolute. After all warlike societies do not exist in the absolute either. Peace can be found at some level in any society. This does not mean that nonpeaceful societies do not exist either. Misperceiving the concept of *peaceful societies* as being an absolute is again a legacy of the nature-nurture debate. We can break free of this and see peaceful societies in relative terms. The societies considered here are defined as possessing relatively low levels of violence. Yet there is more to their identification than this. A relatively low level of violence stems from the active minimization of aggression. This suggests a perception of a *dynamics of peacefulness* rather than an unchanging state. This is the second issue.

Human societies are not static entities; they represent dynamic forces of cultural adaptation and evolution. In other words, what makes up a human society is not just its attributes, but also its sociocultural dynamics (Sorokin 1962; Kemp 1997). Society is not just a social gathering, it is gathering with purpose. It organizes and structures itself to help its members meet changing needs. These structures—made up of cultural values, mores, institutions, and perceptions—form the *cultural technology* of a society. The cultural technology has allowed us to adapt far more quickly than processes of biological evolution would have allowed. In this light, humans within social groups have long since found that they can promote violent or peaceful behavior depending on their needs. The two often coincide within societies (see Davies-Vengoechea this volume), but peaceful societies can be seen as those that successfully minimize violence and are able to promote peaceful behavior. In other words the cultural dynamics of such a society is toward peacefulness. Thus, in a peaceful society, we can see not simply a society in a state of peace, but a society that:

a) desires to be peaceful and seeks to orientate its culture in that direction,
b) has developed cultural means to achieve this aim,
c) and has achieved success in this aim.

In fact, in identifying peaceful societies, we should consider not only their state, but also their orientation. The fact that violent incidents occur in a society does not necessarily deny that it is a peaceful culture. We need to consider how that culture's orientation deals with that violence. Is it capable of minimizing its impact and its spread, and of preventing it from becoming part of the culture? To illustrate this point, let's take two of Fabbro's societies, the Semai and the !Kung. The reader may also wish to consider this point in reference to Norway (Dobinson this volume).

Some men from the nonviolent Semai culture engaged in particularly violent combat when conscripted into the British Army (Dentan 1968; see also this volume). On this basis, some might dismiss the Semai as a peaceful society, but Robert Dentan (1968), who describes the Semai as nonviolent, sees no contradiction when he recounts this observation. The reason is that Semai society isolated the event as a *nonevent* and did not allow it to alter their orientation and culture when this unpleasant incident was over. As Dentan (this volume) reveals, Semai society has had violence forced upon it from outside for centuries, yet its members remain true to their nonviolent adaptation.

In reference to the !Kung, now referred to as Ju/'hoansi, anthropologists' experience with this culture was that they were "harmless people." That was until one study showed that they had a homicide rate per capita as high as some U.S. cities such as Detroit (Lee 1979: chapter 13). This caused some to question the previous perception. One problem with simply citing a homicide statistic is that it focuses on victims in a small population, not murderers. Closer examination reveals that the actions of only two individuals precipitated half the homicides and that half of the victims were bystanders, not intended victims. The question is not that these killings occurred, it is how they affected the culture of the Ju/'hoansi. Did their orientation to peacefulness change? Did a high level of homicide become a subsequent norm? Or did the culture, as with the Semai, close ranks to restore the desired aim of peacefulness? Incidents or nonincidents do not necessarily make a peaceful society; after all, some warlike societies have periods of peace. Thus in identifying a peaceful or nonpeaceful society, one should consider the dynamics of a society and not just its low levels of violence. After all, a society is made up of individuals, and, for varying reasons, not all will find it easy to conform to the social norms. Alcohol abuse is mentioned as one problem in some of the societies referred to in this volume. The success of a peaceful society is how it deals with violence, when, for whatever unfortunate reason, it occurs. The same challenge but in the opposite direction may be true of a warlike society. Warlike cultures too find that unwarlike behavior can develop among their members—incidents of nonviolence occur. In a recent work, *On Killing*, Lt. Col. Dave Grossman (1995) reveals an undeclared problem that militaristic societies face. In engaging face-to-face, a surprisingly large number of soldiers suddenly hold back from killing. Grossman quotes S. L. A. Marshall's (1978) conclusion of a study on U.S. soldiers in World War II, on the actual moment of firing a rifle. " 'At the vital point,' says Marshall, the soldier 'becomes a conscientious objector'" (Grossman 1995:29). The threat of peace breaking out is something a warlike culture needs to attend to in much the same way that the outbreak of violence is something a peaceful culture needs to deal with.

The idea that peaceful societies result from social decisions means that a society can alter itself from warlike to peaceful. For example, Fabbro (1978) referred to two cases he called created societies: the Hutterites and the Tristan da Cunha Islanders. We also have an historical example of societal change toward peacefulness if we compare current day Norway with its Viking past (see Dobinson this volume). Such transitions are liberating and show a lesson that peaceful societies offer the modern world.

Dentan (this volume) argues that peacefulness for the Semai is not the pursuit of a utopian goal, but rather it is cultural adaptation to help the members of the society survive. For the modern world overall this can also be said to be true. For most of the world's societies—or more accurately, dominant societies—warfare and the use of violence to maintain political positions within a society has long been part of the culture.

Maybe in early history, when civilizations first developed as wealthy but vulnerable societies, other societies on their borders adapted by robbing them. Civilizations, then, with great skills of organization, developed military defense. They found it could be used to further enhance their own position by robbing and conquering others and controlling their own large populations. But for whatever reason, such violence—particularly organized and tolerated violence—became part of the culture and its dynamics (see Williams 1981 for a discussion of legitimate and illegitimate violence). Generation by generation, society by society, such "civilized" violence became refined and developed to enhance societal success. This has been a prevalent pattern from the rise of civilization until the present. For example, in late-nineteenth-century Germany it was declared that after the maintenance of internal law and order, "the next essential function of the State is the conduct of war" (Oldfield 1989:7).

In today's world, the security situation has totally changed. What made a real difference was the terrible experience of the twentieth century: the appalling destructive nature of new military technologies that can leave victors not much better off than the defeated. War can no longer be seen as such a culturally attractive institution. With the advent of weapons of mass destruction, war has become a threat not just to the survival of particular societies, but to humanity as a whole. As a result the twentieth century saw war as an instrument of social advancement first declared immoral and then illegal. *Offensive war*, or war of aggression, was only declared immoral in the 1920s and illegal in 1946 (Rifaat 1979). War in pursuit of defense, or *defensive war*, remains embodied in the UN charter. Defense, though, has come to be interpreted as allowing preemptive attacks in the protection of national interest, not simply a nation's territory. Thus the process toward international peace has been undermined by a continuing reluctance to allow war to be outlawed completely.

The culture of violence that we have lived in for so long is still there, but desire to maintain it is rapidly waning. The UN General Assembly has passed a resolution calling for the promotion of a Culture of Peace. The year 2000 was declared the International Year for a Culture of Peace, and the UN–sponsored campaign continues. This move to a Culture of Peace is not merely a utopian desire: survival demands it. As societies of the twenty-first century seek a new orientation—a path to a Culture of Peace—and a move away from the past, the question becomes how to accomplish the change. We need, as peace scientist Theo Lentz called for in the 1960s, a *technology of peace* (Lentz 1972). Herein lies the great value of those societies that have followed this path of peace and proved successful over generations; they may have something to teach the world overall. The problems they have had, their successes, and even failures; the mores, values, and institutions they have set up, all could be of value to the rest of us. Of course, various environmental circumstances may mean that not all their ideas can be applied, but it should not simply be assumed that lessons do not exist without carefully examining peaceful societies.

Before I conclude, there is one final question about peaceful societies that we should be aware of: What is it that is being minimized? For many, *violence* means physical violence. But this is only one way to inflict purposeful harm on others. Violence comes in three forms. *Direct physical violence* most people are aware of, but there are also *indirect violence* and *structural violence.* The former entails inflicting harm by exclusion or by indirect verbal attacks, such as gossip, rumor spreading, character assassination, and so forth (Lagerspetz, Björkqvist, and Peltonen 1988; Björkqvist, Österman, and Kaukiainen 1992; Björkqvist 1994). The latter is inflicting harm on fellow humans via institutions of society, such as slavery, racism, sexism, and class systems, which deny equal rights to members of society (Galtung 1965). This is a crucial point, as some societies may appear peaceful—that is, they have a low level of physical violence—but peace may have been achieved by considerable indirect or structural violence. One needs to be aware of this possibility in considering peaceful societies. Also, some peaceful societies may be more successful in one aspect than another; their value may reflect their success in some of these areas of violence, but not necessarily all to an equal degree. Peaceful societies are not all the same. Some are more successful than others in promoting peace and may address different aspects of the three forms of violence in their social and physical environments. It is possible for peaceful societies to learn from each other, as us from them.

Conclusion

So what do we mean by the concept *peaceful societies?* Well, it is *not* a question about the origins of peaceful or violent human behaviour—as reflected, for example, in the nature-nurture debate. It is *not* only about proving that humans can be peaceful—we can find peace even in the most violent societies, and violence can appear in peaceful societies. A peaceful society is a society that has orientated its culture and cultural development toward peacefulness. It has developed ideas, mores, value systems, and cultural institutions that minimize violence and promote peace—a *cultural technology of peace.* This latter point is crucial, as we can find societies that claim they are peaceful, but in fact maintain a technology and an orientation toward war, as those in power seek to preserve the right of violence as an instrument of power and conflict resolution.

This book though is not about the concept of peaceful societies, but about learning from peaceful societies. We should not think of peaceful societies as something to be used, but as a resource to learn from. For the rest of the world, the value of peaceful societies is in how their experience and cultural ideas might help modern societies achieve their own desire for peacefulness. It is not a question of utopia, but of enhancing the well-being of all the world's people and future generations, even of assuring human survival. It can be summed up in the words of one Yanomami spokesman, who wanted his society to be truly valued. "I David Kopneawa Yanomami want to help white people learn to make a better world together with us, for our mutual benefit" (Survival International 1990:12).

Study Questions

1. According to Kemp, what is the greatest value of peaceful societies?
2. Summarize the views of Hobbes and Rousseau on human nature. Do you characterize your own views as more Hobbesian or Rousseauan? Must reality lie with one or the other type of view?
3. What are the three components to Kemp's definition of a *peaceful society?*

2

A Positive Concept of Peace

XIMENA DAVIES-VENGOECHEA

In examining peaceful societies, there is a need to understand what is meant by *peace*. In this chapter, Ximena Davies-Vengoechea, of the Richardson Institute of Peace Studies, examines thinking in Peace Science over the past few decades on what the concept of peace entails. She reveals peace to be a more complex concept than simply an absence of violence. She shows how Peace Science has come, through the concepts of *negative peace* and *positive peace*, to perceive peace as a culturally active process. In this view, peace and war are no longer seen as diametric states of the human condition. They can coexist as dynamic cultural forces and become issues of social choice.

—GK

The evidence of more than fifty years of scientific exploration of peace and violence shows a pivotal association between these two phenomena; the issues of peace are related to the discourse on war and violence. Efforts oriented toward the elimination of violence and war, or the alleviation of their effects, as a way to peace reflect a general tendency to perceive peace as the negation of violence or war (Wiberg 1981).

In this chapter, I challenge the idea that peace opposes war or violence and propose that peace and violence, rather than being two antagonistic realities, are coexistent aspects of reality. To begin, I shall examine some traditional definitions of peace in the academic field of Peace Studies, looking at the notions of *negative peace* and *positive peace* as popularized by Johan Galtung. I will then introduce the possibility that peace and violence are actually coexistent dynamics, both at micro and macro levels. I will conclude by offering a conceptualization of peace as a positive, life-enhancing dynamic that does not rest upon making an opposition between violence and peace.

Traditional Concepts of Peace in Peace Studies

Early initiatives in Peace Studies, motivated by the need to counteract the growing threat of nuclear war, saw the study of war and its causation as the means to ensure international peace. Pioneering studies, such as those by Theo Lentz (1955) and Lewis Richardson (1960), are examples of this early approach. Richardson (1960:vi), for instance, used statistics and physics to assess war, convinced that "wars arise from measurable conditions surrounding and measurable relations between nations, groups and individuals."

American scholar Quincy Wright, in an approach very similar to Richardson's, also regarded the study of war as the key to its prevention or abolition. "If we are going to eliminate war," for war was seen as problematic, "we must know what we are going to eliminate" (Wright 1965:6). Wright directed his analysis toward the conditions that make wars possible, in the belief that a better understanding of those conditions could then lead to the prediction and minimization of wars.

Based on behavioral and quantitative data, Wright (1965:16) attempted the "isolation of measurable or at least recognizable factors" that influenced the incidence of war, positing that once isolated, these factors could be modified. According to Wright (1965:xiv), certain factors or conditions bring peace into being. It is the loss of balance among these factors that leads from peace to war.

During the late 1950s and early 1960s, peace research started to develop two concepts of peace: negative peace and positive peace. Negative peace, first conceived as "the absence of organized violence between major human groups" (Galtung 1975:224), suffered later alterations and became "the absence of *direct* violence" (Galtung 1975:113). This was how peace had been conceived within Peace Studies. Positive peace was first outlined by Johan Galtung (1975:224) as "a pattern of cooperation and integration" between societies or nations, and later as "the absence of *structural* violence" (1975:130). This move marked a welcomed expansion of the concept of peace, brought an awareness of other forms of violence, and also related peace to social justice (Galtung 1975:23).

Direct violence is the type of aggression that corresponds to wars and other sorts of personal, visible confrontation. Direct violence produces an effect in the body or mind of a person that affects his or her potential somatic and mental realization (Galtung 1975:111). It is physical, observable, and the provoking agent is discernible.

Structural violence is "built into the [political, economic, and cultural] structures" (Galtung 1975:114, 251) and has the same ability to harm but operates at a slower pace. It is related to social inequity and injustice. Structural violence is somehow invisible, although its effects are not. It is not necessarily physical, yet its material effects are tangible. In this sense, structural violence is said to embody a type of "unintended harm done to human beings" (Galtung 1985:145), where responsibility for the damaging action cannot be attributed to individual will. Galtung writes:

> If one person kills another, and more particularly if a group attacks another, these are clear cases of direct violence. [But] what if the social structure, inside and between nations, is made up in such a way that some people are permitted to live full, complete, long, creative lives with a high level of self-realization— whereas others are killed slowly because of wrong nutrition, protein deficiency, inadequate health facilities, deprivation of all kinds of mental stimuli, and so on? This type of reflection [leads] to the distinction between *direct* and *structural* violence. (1975:251)

Structural forms of violence—inequalities, asymmetries, domination, and exploitative systems—also became a concern in Peace Studies. Peace researchers devoted more attention to intrasocietal processes and dynamics affecting a human being's self-realization. Accordingly, the mere lack of confrontational physical behavior between human groups or individuals could no longer satisfy the necessity for "peace," for peace became both *absentia belli* and social justice.

Negative and Positive Peace

Galtung's complex notion of peace as both negative and positive moved Peace Studies beyond the traditional concept of peace as *absentia belli* and incorporated the idea of social justice (Galtung 1985:145). It is unfortunate though that positive peace was defined at times as the absence of structural violence. First, the idea "the absence of (structural) violence" refers to a negative condition, not a positive state. Second, peace is still defined in relation to violence, as if sadness meant "the absence of happiness."

Galtung (1975:226) referred to positive peace as "cooperation, development, pluralism, dynamism, justice, freedom." However, making peace a synonym for a list of values risks turning peace into an irrelevant category of analysis. Justice, pluralism, freedom, and so forth are no doubt related to peace, but they represent different foci of study. Additionally, social justice has many, sometimes contradictory meanings depending on the political and philosophical approach being applied to the idea. Thus, if peace is equated with social justice, it translates into social welfare, equitable distribution of resources and goods, democratic participation, efficiency of the criminal justice system, fairness, and a very long *et cetera*.

Somehow Peace Studies has not defined its central concept in a positive way, that is, in a way that would tell what peace represents without opposing it to violence. This orientation is problematic, because instead of focusing on how to actively build peace, it concentrates only on how to prevent or eliminate violence. If peacemakers simply target violence, then they may remain oblivious to the real issues of peace.

Positive Peace, or Peace as Positive

I challenge the idea that "peace is the absence of violence." In this view, individuals, communities, and nations can only move from a situation of violence to a situation of peace, and vice versa, with no alternatives in between. According to this reasoning, examples of ongoing peace may obscure more subtle forms of violence, and instances of violence—both structural and direct—can cause us to fail to recognize coexistent expressions of peace. On the one hand, for instance, societies could display overt intolerance to expressions of direct violence—what traditionally would be known as peaceful societies—yet at different levels they could succumb to more subtle types of violence. On the other hand, too-frequent manifestations of violence could lead to disregard for the built-in peacefulness within a society's sociological, political, economic, or cultural institutions.

In reality, the peace-violence opposition is misleading. If violence invalidates peace, the occurrence of a single, violent event can obscure manifestations of peace already existing, making peace disappear from the mental panorama of the observer. But if peace is viewed as coexisting with violence, then the presence of violence does not disqualify the existence of peace, as the presence of peace would not rule out the possibility of violence.

In sum, if what we are after is a more accurate conceptualization of peace, then a change of perspective is required. First, we should focus beyond the conditions required for the prevention or elimination of violence; that is, we should concentrate on what peace *is*, rather than on what it is *not*. To this end, a positive definition of peace should be independent of notions of war or violence, and should speak about an existing condition rather than an absence. Second, we should consider peace and violence as coexistent dynamics.

Peace and Violence as Coexistent Dynamics

The thesis that *violence coexists with peace* can be illustrated in reference to Colombia, considered one of the most violent places on earth. Colombia has endured an armed conflict among the army, guerrillas, and paramilitaries for more than fifty years. Statistics show that the rate of assassinations in Colombia has grown as high as 89.5 per 100,000 inhabitants per annum (Comisión Interamericana de Derechos Humanos 1999:34). However, whereas about 250,000 men and women fighters engage in deadly confrontation, the remaining 40 million people go about their work peacefully, raising children, building a home, having a family, interacting with friends and neighbors, believing that a better future is yet to come. In effect, widespread direct violence and many forms of structural and cultural violence coexist with a very strong sense of family, community, and cooperative networks. In Colombia, interpersonal relations are easily established, and people are renowned for their friendliness and warmth.

More impressively, in the face of conflict, entire communities have established themselves as "peace areas," where participants in conflict are not allowed to use the territory as part of the war scenario or involve members of the community in it. Additionally, there are many efforts involving peace building, campaigns for human rights, expanding participation in the public sector, and improving social services. Finally, many other informal forms of solidarity exist among ordinary people as they go about their daily lives. Ultimately, this observation explains why a war-torn society does not collapse.

The existence of peace does not count on the partial or total abolition of violence and war. There is peace amidst great violence; there is violence associated with the fight for peace. In the same way, it is unrealistic to believe that the more likely peace, the less likely violence, and vice versa. In fact, both phenomena can increase or decrease simultaneously, or can be present at the same time and place.

Viewing peace and violence as coexisting has practical consequences. Rather than opposing extremes of a continuum—like different ends of the same cotton string—peace and violence each make cotton strings of their own. And both peace and violence, together with many other social entities, weave the fabric of life.

A Positive Definition of Peace: Peace as A Life-Enhancing Dynamic

Is it the intention behind different actions that makes them peaceful? Or can the peacefulness or violence of an action be determined by its effect? And can inaction ever be violent or peaceful? Let us think of peace and violence as forms of behavior rather than as states. In order to determine whether particular forms of behavior are violent or peaceful, we utilize the perspective (not the perception) of the recipient or victim, that is, the final outcome of the action-effect process. In a violent situation, there would be an active element, an agent, behaving in a harmful way toward a recipient or victim.

In a peaceful situation, we would see the agent acting in a nonharmful, nonpassive way toward the recipient.

Let us now assume that life is the most important value for a human being, and that life represents more than biological subsistence. Mental, emotional, and spiritual processes also count in the process of self-realization. This amounts to the fulfillment of a person's dreams, ambitions, intellectual requirements, and so on. In this perspective, violence is a form of influence that prevents such self-realization. Violence corresponds to whatever is standing in the way of the human possibility to be.

In fact, "Violence attacks the two most universal values of the individual: the state of being and the recognition of the status of being" (Botero 1998:7, author's translation). For that reason, societies subject violent behavior to social reproach, using the methods of moral and legal constraint. Laws, mores, and religious precepts aim to protect the values each society identifies as essential to preserving human existence.

When we witness violence against another human being, it echoes at the deepest levels of our consciousness. Violence reminds us of our fragility. Peace is the behavior that compensates for such fragility. That is why we need peace in order to exist. Peace is then the behavior that enhances life. Very roughly, but not sufficiently, we could identify peace with plenitude in the act of being.

Life is enhanced through abstention and action. *Abstention* implies refraining from action, a nondoing that includes not preventing the process of self-realization in oneself or others. *Action* implies mobilization of resources to enhance the development of people's full potential. Peace, accordingly, is to be found in acts and omissions that tend to preserve or promote life biologically, emotionally, and mentally. This element shall substantiate our definition of peace.

Life strives for its perpetuation, and most of our behavior is peaceful. In effect, "Peace is the normal condition of human life" (Carroll, quoted in Conroy 1971:58). The majority of human activity is peaceful; our daily lives are full of peaceful acts (or omissions). The peacefulness of these acts and of the abstention to act must be measured, as we said earlier, from the recipient's perspective, as the final outcome of the entire process. Otherwise, the act may appear peaceful, while in effect leading to the destruction of life—that is, while actually being violent.

The peacefulness of an action or omission would depend on its ability to enhance human life and promote self-realization. Actions and omissions could be meaningless on their own; their significance depends upon their consequences in terms of human growth and fulfillment. This philosophical exercise enables us to determine the authentic meaning of a particular behavior, and thus ascertain whether it is a form of violence or a form of peace.

An act that seems peaceful but causes destruction cannot be referred to as peace. Equally, acts of destruction conducted in the name of promoting life (such as just wars, terrorist attacks, and revolutionary causes) are not peace. A violent act committed in the name of peace, and a peaceful act that hides a form of violence reflect the coexistence between peace and violence.

For an action to be peaceful, a delicate connection is required between the action itself and its implications for the immediate and longer-term future. Peace is both the peaceful action *and* the peaceful consequences of the act. The same reasoning applies to the abstention from acting. Positive peace, or peace defined in a positive way, is the life-enhancing outcome of certain behaviors.

This implies an extended awareness of the consequences of our actions and our omissions. Violence can come as an effect of our carelessness or ignorance. We can harm a person or a group of people while believing that our behavior is innocuous. As gregarious beings, humans participate in political, cultural, and economic institutions. These institutions affect other human organizations with their own political, cultural, and economic institutions as well. It is worth reflecting on the realities of interconnectedness.

As individuals, we are also part of this human society, and our internal make-up depends in turn on the internal make-up of those people with whom we interact. Interconnectedness refers to the idea that individual behavior has an impact on the lives of other people. In this way, our actions and omissions form part of an intricate web of causes and effects linking people from different parts of the world. The idea of globalization makes this more evident day by day. Peace and violence are our responsibility as "global villagers."

Conclusion

The idea of peace as the life-enhancing outcome of a certain practice or behavior makes a positive statement *about what peace means* that does not link peace to the concept of violence. The idea of positive peace also provides a parameter for measuring the peacefulness of diverse social, political, or religious practices across the global spectrum and at micro-levels of an individual's heart and mind.

At the same time, a positive concept of peace clarifies that peace and violence are both forms of behavior that human beings are capable of. A positive definition of peace places it in the realm of freedom, as a matter of choice. Seen this way, peace represents a way of being, a commitment to the service of life and life-enhancement. It is a possibility that redeems the striving for peace not only in those societies that find themselves buried under the weight of war and internal conflict, but also in those societies that have apparently conquered violence.

Study Questions

1. Explain the difference between *negative peace* and *positive peace.*
2. Define *structural violence.* What examples of structural violence do you see operating within your own society?
3. Davies-Vengoechea states that peace and violence can coexist. Do you agree with this? Present evidence or examples to support your view.
4. Davies-Vengoechea considers two types of positive peace. What are these two different ways of conceptualizing positive peace? Does one way make more sense than the other way to you? Why?

3
Contentious But Not Violent: The Hopi of Northern Arizona

ALICE SCHLEGEL

Alice Schlegel opens this chapter by reviewing how the Hopi have been victims of the "noble savage" ideal. In contrast, she shows them to be "ordinary
people." A people who have known violence in their past, threatened by much
contentious conflict from within and from without, the Hopi, as Schlegel shows,
have created and maintained a "peaceful coexistence." It is how they create and
maintain peace in their society that has real value. Schlegel reveals Hopi peace
promoting mechanisms that most societies would understand—peer pressure,
child-rearing practices, choosing what is socially valued, linking respect and status to nonviolent behavior, and the use of the spiritual to create a society that,
although high in conflict, is low in violence and aggressiveness.

—GK

Hopis have often been depicted as a people of peace. Although Benedict
(1934) was writing specifically about the Zuni when she called the Pueblos
"Apollonian," the rather similar Hopi could also be characterized that way.
How, then, do we explain the pride Hopi men (and now women) and their
families take in their military service, prominently displaying their pho-
tographs in uniform? (There were a few cases of draft resistance in World
War II, but these seem to have been more with the aim of avoiding of involvement in the white man's affairs than pacifism per se [Geertz 1994:139].)

Ever since the Santa Fe Railroad brought the Hopi within easy reach
of visitors, their rituals and way of life have exerted an appeal for those

searching for the exotic or escaping from heartless technological rationality. Frank Waters' (1963) *Book of the Hopi* appeared just when this fascination with the "noble savage," in its 1960s version, reached mass proportions. Erroneously translating *hopi* to mean *peace*, Waters (1963:xvii) gave this audience what it desired: a people dedicated to peace and to maintaining the inherent harmony of the universe, using spiritual forces put into play through ritual. (In fact, *hopi* means "one who behaves properly" [Malotki and Gary 1999]; most of the Hopis considered what they called "hippies," who invaded their territory in the wake of Waters' book, to be decidedly *ka*[un]*hopi.*)

In contrast to the popular image of Hopis as living in harmony, most anthropologists and others who have had long contact with them have written about the contentiousness that is pervasive in Hopi village life. The events of 1906, when the village of Oraibi split into two factions, and the losers had to leave and found a new village, has its own large bibliography. Scholars have taken various positions on the causes of the split, from ecological stress to a planned destruction of traditional life in keeping with ancient prophecies (see Whitely 1988). Most of them have acknowledged that the factionalism that precipitated the split was the direct result of a rapid dislocation of traditional political and economic systems under U.S. rule. However, construction and dissolution of villages may have a more ancient history, as suggested by the many small Pueblo ruins throughout the region. I have written of the fragility of the political system of the Hopi as an internal frontier society (Schlegel 1991). Far from being a seamless harmonious whole, such a society has to work hard to form and maintain a coherent structure, and external stresses or internal political machinations can deepen the ever-present fracture lines to the point of breaking.

Are the Hopi, then, peaceable or are they not? Before we can address this question, we need to take a look at the cultural setting in which peaceful or disruptive behavior occurs. The time under consideration, from about 1880 to shortly after World War II, is the period when the Hopi were acquiring their reputation as a people of peace, as well as a people whose factionalism made concerted political action almost impossible. Many of the activities, beliefs, and cultural themes were still extant when I did my field research, mainly in the 1970s and early 1980s.

An Ethnographic Sketch of The Hopi in the Early Twentieth Century

Each Hopi village was an independent polity with its own chief and ceremonial system, with the exception of one or two outlying farming hamlets. Although clans of the same name, and usually with similar civic responsibilities, existed across villages, there was no overarching clan system uniting them.

These villages, strung out along the mesa tops that rise above the dry plains, were indistinguishable at a distance from the rocks on which they were situated. Small rectangular houses, built of the rock and seeming to grow out of it, formed a square around a central plaza, where village ceremonies took place. Men planted beans, squash, and a few other vegetables, but the principal crop was the native corn. They also grew native cotton, from which they wove the family's clothing and textiles for trade with other Indian peoples. Men hunted regularly, but most meat consumed came from the small flocks of sheep owned by the men. Herding took men and boys out to their sheep camps away from the village for one to several days a week. Women's principal activities were domestic, including laborious corn grinding and preparation. Their principal crafts were pottery and the baskets they wove from native grasses.

Every village had two or more *kivas,* the ceremonial buildings in which the men's and women's religious societies held their private ceremonies. When they were not used for religious purposes, the kivas served as men's clubhouses, where men gathered to discuss village affairs while they occupied themselves doing handicrafts.

Women's lives were centered in the matrilocal stem—or extended—family household. The houses belonged to women, and, as the Hopi say, "The man is a stranger at his wife's house." This is an exaggeration, for women depended on men to provide the food and clothing they required. Nevertheless, female ownership of the house and its contents is still well recognized by the Hopi. A typical family consisted of an elderly female household head and her husband, one or more married daughters and their husbands and children, and unmarried sons.

Each village was divided into a number of matrilineal clans. Most of them owned farmland and apportioned it out among the women members for their husbands to farm. Each clan had two leaders, a Clan Mother and a Clan (maternal) Uncle, a sister-brother pair who passed on their offices to a daughter and son of the Clan Mother. Clan decisions, generally concerning land, were arrived at through discussion among clan members. Final authority over matters concerning the clan's role in the village rested with the Clan Uncle, while the Clan Mother had final authority over clan land and cared for clan ritual objects.

Each clan played its part in the ceremonies that made up the elaborate Hopi ritual calendar. Priestly offices were controlled by clans: the village chief, who was the spiritual "father" of the village, came from the Bear Clan; the leaders of the important *Powamuya* ceremony came from the Badger Clan; the head priest of the Snake Society and leader of its ceremony came from the Snake Clan, and so on. The village was organized around its ceremonial calendar, which provided the rhythm of the year and brought the clans together into a cooperating body. The leaders of the most important ceremonies, plus a few other officials, made up the village chief's council.

The dual role of the kiva, as ceremonial chamber and men's clubhouse, also points to the integration of church and state. During the times when ceremonial participants were secluded in a kiva, men's and women's minds must be on spiritual matters, allowing unity and brotherhood to prevail over clan and factional politics. But at other times, when kivas served as informal gathering places for men, political issues were aired, and positions, formed in homes or clan meetings, were taken. Village council members, as kiva participants, listened to these discussions and were able to get a good reading of village opinions. Supported by this information, their council decisions reflected village consensus or at least the most widely held positions.

Hopi Ceremonies From The Late Nineteenth Century to the Present

To the traditional Hopi, there is no distinction between the ethical life and the religious life. If people meet their responsibilities with a cheerful heart and avoid selfish and sorrowful thoughts, the supernatural beings are pleased and pour blessings on them. Hopis do not so much ask for blessings as fulfill their part of a contract with the deities, maintaining harmony in the world so that the blessings can flow freely.

There are several types of spiritual beings, but the most important are the gods and the *kachinas*. The gods and goddesses of the Hopi pantheon include such figures as *Masau,* the god of the earth and the underworld of the dead; *Muingwa,* the young corn god; and *Talautumsi,* the mother of the game animals. These deities are worshipped with prayers and offerings, and they might appear to someone, but they are generally rather distant.

The kachinas, somewhat analogous to angels, are very close to people. Hopi legends recount that they once lived on earth and danced in the plaza for the delight of the villagers. But they took offense at human evil and corruption and left, promising to return in spirit whenever the kachina dances are held. When a man dancing the part of a kachina puts on the mask of that kachina, its spirit enters his body. In this way the kachinas have remained with the Hopi people, sending rain and other blessings. Unlike the calendrical ceremonies of the ritual cycle, kachina dances are not under the authority of specific clans. Rather, they are organized through the kiva groups. These groups engage in good-natured competition to produce the best songs and dances.

Ritual clowns, organized into societies, take part in kachina dances. They perform skits between dance sets, vividly demonstrating kahopi behavior.

These are explained as teaching Hopis how *not* to behave, but it is obvious that the spectators greatly enjoy the improper and even outrageous antics they witness.

The ceremonial year begins in late November with *Wuwucim,* which celebrates the emergence of the Hopi people from the underworld. The next important public ceremony, *Soya,* takes place in early December. It celebrates the founding of the Hopi villages, and the village chief is its leader.

The third major ceremony, *Powamuya,* is the great kachina festival. Occurring in mid-February, it anticipates the planting of crops. Beans are sprouted in the kivas, and each participant takes home a bundle of bean sprouts from which a special soup is made. The festival itself consists of several separate rituals. The most dramatic is the great kachina parade, when many different kachinas march through the village.

Kachina dances begin after Powamuya. At first they are held in the kivas. Later, when the weather permits, the kachina dances are held in the plaza. By mid-July, it is time for the kachinas to leave. The *Nina* is their farewell dance.

The dances of late summer and fall are put on by individual religious societies. The Flute Dance, celebrating life and fertility, alternates annually with the Snake Dance, a somber reminder of warfare and death. The former is performed by the Blue and Gray Flute Societies, the latter by the Snake and Antelope Societies. The three women's societies, whose themes are permutations of themes in other ceremonies, hold their ceremonies in September and October. All of the calendrical ceremonies, unlike the kachina dances, are held by a particular clan, which provides the officers. However, any Hopi can join any society appropriate to his or her gender.

Forms of Conflict

War

Hopis relate tales of two types of armed conflict. The one most salient and most relished in the telling consists of battles with Navajos and other peoples who raided their farms or encroached upon their land. Titiev (1944:162) was told that the Hopis regularly went to war after the harvest was gathered, celebrating their return by dancing with the scalps they had taken. There is also mention of returning with sheep or other loot. Although prowess in battle was not necessary for social or political success, it was admired as a contribution to the welfare of the people.

Another type of armed conflict, warfare between neighboring villages, disappeared well before the time discussed here. Tales, probably based on historical events but undoubtedly much elaborated over the years, describe battles between villages over slights and other causes. The real cause of intervillage conflict was probably the same as much intravillage conflict, as we shall discuss: disputes over land claims and land boundaries. Since there was no higher authority of either a political or a religious nature to appeal to for judgment or mediation, it was almost inevitable that serious disputes should result in force of arms.

There were two times in Hopi oral history when villages did unite in concerted political action. The first was at the time of the general Pueblo revolt against the Spanish in 1680. The Hopi had not felt the full brunt of Franciscan missionization as had the eastern Pueblos; nevertheless, it is clear that Christianity and the social and economic systems that maintained it were a threat to the local political establishment in all of the villages. Any Christians loyal to the new system—and there must have been some, just as there were in the eastern Pueblos—were overridden. The two mission churches, in Oraibi and Awatovi, were destroyed, and the priests were murdered.

The second event took place twenty years later, after the Spanish had retaken control of the other Pueblos and rebuilt Santa Fe, their northernmost town in New Spain. Awatovi, the easternmost of the Hopi villages and the one most likely to benefit from trade contacts with Santa Fe, was believed to have invited the Spanish to reestablish a mission there. Other Hopi villages, under the leadership of Oraibi, united to attack Awatovi. While the alleged invitation gave moral justification to the attack, an underlying cause may have been the rivalry between Oraibi and Awatovi for control of the trade in raw cotton and textiles, which intensified after the Spanish increased the market demand for textile production.

According to legend, partly corroborated by archaeological evidence from that ruin, they killed all the men and captured the women and children. While some of the captives, probably young women and children, may have been adopted into victorious villages, many of them were killed at a place outside the village for reasons unknown, possibly because they were members of the clans believed to be friendly to Spain and the Christians. This is still viewed as a shameful event, and Hopis do not like to talk about it.

It is interesting that the story of the massacre at Awatovi is not related as a tale of triumph. The Hopi attitude toward war seems to be that it is a necessary evil. While men were (and still are) recognized for their prowess in war, warfare and violence were not a path to glory. Leadership was achieved through inheritance of a position through one's clan and through personal political skill.

However, warfare was given cultural recognition in several ways. Many of the ceremonies include a warrior figure, there as a guard to protect the ceremony and the people. The famed Snake Dance consists of snake priests dressed as warriors, who dance holding live snakes, often rattlesnakes, in their mouths. Snakes—which the Hopis normally fear—are associated with war, and after the dance these animals are deposited at the ancient war shrines at the edges of the village to carry the prayers of the people to the deities. I cannot go into a detailed interpretation of this ceremony here, but its major point seems to be the control of violence and the transformation of violent energy into protective energy: killers become guardians, and predatory snakes become messengers to the gods, among other transformations.

Another ceremonial activity that transforms violence in warfare into a form of benevolence was the treatment of the scalps of slain enemies. The scalp was ritually purified, after which it became the "son" of the scalp-taker. He kept it in his home and was buried with it (Titiev 1944:161).

It is clear from the various rituals and expressions that Hopis did not glorify violence, even the necessary violence of warfare. While they identified the Apaches, Utes, and Chimahueves as their enemies in war songs, they presented themselves as defenders rather than aggressors (Titiev 1944:162). (In the late nineteenth and early twentieth centuries, Navajos were more of a threat than other neighboring peoples; however, the Hopis considered them to be inferior and held their scalps to be ritually worthless.)

Anger but No Violence in Village Dissolution

The single most salient feature of Hopi history over the last hundred years is the split of the village of Oraibi in 1906. This village was divided into two factions that were bitter rivals for political control. Feelings were strong, and there were mutterings about chasing one or the other out, by violence if necessary. The leaders of these factions met and agreed to hold a pushing contest in the plaza, the losing faction then being obliged to leave the village. The leaders drew a line in the sand, with the members of one faction on one side and their enemies on the other. Then the two groups of men confronted each other until one was able to push the other back and surge over the line.

The losers, with their wives and children, packed up their belongings and left Oraibi as agreed. For a short time, they camped outside the village. After suffering much hardship, they eventually built their own village a little to the north. At no time, as far as reported, did any brawling break out or were guns or other weapons used defensively or offensively. This is self-control on a massive scale.

Homicide

Intentional homicide seems to have been quite rare, but it is impossible to estimate the rate. Deaths reported as accidents while hunting or out in the fields or sheep camps might at times have been suspect, but even if suspicion were strong, there was no obligation on anyone's part to seek retribution. Brandt (1954) believes that in earlier times, before the Hopi came under U.S. law, the victim's clan might have demanded some payment or killed the perpetrator if he were known, but once the score was settled, the matter came to an end. There are no reports of feuds between clans over this, and relatives were not dishonored if they failed to avenge a death. In cases of unintentional homicide and personal injury, some payment in the form of food or goods from the relatives of the perpetrator to the family of the victim was expected.

Rape

It is difficult to estimate the incidence of rape in earlier times, although there are accounts of it (Brandt 1954). As reported to me, an adolescent girl was told not to be alone with a boy or man, because he might not be able to control himself. Premarital sex for girls was discouraged because pregnancy might result, although there was no particular value placed on virginity. (An illegitimate child, if unacknowledged by the father, was deprived of important paternal kin.) Men were believed to be easily aroused, and persuasion could slide into coercion. The few rapes I heard about were those of coercion or taking advantage of a drunken or mentally disturbed girl or woman, not violent attacks. No one mentioned any lasting psychological damage to the victim, although this lack of mention does not necessarily mean that it did not exist. Sexual favors were a woman's to give as she chose, and rape was viewed in part as theft.

Public Fights

Public brawling is considered disgraceful, indicating a total lack of self-control, and there are very few accounts of it. One cause of fighting that everybody acknowledges is sexual jealousy. Women are alleged to be more likely than men to engage in public fights, which usually involved a wife pulling at the hair and clothing of the supposed mistress. However, fights between men, when they occurred, were more serious.

One incident of fighting over adultery was reported to me with great relish. Two men who belonged to the same ritual clown society were in conflict over a woman, the wife of one and the alleged lover of the other. One of the skits that the society devised to be performed at a kachina dance involved a wrestling match between two of the clowns, who happened to be the rivals. Once they got into it, they forgot their ceremonial roles and began fighting in earnest, rolling each other into broken glass that was lying in the plaza. The crowd, well aware of the rivalry, roared with excitement as it egged them on. If the moral of this skit was that one should avoid kahopi violence, it did not get its message across very well.

I only witnessed one fight between two Hopi men, a drunken brawl outside the plaza on a day that a ceremonial dance was being held there. This event was triply disgraceful: the drunkenness, which Hopis abhor (even though a fair number of men drink heavily in secret); the public violence;

and the fact that this was a desecration of a ceremonial time. I came upon the fight just as it started, before onlookers had a chance to separate the contestants. They were staggering back and forth at one another, yelling and pushing. I saw no attempts to punch or kick. I was told that pushing was the major form of violent contest between men, a minor violence when compared to some other forms.

Violence against Animals

While hunting did not entail the spiritual danger that accompanied the killing of humans, it was not undertaken without ritual preparations and precautions. An important element was the ritual treatment of the killed animal, whose spirit was sent back to its spiritual home under the care of the goddess of wild animals. This was an apology for killing it and thanks to it for having willingly sacrificed its life for the benefit of the people. It was also a prayer that this type of animal would increase.

One type of hunting was closely connected to warfare, the hunting of coyotes for their skins. Slain coyotes were addressed as "child," like the scalp of a slain enemy, and the skinned body, which is inedible to humans, was "buried" in a crevice where it would not be eaten by birds or other predators (Titiev 1944:192). One member of the Coyote Clan told me that his clan's duty to the village is to stand between it and its enemies, both as actual warriors and as go-betweens to the outside world. This replicates the behavior of coyotes, who patrol the village by walking around it without entering.

The respect with which hunted animals were treated was not, however, granted to domestic animals. Donkeys had their ears cut off as punishment for eating corn in the fields, until an early missionary persuaded people to cease this cruel treatment. There are accounts of the mistreatment of animals, particularly birds and young dogs or cats, by Hopi children, unreproached by adult bystanders. I once witnessed a Hopi toddler repeatedly picking up and throwing down a whimpering puppy in the presence of two women who ignored the behavior.

The worst cases of animal mistreatment in the literature on the Hopi are accounts of wanton cruelty to such creatures as sheep and dogs during the ritual clown performances. (This sort of mistreatment has not occurred for many years.) As reported in earlier accounts, the spectators laughed at the suffering of animal victims. This was one arena where violence and deliberate infliction of harm was permitted.

Conflict in Everyday Village Life

Domestic and Kin Conflict

The major form of domestic conflict reported in the literature is tension between spouses over suspected or acknowledged adultery. In some of the myths, village chiefs, despondent over their wives' adultery and other kahopi behavior by the people under their spiritual charge, caused the destruction of their villages by inviting enemies to invade when the villagers were unaware. Joking allusions to adultery are part of the stock-in-trade of men's bantering when they are in the kivas. Sly mentions that a man must be "hunting for two-legged deer" always bring a laugh. Since almost all adults are married, gossip about sexual matters, a favorite Hopi topic, frequently focuses on adultery.

One elderly person told me about a specific case, in which a man reasoned and then pleaded with his wife to give up her extramarital affair on the grounds that it was harmful to the children. This is the correct, hopi, way of handling spousal adultery by either sex. If that does not work, the husband might leave, or the wife might insist that he leave. Spousal violence is never excused, nor should jealous husbands or wives fight with their competitors. Nevertheless, as noted above, fights with rivals have occurred, even in public.

Why is there so much concern about adultery? Although people are supposed to marry for love and remain faithful, in fact marriages are often tense, at least until the older years, when many couples seem quite devoted. Marriage traditionally validated a girl's womanhood; she was referred to as a *wuhti*, or woman, only after she married. For young men, however, the transition to manhood was made through initiation into one of four ceremonial fraternities. Marriage brought an end to the carefree life of young bachelors in the homes of their often indulgent mothers. They moved into the homes of their wives, under the authority of the parents-in-law. They were expected to prove their worth through diligence and fortitude, earning their place in the new home by providing food and children for the wife's family. Unsurprisingly, men spent much of their time when not herding or farming in the kivas, away from their in-laws. In this case as in many others, the response to tension and the possible conflicts it might cause was primarily to leave the scene. It is likely that adultery provided one of the few social arenas removed from the duties and constraints of marriage and kinship relations. This may account for the keen interest in adultery, even among those who lead blameless marital lives.

Overt conflict between other persons related by kinship or marriage are not widely reported. Witchcraft beliefs suggest that unresolved tensions may "go underground." A common assumption is that a witch must kill a close relative by stealing his or her heart in order to extend his or her own life, which has been bargained away for witch power. Although anyone may be a witch, a frequent suspect is one of the clan uncles, an older man who stands in a brother or mother's-brother relationship to the victim or the mother of the victim (see Schlegel 1979; Simmons 1942). The very ties, then, that should be most supportive are clouded by an undercurrent of suspicion when deaths or illnesses strike without ready explanation. These fears have receded with improvements in health and sanitation and widespread education in the germ theory of disease.

Conflict between Clans

Hopis told me that the primary source of conflict between clans was disputes over land boundaries. In earlier times, when Hopis farmed lands close to the village and depended on them for subsistence, most good land was allocated to clans. Clans marked their plots with boundary stones. Accusations of moving the stones, or of encroaching on land claimed by another clan, led to conflict. If the male heads of the contesting clans could not resolve the dispute, the village chief made the final decision in his role as father of the village and all its lands. It was also the village chief to whom the few low-ranking landless clans appealed for the right to farm village land unclaimed by any clan.

The chief's authority over land and the power this gave him may explain why there were sometimes disputes between clans over which one should "own" this office, for in theory the chief should be a humble man who abstains from conflict and spends most of his time in prayer and ritual for the benefit of his "children," the villagers. Clans sometimes also disputed about which one held other ritual offices as well. Once again, land was at issue, for plots of farmland accompanied important ritual offices. If this office was headship of a ceremonial society, the members of the society planted and harvested the fields of their leader. Thus, an important ceremonial office had considerable economic benefit to its holder and his (actually his wife's) household. The young heir to such an office was a desirable husband and son-in-law.

Each clan preserved its identity through clan origin myths and lore, some of it secret. Much of this explained and justified the clan's holding of its ceremonial-political offices, if it had any. There was always the possibility of competing claims. When Titiev (1944) was doing his fieldwork in 1934, he was given an account of the ongoing dispute between the *Pikyas* and *Patki* clans over land that each clan claimed. Probably sometime around 1910, the Patki temporarily filled an office held by the Pikyas clan until the heir to the position was old enough to fill it himself. They took the land that went with the office, but then they refused to return it. That is the Pikyas version; the Patki claimed that the Pikyas did not deserve so much land because they were originally Tewas from one of the eastern Pueblos and not true Hopis. Even though the village chief sided with the Pikyas clan, thus settling the dispute, there was still bad feeling between the clans twenty years later.

Factionalism

The conflicts discussed above all arise from indigenous causes. The structure of the household and kin group leads to tensions between spouses and relatives of different kinds. The very strength of clan affiliation means that each identifies as an interest group, frequently in competition for land or power with other like groups. Warfare and raiding were probably endemic when there was no higher authority to adjudicate disputes or squelch aggressive action. The final kind of conflict I shall discuss, however, is the result of the U.S. presence and is similar to the factionalism found in other native peoples of the Southwest. This kind of factionalism probably occurs wherever a colonial power has undercut indigenous power structures, while at the same time offering many kinds of attractive opportunities to those who cooperate with it. Factionalism appears quite early in the Spanish colonial accounts of the Pueblos and other peoples subjected to Spanish control and Catholic missionization. It reappeared among the Hopi when they confronted the power of the United States.

Beginning in the late nineteenth century, Hopi villages were divided into those who were willing to cooperate with the U.S. government and accept modern improvements and those who wanted nothing to do with outside ways. These factions were initially called Friendlies and Hostiles. Sometime after World War II, these changed somewhat and called themselves Progressives and Traditionals. The former portrayed themselves as those open to modern life, while keeping the best of Hopi ways; while the latter argued that Hopis should be left alone and have nothing to do with the U.S. government or its agent, the Tribal Council (see Geertz 1994; Clemmer 1995). This bitter factionalism, which reached its apogee in the Oraibi split of 1906, withered away by the late 1980s after a life of about one hundred years. Nevertheless, there is still no consensus on how much to involve outsiders in Hopi life and on what terms.

Much Conflict, Little Violence

I have indicated some of the roots of conflict among the Hopi. There are the structural causes well known to students of kinship and family. In the Hopi case, the unenviable position of the husband in the home until he has earned respect creates tensions between spouses and leads to fears of adultery and abandonment. That, in turn, can cause suspicion among men or women: young widows, who needed a husband to farm for them, were often a target of the suspicions of other women (Schlegel 1988). The brother-sister relationship was too important in this matrilineal society to be marred by overt disagreement, but the witchcraft beliefs discussed above suggest that it too was not without undercurrents of antagonism (Schlegel 1979).

The village also had its fault lines. The ideology is for each clan to contribute to the welfare of the village and play its necessary part in maintaining the whole. However, each clan has its distinct legendary history, and the Hopi see themselves as a composite society consisting of clans that came into the present location at different times and from different places. This strong clan identity, reinforced by clan ownership of land, created divisions between clans and competition over land and political power before the Hopi became incorporated into the larger U.S. political system.

In spite of all these settings in which violence might occur, there is actually very little of it. How can we explain this?

The Use of Ritual

The high level of ritual activity seems surprising for a small-scale society that had no full-time ritual specialists. The older an individual, the more time he or she was expected to devote to participation in rituals. From the writings of Stephen, who chronicled life among the Hopi in the 1890s (Parsons 1936), it seems that almost every day saw at least one kiva ceremony or public ritual, although some of these rituals were short and had few participants. Hopis worked very hard to maintain their complex ceremonial calendar.

One interpretation of all this ritual activity is that it was an attempt to hold together a society that was not well integrated in other ways. At the same time that each clan acted as an interest group, potentially competing with other clans, most clans controlled at least one ritual office or had a specific role in one or more ceremonies. In Hopi terms, each played its necessary part in the ritual calendar that kept the world in balance. Any kind of "bad thought," including anger, jealousy, bitterness, or even sadness, could pollute a participant and thereby weaken or invalidate the ceremony, particularly if the person with these emotions was a key figure. Thus, negative emotions were morally reprehensible, and a person who exhibited them was reproached as a danger to all. This undoubtedly helped suppress angry words and rash actions.

Shame

Far from glorifying boasting and excess, Hopis abhorred such displays. These were the marks of individuals who wanted to put themselves above others. In spite of having a system of ranked clans, so that some were elite while others were middling and still others ranked low (Levy 1992; Schlegel 1991), Hopis did not respect those who tried overtly to exert control or demonstrate superiority. Even the most highly placed man or women should assert that "I am only a humble person." In addition to being valued, humility helped guard against witchcraft accusations, because anyone with ritual power could be using it for personal gain rather than to benefit the people as a whole. (For a thorough discussion of the Hopi value on harmony and self-control, see Brandt [1954].)

In these small villages where everybody knew everybody else and there was no material basis for class distinctions, there was tension between an ethos of equality and the reality of social inequality of the ranked clans

(Schlegel 1991). The ethos of equality included recognizing the autonomy of the individual, and one often still hears the phrase "it is up to you" to decide this or that. Anger and violence have no part in the life of a humble person who respects the autonomy of others. To be known as an angry or violent person brings shame on the individual and, to some degree, on his family. Alcohol was feared, and now it is prohibited on the Hopi Reservation, because it can loosen the repression that keeps anger and violence in check.

The major ways of shaming people were and still are through gossip and the clown skits given as entr'actes at the kachina dances. Often, gossip seems to focus on people's shortcomings, so that it is as much a means of social control as a way of circulating information. It is also a way of relieving frustration when action is impossible or unavailing (Cox 1970). However, Hopis can become quite thick-skinned about gossip, and unless there is a confrontation, which rarely happens, they can simply ignore it.

It is harder to ignore clown skits when one is the butt of the joke. I have been told of people who fled the plaza when the clowns, in their outrageous words and actions, made thinly veiled allusions to whatever kahopi acts their victim was guilty of doing. Teasing, some of it very pointed, is a normal part of Hopi daily life, especially among men in their kiva circles. (The person a man is told not to tease is his wife, although when couples are old and comfortable with each other, they may tease gently.) However, the clown play went beyond teasing to harsh mockery. It must have been very painful to have the entire village, gathered around the plaza, laughing at you.

Witchcraft

I have already spoken about witchcraft beliefs. Kin were often suspected, but anyone could be a witch and try to steal one's heart or, better yet, the heart of one's child, because children's hearts are strong and innocent and can give the witch a longer life. The recognized way of handling suspected witches was to be nice to them so they would not harm the person who suspected them. (It is possible that, in earlier times, when suspicions grew strong, the aggrieved party resorted to self-redress, but no one talks about that.) The best way of avoiding suspicion as a witch was to be cheerful and humble. The prime suspect was a person who behaved erratically or in a kahopi manner. Witchcraft beliefs and fear of mockery were powerful deterrents to violent behavior.

Origins of Hopi Peacefulness

As we have seen, Hopi peacefulness extended to village boundaries, but not necessarily beyond them. It is likely that strong self-control of aggressive impulses is a survival strategy when the community is the polity, for there was nowhere in earlier times for dissidents to go—expulsion from the village would have been a death sentence.

Self-control was as necessary for the survival of the village as for the individual. Without any locus of control over force, like a policing system, there was no one to enforce peaceful resolutions of conflict or to punish miscreants. Ritual authority was so dispersed that no single individual or institution had the power or authority to adjudicate or mediate in cases of serious conflict, although the village chief did make decisions over land. The extreme emphasis on harmony and control of aggression and violence suggests that the Hopi were working very hard to counter the centrifugal tendencies of a society made up of strong and often competitive interest groups. They did this in part, as I have indicated, through ritual and through social control by means of shaming and fear of witchcraft.

However, there is another more positive factor that contributed to low aggressiveness: the strong value placed on harmony and "good thoughts." This value may have its origin in social and individual necessity, but it becomes a force in its own right when it is internalized through child-rearing practices and constantly reinforced through approval of those who act in hopi ways. The value on harmony and good thoughts paid off in helping to promote social peace even in the face of tensions and disputes. It is worthy of note that when Oraibi split in 1906, the winning and losing factions were determined not through brawling or murder but by a pushing contest. The losers, those who were pushed over the line in the sand, accepted their loss and sadly left the village. This says a great deal about the success with which the value on nonviolence was internalized and put into practice.

Study Questions

1. How do the Hopi perceive aggression and violence? How does this relate to their peacefulness?
2. In what ways do the Hopi utilize religion, ritual, and supernatural beliefs to maintain peace in their society?
3. What lessons from Hopi society might be applied to your own society to reduce violence?
4. Explain what Schlegel means when she writes that the value placed on "non-violence was *internalized* and put into practice."

4
Restraint and Ritual Apology: The Rotumans of the South Pacific

ALAN HOWARD

Halfway around the world from the Hopi, the Rotuman people have a society whose maintenance of peace can be seen to have many features in common with the Hopi. Alan Howard discusses four components to their *cultural technology* of peace: patterns of socialization, social provisions for mediation, culturally sanctioned beliefs that promise immanent justice for wrongdoing, and the role of the "custom of *faksoro*"—a ritual of apology. In reading about faksoro, one cannot help being reminded of occasions when victims in other societies, even after having suffered some horrific atrocity, argue they want a public apology more than just some form of retribution or litigation. Howard reveals too that this is not a society in isolation; it faces the political and economic forces imposed from without. It is of interest to note how Rotumans deal with these influences and maintain peacefulness.

—GK

The island of Rotuma is located some 500 km north of Fiji in the South Pacific. Although politically part of the Republic of Fiji, the Rotuman people resemble their Samoan and Tongan cousins to the east, both physically and culturally, more than their Fijian countrymates. Rotumans are remarkable for their gentleness—physical violence is a rarity on the island—yet disputes are not infrequent and in rhetoric, at least, can be quite bitter. This chapter

focuses on the cultural mechanisms Rotumans employ in constraining physical violence and containing, if not always resolving, disagreements.

The Extent of Violence

During my initial fieldwork, I copied the birth, death, marriage, and divorce
registers from 1903 to 1960. In that period, three murders and nine suicides
were recorded as cause of death on Rotuma. This was for a population that
averaged about 2,600 over the 57-year period, yielding rates per 100,000
equivalent to 2.02 for murders and 6.07 for suicides. I also recorded 2,216
marriages and 200 divorces for these years; 13 of the divorces were entirely or
partially on grounds of cruelty by the husband (no instances of cruelty were
claimed by a male petitioner). In one additional case, cruelty was mentioned
in the testimony, although the grounds were desertion and adultery. The
most prevalent grounds were adultery (68.5 percent), followed by desertion
(25.5 percent). Cruelty accounted for just 6.0 percent of the total. In each of
these instances, claims of cruelty referred to physical abuse.

In the cumulative three years or so that I have lived among Rotumans
(1959–1961, plus nine visits of varying duration since 1987), I have witnessed only two instances of physical assault. Both cases involved young,
unmarried men; in one case, the man who initiated the fight was drunk.
I witnessed several other instances in which a fight between youths who
had been drinking appeared imminent but was stopped through interces-
sions by others present. While drunkenness among the young men is not
uncommon, my field notes from 1960 are instructive:

> People continually apologize to me for their own behavior, or the behavior of
> other Rotumans, when they are drunk, although Rotumans, when drunk, are as
> inoffensive as a drunk person can be. They generally get very happy and playful.
> They may at times use obscene language, but rarely in an abusive way.... People
> refer to this form of behavior as being very bad ... [but] by our standards this
> "bad" behavior is just the kind that generally is the goal of a successful party.
> (Rotuma field notes 1/19/1960)

I have also seen tempers flare during athletic competitions between spirited youths, and although they sometimes involved a lot of pushing and
shoving, they rarely resulted in physical assault. On occasion, gossip included reports of physical violence, almost always with a strong degree
of disapproval attached. In general, the overwhelming impression I have
formed is that Rotumans manage anger well, both personally and socially.
That their nonviolent disposition is not a post-missionary phenomenon is
attested to by the remarks of visitors in the first half of the nineteenth century, prior to missionization. Many comment on the gentle disposition of

the Rotumans. (See, for example, Mariner, cited in Gardiner 1898:404; and Lesson 1838–39:430.)

This is not to say that Rotuma has always been a peaceful island. Oral histories recount tales of warfare between districts, usually in the context of rival chiefs competing for dominance. In historical times (prior to cession to Great Britain in 1881), at least three skirmishes took place between groups that had aligned along religious lines (French Catholic, English Wesleyan, and pagan; see Howard and Kjellgren 1994). The evidence, however, suggests that the encounters were not particularly bloody, with only a few people killed on each side. Indeed, the mode of warfare was largely ritualistic, with one side accepting defeat when their leader was killed or seriously wounded. In acknowledgment of their relatively peaceful disposition, Rotuman soldiers who served with Fiji's military forces in the Solomon Islands during World War II were assigned to a medical unit as stretcher-bearers.

An Overview of Disputes ·

Ironically, two of my visits to the island, nearly three decades apart, occurred when the rhetoric of violence was rampant. In 1959, when I headed for Rotuma to do dissertation research, I was almost prevented from going by a colonial administration (British) that was trying to pick up the pieces of an ill-fated land commission. The colonial government, in consultation with a few Rotumans resident in Fiji, decided that it would be desirable to legally codify the Rotuman system of land tenure and to survey boundaries. In order to simplify what they considered a confused situation, an ordinance was passed (Fiji Ordinance No. 13 of 1959), changing the system of land tenure from bilineal to patrilineal inheritance. In their rationale, the authors of the ordinance pointed to a large number of unresolved disputes and the difficulty of arbitrating them when individuals were able to make claims to so many parcels through so many routes. The ordinance authorized a commission to be sent to Rotuma to register owners of land and to survey land holdings. The response of the Rotuman people was dramatic. They refused to cooperate with the commissioners. Threats of violence were made, and in short order the commission was withdrawn.

There are several reasons why disputes over land were particularly intense at that time. For one thing, the population of the island had surpassed 3,000 people, and the people-to-land ratio was creating increasing pressure on resources. Since the main source of money—indeed virtually the only source for most people—was copra (the dried meat of coconuts), control of land was vital. Problems were also created by the fact that Rotumans had begun to emigrate in substantial numbers to Fiji, where wage employment, educational opportunities, and other advantages of urban living were available. Most of these émigrés wished to retain land rights in Rotuma, so issues of genealogical precedence versus occupancy came to the fore. When persons who had been away for some time returned to claim their rights, they were often met with stern opposition by those who had stayed behind and occupied, and often improved, the land. In addition to these pragmatic issues is the symbolic significance land has for Rotumans, as it does for all Polynesians. Being associated with one's ancestors, land is at the very heart of one's sense of identity. To deny people's claims to land is to threaten the very core of their social essence, and by implication, their social worth. Given this mix of practical and symbolic considerations, it is no wonder that disputes over land became passionate.

Complicating the picture still further is the ambiguity of boundaries. Rotumans have traditionally used natural features such as trees and rocks to mark boundaries, and this vital information is transmitted orally. Given normal propensities to interpret ambiguous information in one's favor, it is not surprising that disagreements over boundaries occur with some frequency. At times, when land is plentiful vis-à-vis human needs, potential disputes may be sidestepped, but when land pressure intensifies, boundaries are of critical concern. Such was the case in 1959, and surveying the lands and fixing the boundaries was a major priority of the ill-fated commission.

I did not return to Rotuma until 1987, when my wife and I visited for two weeks during a sabbatical leave. Many things had changed. A wharf had been built in the late 1970s, and an airstrip was inaugurated in 1981 as part of the centennial anniversary of cession. These made the island much more accessible than it had been previously. Hurricane Bebe had destroyed most of the Rotuman-style thatched houses in 1973, and they were mostly replaced by concrete and corrugated-iron structures. An underground freshwater source had been tapped, and most houses now had running water; many had flush toilets. There had been significant social and economic changes as well, but I found that life on the island retained much of the charm and allure that made my first experience such a marvelous adventure. I decided to resume my research, focusing on the history of changes over the past three decades.

As my wife and I prepared to return to Rotuma in the spring of 1988, we were startled to find, just a few days before departure, that this remote little island was the subject of the headline story in the *Honolulu Star-Bulletin*. The headline read, "Fiji 'King' Vows to Secede." The story focused on a part-Rotuman man by the name of Henry Gibson, a resident of New Zealand, who claimed to be "King of Rotuma." Following the second coup in Fiji and the declaration of Fiji as a republic, Gibson pronounced Rotuma independent and petitioned the English Crown (to whom Rotuma had originally been ceded) for recognition. A karate expert with some charisma, Gibson had a small but dedicated following on Rotuma, including many of his kinsmen and a variety of dissidents. Following his lead, they disputed the legitimacy of the Rotuma Council's decision to stay with Fiji following the coup. Tempers flared, and there was talk of violence. In response, a gunboat was sent to the island from Fiji with a contingent of armed soldiers to quell the "rebellion." My friends in Hawaii feared for my safety and assumed I would cancel the trip. Anyone who knew Rotuma (and had a healthy skepticism regarding journalistic sensationalism) would have realized how ludicrous the situation was. When I arrived a week later, the gunboat was still anchored offshore, but the soldiers were enjoying a pleasant holiday. No violence had occurred, and none seemed likely.

Yet the story did signify a shift in the nature of disputes, from land to political issues. During my first visit to Rotuma, in 1959–60, Fiji was still a colony of Great Britain. As part of the Colony of Fiji, Rotuma was governed by a district officer appointed by the governor of Fiji. The district officer was very much in charge. He had the authority of the Crown behind him, and his decisions had the force of law. He was assisted by the Rotuma Council, composed of the chiefs of the seven districts, a representative from each district nominated by the district officer (but in fact usually chosen by the chief), the headmaster of the high school, and the resident assistant medical officer. The council served strictly in an advisory capacity; they had neither policy-making nor legislative authority.

For the most part, the chiefs and representatives served as conduits for communication between the district officer and the people in the districts. They relayed the district officer's orders and were responsible for seeing to it that the orders were carried out. Then they reported back to him, often explaining why his orders were not followed. Rotumans learned to cope with this system by becoming masters of passive resistance—the chiefs agreed to anything the district officer wanted in order to avoid offending him, but the people generally ignored unpopular demands on their time or resources. During the colonial period, Rotuma was therefore a rather apolitical society. Most individuals were extremely cautious about expressing their opinions, especially if they contradicted the district officer's. Being a chief, or a representative, held very few privileges aside from ceremonial ones, and often put incumbents in awkward positions in relation to both their district constituents and the all-powerful district officer. Given the burdens of office, competition for chiefly titles was not particularly keen. However, following Fiji's independence in 1970, the situation changed dramatically.

During my return visits, I have been struck by the degree to which Rotuma has become politicized. The roles of the Rotuma Council and the district officer have been reversed; the district officer is now advisor to the chiefs and representatives (now elected by popular vote), who hold policy-making and legislative authority. Now that the chiefs control resources and have political power, competition for titles has increased markedly and has become the focus of disputes. Relieved of the burden of a supreme decision maker with extraordinary status, people are no longer reluctant to voice their opinions in public. Passive resistance has been replaced by vigorous and sometimes quite bitter debate.

Although disputes involving land still occur, they have receded into the background. The passion is still there, but the occasions for disputing have diminished, primarily as the result of two factors. For one, despite a high rate of natural increase, the population of the island has actually fallen by approximately 10 percent to around 2,700, reducing the pressure on land resources. Furthermore, a substantial portion of the population now either earns money from wages or receives remittances on a regular basis from relatives overseas. Income from copra accounts for a minor portion of the money obtained by contemporary Rotumans; correspondingly, the economic value of land has been greatly reduced.

Control Factors

A number of factors keep disputes from escalating into violent confrontations, including: a pattern of socialization that minimizes aggressive dispositions; a set of culturally sanctioned beliefs that promise immanent justice for wrongdoing; the social provision for mediation when impasses occur; and perhaps most importantly, the custom of *faksoro*—a ritual of apology that under most circumstances must be accepted by the aggrieved party. In addition to these customary beliefs and practices are sanctions imposed by the political-legal system of the nation of Fiji.

Socialization for Nonviolence

In contrast to their Polynesian counterparts in Samoa and Tonga, as well as to their Fijian countrymen, Rotumans are noticeably gentle in their treatment of children (see fig. 4.1). Gardiner made such an observation during his visit to Rotuma in 1896:

> Their kindness and attention to all children is extraordinary. Nothing is too good for them or too much trouble to do. Castigation is unknown; their sole method of correction is by laughing and making fun of them. (Gardiner 1898:408)

My observations more than six decades later were the same. Whereas all Polynesian peoples are noted for indulging infants, in Rotuma older children are honored as well. They are generally fed first, before adults, and are given the choice foods. In Methodist churches, children sit in special pews in

Figure 4.1. A father and daughter on Rotuma. Photograph by Alan Howard.

front, as do the chiefs and dignitaries. While parents, when exasperated, will physically punish their children, the blows are almost always restrained—more on the order of a light slap or two on the legs, a flick of the finger on the top of the head, or a pinch of the ear. Only a couple of times in the nearly three years I have spent in the company of Rotumans have I witnessed a child being struck with force that seemed meant to hurt. Among themselves, children are discouraged from fighting with each other, and a child who acts the role of bully is likely to pay a heavy price in ridicule from adults and ostracism from peers. There are specific injunctions against potential violence as well, as in the expression, "*Ha' 'e 'ap ser*" (It is forbidden to raise a knife [toward another person, even in play]).

The most effective mechanism for teaching children to behave properly is shaming through ridicule—a technique that is adopted by peer groups early on. Children are also warned to behave in order to avoid the wrath of strangers and authority figures such as doctors, chiefs, and ministers. I was puzzled why small children were so restrained in my company until I discovered that parents were telling their children to behave properly or the white man would get angry with them. The overall effect is to produce individuals who are shy with strangers, are overtly respectful of authority figures, and are strongly drawn to those with whom they are familiar.

In dealings with people, the great concern is not making others angry. This derives from the extreme social sensitivity such a child-rearing pattern produces. One is constantly on the alert for signs of anger or incipient displeasure that might lead to anger. Depending on circumstances, people take steps either to alleviate the conditions or to avoid those whom they perceive as angry or as likely to become angry. In describing their own emotional responses to frustration and mistreatment, Rotumans almost never use the term *feke* (angry), since feke implies being out of control, hence prone to violence. Rather, they describe their feelings with the term *kokono* (disappointed or sad). People also generally precede utterances that might conceivably give offense by saying, "*Se fek*" (Don't be angry).

Although socialization proceeds more by rewarding proper behavior than by punishing misbehavior, the power of shaming is such that fear of failure often becomes a dominating motivational force. Thus, Rotumans are reluctant to engage in activities, including disputes, where they do not feel reasonably assured of success. Avoidance of vulnerability, both socially and emotionally, is the rule.

By Western standards, Rotuman children are granted an astonishing degree of autonomy. Parents rarely force children to do things they do not want to do. I have witnessed innumerable instances in which children who were asked to do something by their parents have simply ignored the request, without apparent consequence. The overriding principle is that it is undesirable to force people, children included, to do things against their will. One expression of this emphasis on autonomy is the frequently heard phrase, "*Puer se aea/irisa*" (It's up to you/them), when people are asked about expected behavior, contributions, and so on.

The principle of autonomy operates throughout the social structure. Not only do individuals exercise autonomy within their households and communities, but villages are also autonomous in relation to one another, and districts are essentially independent political units. Rotuma's relationship with the government of Fiji is likewise colored by this principle. For example, following the 1973 hurricane, in which Rotuman crops were badly damaged, the government sent a relief ship with supplies to the island. Before the ship could unload, the Rotuma Council met and decided to send the vessel back, with the message that Rotuma could take care of itself. They suggested that the supplies be sent elsewhere.

The results of this socialization pattern are a people who are socially sensitive, ready to react defensively when their sense of autonomy is threatened, but nonviolent in disposition. In defense of their autonomy, people are prepared to stand up for what they perceive to be their rights, even against their own chiefs. They may even talk a good fight on occasion—verbal skills are encouraged and rewarded—but talk rarely translates into violent action.

Immanent Justice: The Spirits' Revenge

Rotumans, including many with advanced education, express a belief in immanent justice. Just about everyone can tell a story about someone who had committed, from the teller's standpoint, some kind of egregious act, only to receive his or her just deserts soon thereafter. The cultural roots of this belief precede Christianity; it is based on ancestral spirits who, when offended or otherwise angered, make their wrath felt. Prototypical are the presumed consequences of land disputes between close relatives. The underlying assumption is that the spirits of one or more common ancestors of the disputants will be upset and punish the person in the wrong, or perhaps both parties if they share the blame. Justice is distributed in the form of luck—those in the right prosper, while those in the wrong suffer ill fortune. The consequences of wrongdoing may simply follow from the acts, recognized retrospectively, but an aggrieved party often calls for them. Curses of immanent justice are generally made without overt rancor by the party who has been forced to yield, in the form of public statements like, "The land has eyes and teeth," or, "We shall see who is right."

The most powerful curses are from the lips of chiefs, who were traditionally perceived as intermediaries with the spirit world. When a chief calls for immanent justice, it is usually because an unknown person within his district has committed a serious offense and refuses to confess and put things right. Almost all Rotumans are aware of some classic cases. For example, Chief Fer's son presumably killed a cow with his cane knife without his father's knowledge. When his father called a meeting to seek out the culprit, he did not confess. Shortly thereafter (I do not know the actual time lapse involved, but it is usually spoken of as short), the son threw his knife up into a tree; it rebounded and hit him just below his shoulder, blade first, and killed him. Storytellers invariably point out that he was struck in precisely the same place the cow was struck. The chief was extremely grief-stricken and reportedly vowed never again to use a curse for justice.

This belief in immanent justice affects the dynamics of disputing in several ways. For one, it tends to restrain individuals from making spurious claims that might backfire. But for those who are more sure of themselves (especially those whose claims are based on information from deceased grandparents), immanent justice provides a backup position. A party may lose initially, but if his position is truly justified, he will at least be vindicated. In numerous instances, the victors in a dispute have apologized and abandoned their claim after a period of horrendous ill fortune. Thus, hovering over any dispute or potential dispute are supernatural sanctions that can compensate for secular social impotence. There is more at stake in most disputes than the immediate spoils of victory.

Avoidance: Out of Harm's Way

As pointed out above, Rotuman socialization practices tend to produce individuals who avoid strangers and authority figures. When forced into interaction with such individuals, their behavior is restricted to formalities and is guided by polite etiquette. Aside from serving the purposes of social decorum, such behavior insulates individuals emotionally and serves to diminish vulnerability.

In similar fashion, a typical way of dealing with individuals with whom one has quarreled is to avoid them. This serves the same purpose; it reduces emotional vulnerability. I have come across many examples of individuals changing their allegiance from one subchief to another following a quarrel. Even more drastic are instances of families moving to another district, or leaving the island altogether. The value placed on autonomy, exemplified in the child-rearing pattern, allows disgruntled individuals to dissociate themselves from others for as long as they like without any formal penalties being imposed. They simply do not reap the rewards of mutual exchange that mark positive relationships. Most Rotuman families are self-sufficient, at least with regard to subsistence, so economic costs are likely to be minor.

In those instances in which disputants remain within the same community, avoidance seems to allow emotions to cool, and ruptures are likely to heal over time; but it may take a long time—years in fact. By its very nature, avoidance removes individuals from the mechanisms, such as apologetic discourse, that may be utilized to bring about reconciliation. It often takes some kind of dramatic event, such as a death, wedding, or community celebration, to get disputing parties back into contact.

Mediation and Arbitration: The Role of Problem Solvers

One of the most important functions of a chief is to act as mediator between disputants within his domain. For lesser issues, confined to a couple of households within the same *ho'aga* (a work unit composed of neighboring households under the direction of a subchief, or *fa 'es ho'aga*), the subchief may talk to the individuals involved, try to calm irate tempers, and suggest an equitable solution. If he appears to be partisan, however, he may exacerbate the problem and prompt the unsupported disputant to switch his allegiance to another group. This has the effect of weakening the ho'aga, to the subchief's disadvantage. He is therefore likely to be motivated to seek equitable solutions whenever possible (unless, of course, one party has been a constant troublemaker and a disruptive influence, in which case a move might be welcomed).

In more extensive disputes, those involving land matters and families from more than one ho'aga, district chiefs are mediators, and, if the parties cannot come to an agreement, the chiefs have the authority to arbitrate. A district chief's reputation is based to a significant degree on the success of his mediations and the perceived fairness of his arbitrations. If he is seen as favoring his own parochial interests in disputes, the district is likely to factionalize, diminishing his authority; if he is seen as impartial and balanced in his judgments, his stature is enhanced. But in matters of land, the main source of disputes in the past, impartiality was neither easily attained nor readily recognized. Disputes over land, therefore, often went unresolved, or, more accurately, were only temporarily resolved, despite a chief's mediation and/or decision. The installation of a new chief was often the occasion for grievances to be resurrected, with the hope of a more favorable decision by parties who felt shortchanged on prior occasions. If an individual was dissatisfied with justice at this level, he could make a final appeal to the resident colonial administrator, who served as magistrate (see below).

The Christian churches also play an important role in providing mediation. Each Methodist congregation has a catechist attached, and one of his or her foremost responsibilities is to calm troubled waters within families as well as between them. A deaconess is also assigned to the island; her main job is to meet with troubled individuals and to help them solve problems and disputes amicably. The priest and lay brothers play similar roles on the Catholic side of the island.

In recent years, Rotumans who have distinguished themselves in government service in Fiji have made special trips to the island for the express purpose of resolving long-lasting disputes, often with considerable success. They generally address disputes that arise in their home district where they have insider status but are not party to the disagreements.

In addition to chiefs, church personnel, and distinguished visitors from Fiji, any respected elder related to the disputants may intercede. Mediators appeal to common sense and common interests, to community and kinship loyalties. Their goal is more often to disentangle the knots of anger and hostility than to bring about any particular solution. Prolonged and bitter disputes, it seems, are as disturbing to living elders as they are to spiritual ancestors.

Faksoro: *Apologies with Weights Attached*

Possibly the most powerful conflict resolution mechanism available to Rotumans is *faksoro,* which is translated by Churchward (1940:193) as "to entreat, beseech; to apologize; to beg to be excused." But it means much more than this because of the weight of custom that it carries. Although the term is used in reference to a verbal apology following an inadvertent accident, this is only one end of a spectrum that includes entreaties that are more formal. At the other extreme is the symbolic offer of one's life to atone for a grave injury or insult. At least five gradations can be distinguished:

1. A verbal apology in private following an accidental occurrence in which one individual was in the wrong. In general, it seems that for most Rotumans, the inconveniences caused by such an occurrence are of less significance than the expectation of an apology. An apparently sincere apology following an accident usually offsets damages. For example, if someone accidentally injures another or damages property, monetary or material compensation is generally not expected; a proper apology sets things right. A negative example may be instructive. When a ship arrives (quite irregularly), traffic at the wharf is rather chaotic since there is so little room for vehicles to maneuver. On one occasion, the driver of a truck, rather than yielding to permit another driver to pass, forced his way through, scraping some paint off the other fellow's new, previously unblemished, truck. When the victim called the offending driver's attention to the damage, the latter simply protested, "I couldn't help it." It so happened that a policeman on duty witnessed the incident and suggested to the victim that he file a complaint. When telling the story, the victim said he would not have done so if an apology had been offered, but since none had been forthcoming he decided to pursue the matter. After being called to the police station, the offending driver came to apologize and asked how he could compensate. The victim settled for a can of white paint to repair the damage. In fact, the compensation was more symbolic than real because the paint was not the right type or color for the car.

2. A verbal apology made in public. This lends greater weight to an apology, since it constitutes a public admission of culpability. Typically, such an apology is made at a village or district meeting. Public apologies of this type are appropriate for various forms of verbal insults. In the heat of an argument, someone might demean another's character. Such offenses threaten community solidarity, and mediators are likely to pressure the offender to faksoro. If the insults are not too grave, a public apology is usually sufficient to restore relationships to normal.

3. A formal presentation of a *koua* (pig cooked whole in an earth oven; see fig. 4.2). Prepared this way, a pig is a sacrifice to the gods. Furthermore, a pig is a substitute for a human being (Rotuman myth is specific on this point; see Titifanua and Churchward 1995:116–23). In such a circumstance, a koua is brought to the aggrieved party's

Figure 4.2. Young men take a break while preparing food from an earth oven. Photograph by Alan Howard.

home and formally presented, with appropriate speeches admitting culpability and begging forgiveness. To lend weight to such an occasion, a chief or other respected elder might be asked to make the apology on the offender's behalf.

4.   A formal presentation of a fine white mat (*apei*) and kava plant in addition to a koua. Fine white mats and kava plants are of central significance in Rotuman ceremonies (see Inia 2001). As elsewhere in Polynesia, fine white mats are a traditional form of wealth. They are mandatory prestations at weddings, funerals, and other ceremonial events, and they lend great weight to any ritual presentation. Kava, a drink made from the pounded root of the *Piper mythisticum* plant, is consumed ceremonially on special occasions. In the past, only chiefs took part, although today it is drunk more generally as a social beverage. Ceremonially presented, however, kava signifies life fluid and is symbolically associated with blood. A gift of kava is therefore comparable to a blood sacrifice. Likewise, a white mat is symbolically comparable to a life, insofar as the making of a koua must precede the manufacture of an apei. Thus, kava plants

and white mats contribute much customary weight to a faksoro presentation, even more so if a chief or respected elder makes the presentation on behalf of the offender.

5. The strongest faksoro an individual can make is called *hen rau'ifi* (to hang leaves). This refers to a garland of leaves that the person who comes to apologize wears around his neck. A person coming hen rau'ifi is symbolically offering his life in a plea for forgiveness. Here, too, it may not be the offender, but a chief or distinguished elder who comes in his place.

   Hen rau'ifi are only performed in the gravest circumstances, especially when a life has been taken. A koua, fine white mat, and kava plant are expected to accompany the plea. Theoretically, the offended party is entitled to take the life of the presenter, whether the offender or a stand-in, or he can offer forgiveness by undoing the knot by which the garland is tied around the presenter's neck.

What makes faksoro such a powerful custom is that, when done properly, acceptance is virtually mandatory. Furthermore, even while the person soliciting forgiveness admits culpability and accepts blame, and is thus humbled, he gains compensatory status; for to go faksoro, particularly in formal fashion, is an honorable act. Should the aggrieved party refuse a proper apology, he may be subjected to severe criticism, while the offender might be socially exonerated. As far as disputes go, faksoro thus provides a means by which someone who finds himself in a weak or untenable position can escape the social effects of losing a confrontation, and perhaps even gain a degree of status in the bargain.

The Apparatus of Government: Law and Enforcement

Following cession in 1881, a resident commissioner was sent to govern Rotuma and, with some allowance for customary practice, to administer British justice. In addition to the Rotuma Council, which advised the commissioner, another body, the Rotuma Regulation Board, was charged with constituting (and periodically reconstituting) a set of regulations governing land matters, public health, marriage and divorce, road maintenance, and criminal violations, among others. A system of fines was imposed and a small jail constructed to incarcerate wrongdoers. The resident commissioner was also appointed magistrate, with the power to pass judgment on all but the most serious crimes (Eason 1951).

Resident commissioners, and the district officers who succeeded them following an administrative reorganization in the 1930s, provided recourse to individuals who were dissatisfied with resolutions to disputes arrived at by customary procedures. They could bring their case to the commissioner, who would conduct a hearing and make his own judgment. Since commissioners usually held the post for only a few years, if a disputant was dissatisfied with the judgment of one man, he could wait until another took office and try again. This was particularly the case with long-standing disputes over land (Howard 1963, 1964).

This situation prevailed until 1970, when Fiji gained independence. At that point, the Rotuma Council pledged their loyalty to the new nation and its laws. The governance of Rotuma continued to be in the hands of the Rotuma Council and a district officer, but with the reversal of roles described above. The council now has decision-making authority, and the district officer is an advisor. Although he retains the power of a regional magistrate, the district officer is less able to directly intervene in disputes than before. To compensate, individual Rotumans can now take their grievances directly to government agencies in Fiji if they are dissatisfied with judgments rendered on Rotuma.

Summary

Rotuma is a good example of a society that is disputatious but nonviolent. Socialization is low-key with regard to physical punishment, and aggressive models are few. Individual autonomy is respected, and even children learn to assert themselves in defense of their own interests. As a result, people stand up for their rights; while gentle in comportment, they are not necessarily docile in disposition. Disputes are therefore endemic in Rotuma. What is remarkable is that they so rarely escalate to violent encounters.

One mechanism that acts to contain disputes is a widespread belief in immanent justice. This belief—that wrongdoers will get their just deserts in the form of ill fortune—restrains individuals from making claims they know to be spurious. It helps keep people from being overly aggressive in their pursuit of self-interest.

A second mechanism for dealing with conflict is avoidance. Unlike many other island peoples who have institutionalized procedures for getting disputants to discuss their grievances in controlled circumstances (Watson-Gegeo and White 1990), Rotumans avoid such confrontations. They therefore rely less on *resolving* disputes than on *containing* them. Avoidance is a workable strategy because of the degree of economic self-sufficiency and mobility enjoyed by most Rotumans. It allows time for tempers to cool, for hurts to be forgotten, and for vulnerability to be minimized. Relationships are sometimes, but not always, renewed under more favorable circumstances. Avoidance has costs, however, in the form of diminished possibilities for social and economic support.

A third mechanism for managing disputes is institutionalized mediation. Ideally, mediators are trusted elders who have an important stake in maintaining harmony between adversaries and who are free of parochial interests. It is their job to soothe ruffled feathers and to promote compromise in the interest of community solidarity. Chiefs are expected to be arbitrators as well as mediators. They have the right to make judgments in disputes that cannot be settled by the antagonists. If a disputant is sufficiently dissatisfied with a chief's judgment, he can appeal to the district officer, or to other government officials. The fact that the most passionate disputes are over land and chiefly prerogatives—essentially long-term issues—means that current setbacks may be reversed when new chiefs or government officials are in place. This encourages patience, as does the belief in immanent justice.

Perhaps the most effective mechanism available to Rotumans is the custom of faksoro. By construing apologies as honorable, persons who have offended others can gain compensatory status for admission of wrongdoing. The fact that acceptance of such apologies, given under proper circumstances, is virtually mandatory makes them especially effective as strategies for ending disputes.

Finally, one must not lose sight of the important role played by the government of Fiji as final arbitrator in Rotuman disputes. While sending gunboats to quell political protests may be somewhat overzealous, the point was not entirely lost on Rotumans. They were made acutely aware that what happens on Rotuma is watched abroad, and that they will pay a price if matters get out of hand. When the dissidents were brought to trial for sedition on Rotuma before Fiji's chief magistrate, even the chiefs were made to feel the power of the law to intimidate. They were shown no more respect by the lawyers and magistrate than were the dissidents. The process of the trial itself conveyed the most powerful message—that even the threat of violence on Rotuma puts everyone's dignity at risk. The magistrate, on finding the defendants guilty of sedition, wisely imposed an extremely light sentence. He fined them 30 Fijian dollars each (20 dollars less than the fine for riding a motorcycle without a helmet) and placed them on two years' probation. Many observers thought this was too light and would like to have seen them sent to jail. The dissidents thought otherwise and vowed to keep up their struggle for Rotuma's independence. But talk of violence had passed, and calm prevailed.

Study Questions

1. List the diverse mechanisms that Rotumans use to handle disputes without violence.
2. What is faksoro? How important is faksoro in maintaining the peace in

Rotuma? Are apologies also important in your society? How are they similar to and different from the Rotuman faksoro?

3. What is immanent justice? How do beliefs in immanent justice prevent violence?

4. What aspects of Rotuman cultural ideas, values, and institutions for maintaining peace seem to be most affected by social changes? To what extent, if at all, are social changes undermining the ability of Rotuma to remain a peaceful society?

Respect for All: The Paliyans of South India

PETER M. GARDNER

In the south of India, Paliyan society shares many of the conflict management features that other peaceful societies utilize—for example, avoidance, nonviolent values that emphasize respect and condemn disrespectful actions, mediation assemblies to resolve conflicts, and religious ideas that promote nonviolence. Peter Gardner analyzes the Paliyans' day-to-day conflicts in light of these features. Of added and significant interest, Gardner compares a traditional nomadic Paliyan band with a band that recently switched to a sedentary lifestyle, bringing them in closer contact with mainstream Indian society. Economic and political forces from without are forcing major changes on Paliyan society. Gardner reveals how the Paliyans are dealing with such changes, thus allowing readers to see the resilience of peaceful Paliyan culture.

—GK

Peaceful societies are more than just a fascinating human oddity, more than just material for another coffeetable book to feed public curiosity about such exotica as ceremonial masks, neck elongation, human sacrifice, and pyramids. The very existence of peaceful societies is significant because it tells us about fundamental human possibilities. Although social philosophers since Lao Tsu have written about hypothetical systems in which each person respects all others, other thinkers tell us that, in our species, power plays and conflict are inevitable, that they derive from human nature, that they are a product of our having desires and being smart and capable. In 1651

Thomas Hobbes explained human behavior in terms of our desire to acquire dominion over others, with an original state of war being replaced by social contracts and the creation of authorities. A chorus of recent voices insists that there is biological support for such a stance. Edward O. Wilson (1978:14) tells us that human aggression is innate, Wrangham and Peterson (1996) argue that aggression is our evolutionary heritage, and Ghiglieri (1999:197, emphasis in original) contends that evolutionary processes "*compelled* human males . . . to wage war." In other words, by this reasoning, peaceful societies should not even exist.

I have been documenting the extreme peacefulness of south India's Paliyan hunter-gatherers for a number of years, paying special attention to traditional techniques for dealing with conflict (Gardner 2000b: esp. 83–100, 122–33). I have also just detailed the persistence of effective conflict management in a Paliyan community that settled down to village life in the early to mid-nineteenth century (Gardner 2000a). That persistence is unexpected; evidence from other continents tells us that as hunter-gatherers settle, due partly to the increased human contacts, sedentary village life generally brings with it intensified interpersonal difficulty (Bender 1978; Kent 1989; Rafferty 1985).

My previous accounts of Paliyan peacefulness and persisting nonviolence derive from fieldwork conducted some years ago, and the Paliyans' circumstances are changing rapidly. Has their ability to wage peace been undercut? While a brief revisit to the region during December 2000 and January 2001 demonstrated a continuation of the general pattern reported earlier, some new challenges and responses were found to have arisen, making it a good time for an updated overview. I shall begin with the earlier picture of respect, disrespect, conflict management, and responses to disrespect. This will provide a context for understanding the present picture. The last section of the chapter will show how Paliyans are coping with the new challenges.

In the 1960s and 1970s, Paliyans lived by digging wild dioscorea yams, hunting small game, fishing, and collecting honey in relatively open monsoon forest on the lower, eastern slopes of the ranges of hills that reach into the southernmost tip of India. They were able to live quietly and evasively, side by side with ancient Indian civilization. Their habitat was sufficiently dry, stony, and thorny to keep away all but the most intrepid outsiders. But Paliyans did engage in modest, sporadic trade of forest produce—including honey, medicinal plants, condiments, incense, toiletries, and sandalwood—with licensed forest produce contractors, forestry staff, and private individuals from the Tamil-speaking plains below. Such trade was documented in the mid-nineteenth century and may be many centuries old. I found that most Paliyan bands dwelt relatively near the forest edge. Individuals, families, or whole bands withdrew into deeper forest for weeks, months, or even years at times of social friction or when they felt threatened by their loud, sometimes violent neighbors.

Even the world's most peaceful peoples face intrasocietal conflicts and external threats. It takes an extraordinary individual in any society to be immune to feelings of envy, jealousy, resentment, annoyance, or outright anger. That is the way humans are. In the case of so-called nonviolent peoples, such as Paliyans, we must explain how they manage to deal with distressing situations in ways that prevent negative feelings from escalating into open social disruption and how they cope with open conflict when it does occur.

Respect for All as a Key Value

Any description of Paliyan social relations has to begin with consideration of beliefs and values. Everything pivots around those. To begin with, we are talking about a truly egalitarian system: Everyone deserves respect, regardless of maturity, relative seniority, gender, and degree of relatedness. A seventy-year-old man must respect the rights and needs of a totally unrelated four-year-old girl. As they would say, emphatically, "She is a person." This is not one of those societies about which anthropologists sometimes write that "they are egalitarian except, of course, in regard to age or sex." For Paliyans, that would not be egalitarianism at all.

The way they actually express their social goal is to say that one must "avoid disrespect" in one's relations with everyone, and they mean absolutely everyone, including outsiders. However, they use a figurative term for *disrespect*; when we analyze this term and examine examples of improper behavior, we find that they are saying it is disrespectful to place oneself above or below another person. In their view, either kind of asymmetrical relationship constitutes an imposition on the other party. This helps us to understand why any sign that people are pursuing power or prestige is offensive to their fellows; so, too, is unnecessary pursuit of dependence. A premium is placed on everyone who can physically do so achieving self-reliance and noninterference. This clearly does much to shape appropriate behavior in their economy, social organization, conflict management, religion, treatment of illness, and play. We should not expect to see recognition of leaders or technical specialists on whom others might rely. Indeed, Paliyans firmly deny the very existence of all but one kind of specialist (which is described below), apparently on principle. In sum, dependence on other people is acceptable only for the very young, those decrepit with age, and those seriously disabled by illness.

To say that respect for others is valued does not mean that one sees such proper behavior only sometimes. The rules are far more compelling than this. It is more realistic to state that only now and then can one see violations of propriety, and these are generally all mild instances. To employ Raymond

Firth's (1951) distinction, the everyday organization actually achieved by Paliyans is very close in form to the structure that is prescribed. This underlines clearly that we are dealing with a key value.

The rare self-elevating individual, such as Old Ponnan, who harangued others about what he took to be their misdemeanors, was ignored or informally shunned. Old Ponnan did this only once during the time of my formal study of disrespect, but I have witnessed other such outbursts from him, including one against me. He also had a reputation for being insufficiently self-controlled and was said by outsiders to have had a brawl some years before with a contractor's agent. In turning away from Ponnan's accusations and insinuations, his fellows rendered him peripheral and uninfluential. Sickly behavior was also negatively sanctioned, unless the disability was being handled properly. When a different man, thirty-eight-year-old Ponnan, responded to a boil on his ankle by hobbling around in a fragile way for nearly a week with a specially made cane, his exaggerated display of incapacity was *not* directed toward his fellows, and they knew it. No one acted as if his behavior was problematic. He was sending a stereotyped message to the Paliyan gods, whose parent-like protection he sought, dependence on gods being stylized and specially sanctioned. Indeed, he petitioned one of the gods for help during a possession ceremony. By contrast, there was no evidence that the slow, pathetic behavior of twenty-five-year-old Nallamma was a message to the gods. I took her lack of inclination to work as being disrespectful toward her husband, yet he appeared to disregard it. She suffered from a degree of social exclusion by most others, suggesting to me that many took her to be a malingerer, as did I. Although Nallamma elicited odd gifts of food for her two thin young daughters, she rarely received anything for herself, even from her productive and abnormally generous female cousin or her sexually entranced father-in-law.

Independence may be treasured, and self-reliance may be expected of all who are capable, yet the social world of Paliyans is warm in tone and laced with light humor. It has little resemblance to the bleak way of life of individualistic people, such as the Ik, who act in an alienated, self-centered manner even in relation to primary relatives (Turnbull 1972). Paliyan husband and wife characteristically accord each other a lot of freedom without being aloof; again and again, I noted conspicuous signs of affection and play between them.

Types of Disrespect

Everyone's best intentions notwithstanding, disrespectful acts can and do take place, and disrespect has many faces. The thirty-one physical and verbal offenses recorded by me were of ten different kinds. (1) There were ten cases of a mother slapping, striking, or attempting to strike her child due to its misbehavior. Usually this was done with a slap of the open hand, but two mothers just swatted at a child with soft plant fiber, and one mother waved a stick ineffectively as she chased her son. It is not that I, as a comparative scholar, would label this mild punishment "disrespectful"; let me be clear that we are talking about Paliyan definitions. There was also an instance of an annoying girl being struck by a nearby twenty-year-old man. (2) I saw five instances of children hitting at other children with their hands (or, in one case, with a piece of limp cloth), these episodes varying from single slaps to intermittent, day-long quarrels. Children always struck each other lightly. (3) Three adults hit their spouses, one woman doing so twice. I believe three of these cases entailed a single blow with the hand, the other involved one swat with a soft, handleless broom. (4) Four instances of verbal disrespect took the form of jealous accusations concerning what a person imagined to be actual or desired adultery by a spouse. (5) In addition, one young man offended another by asking about his apparent liaison with the questioner's married sister. (6) An older man, whose straying eye suggested that he was motivated by sexual desire for a certain young woman and was jealous of her chosen companions, complained loudly about teenagers engaging in excessive intercourse. Young people corroborated my interpretation of this. (7) A statement about differing pay rates of two forest produce contractors offended some who worked for the lesser amount. It was claimed afterwards that the person who made the initial remark intended it as a joke; however, the quip was offensive enough to cause weeping and temporary fission of the community. The remaining cases were diverse. (8) Two men had given household food away, one to his needy mother, the other to his grandchildren, thereby upsetting their wives. Then, there were a case each of (9) petty theft and (10) malingering.

This was not the sum total of social discontent. Four people told me privately that they believed certain community members had used sorcery against others, but none of these beliefs resulted in any open accusation or social disruption. And, although this did not happen during my study, I have information that two men had fussed, some months earlier, about suspicions that each man's wife had given birth to a lover's child. Both couples had separated temporarily.

It is conspicuous that no murders were known to have occurred within Paliyan society, nor was there acknowledgment by the people of murders happening in other Paliyan communities, even distant ones. In light of how private they are, especially about sensitive matters such as violence, it would be irresponsible not to ask if Paliyan claims in this regard are correct. But they may well be. While aging forestry officers, experienced forest produce contractors, malaria eradication workers, and teachers who knew Paliyans well alerted me to four instances of Paliyans being killed by outsiders, they were all in agreement that murder was absent within the tribal society. Understandably, I can report a complete absence of feuding within Paliyan society and a corresponding total lack of warfare.

Techniques for Conflict Management

Self-Restraint

The primary response to disrespect has to be self-restraint; my history of actual conflicts shows it to be primary in both time and importance. There are three prominent forms of self-restraint: simply ignoring an affront, taking steps to control oneself, and separating physically from a disrespectful person to allow time for upset feelings to subside.

Ignoring disrespect could be so total that, at times, it was hard for me to tell whether members of the community thought that disrespect had occurred. And, because it offended most adult participants and nonparticipants for me to inquire about cases of conflict, no matter how delicately, it was difficult to tap peoples' views later as to what had been transpiring. When twenty-year-old Kritnan stole items from four different people—a billhook, a chicken, a rupee, and a piece of cloth—and ran off for two weeks, there were no angry complaints. Nor were there any when he returned. No restitution was requested, offered, or made. It was only thanks to being present during some matter-of-fact initial conversation among young people that I could ascertain that disrespect was thought to have taken place. Raaman's difficulty with the behavior of his wife and Kritnan, the thief just mentioned, was quite another matter. Raaman was aging and ill. When his twenty-eight-year-old wife, Lacmi, brought young Kritnan home, Raaman accommodated his new cohusband and raised not a murmur of protest. Indeed, not long after this, he spoke *against* Kritnan leaving the household in order to marry the maturing young Cellamma, Raaman's explicit grounds being that, if Kritnan left to marry Cellamma, Lacmi would probably leave too and join the young couple polygynously. As the old man expressed it to me, with a smile, "If I have caught hold of a branch, I should not leave it." While the original polyandry was not really to his liking, I concluded that he saw benefit in not treating the unilateral imposition of a cohusband as disrespectful.

Two steps can be taken to ensure calm control of oneself: the first as prophylaxis, the second as treatment. Prevention of outward expression of anger can be aided in the first place by avoiding alcohol. Palm toddy was readily available from outsiders, but most Paliyans abstained from drinking it. They would not even handle a container of it and spoke of fearing the way that it interfered with self-restraint; as they saw it, drinking alcohol could result in the unleashing of pent-up anger. If anger did arise, it was said that the feeling could be subdued or dispelled by smoothing on one's forehead the crushed blossoms of a ubiquitous flower. They described it as having an immediate tranquilizing effect.

Separating physically from a disrespectful person is motivated either by desire to ensure self-restraint, or by a need for protection from someone who lacks self-restraint. To give instances of both, annoyed and offended individuals tend to stalk off, if only for a few hours, until they calm down, and Paliyans flee immediately from aggressive or threatening outsiders. The latter practice gives rise to their reputation for timidity. Children who are too young to withdraw by themselves are either put in the hands of others by those who are attacking them or led away by a convenient, nearby third party. This is done in the name of each child's right to protection.

An agitated woman who is leaving her husband on account of his disrespect may also have her infant or toddler lifted from her arms temporarily by others (she will cooperate with them in this), or she herself may voluntarily hand it over for its safety. Although the child is not directly involved in the conflict, disturbed circumstances and parental distraction leave it vulnerable. What may be a functionally similar protection of a woman or girl by her brother was seen several times. A brother tends to be the first to step forward when a female is struck by a male. In such instances, a single question by the brother is usually enough to ensure an adequate degree of disengagement by the parties to the conflict. I say "usually" because of a case already mentioned (and described more fully below) wherein a brother's protective question precipitated a fight. My reason for calling this functionally similar to protection of babies is speculative. I infer that it may be a common Paliyan view that females of all ages are somewhat vulnerable when faced by a physically violent or pushy male.

Shunning

It is unclear to me whether the tendency to shun habitually disrespectful people, such as Old Ponnan, is better viewed as a separate technique for conflict management, or as a modest, informal extension of separating physically from someone who is unrestrained.

Conciliation

In most bands, when social tensions arise, some members of the group prove to be skilled at stepping forward with playful, witty, or soothing words. There are usually one or two people who can do this. Their styles cross the spectrum from that of clown or stand-up comedian to that of calm diplomat. Such conciliating is the one specialty that Paliyans allow. I witnessed skilled people responding to building tensions due, for instance, to disagreements and jealousy, to gods not possessing anyone when Paliyans called them to a

Figure 5.1. A Paliyan woman named Lacmi and one of her husbands extract yams from between slabs of granite. Though not called a "head," Lacmi's soothing tone, social finesse, and prompt attention to a disrespected child showed that she functioned in that role. Photograph by Peter M. Gardner.

ritual, and to the shock of a group member's death. Particularly when tension is serious, the conciliators tend right away to distract, calm, or reassure the upset. During simple interpersonal difficulties, these voluntary, informal conciliators may intervene, but their involvement is not inevitable. Some referred to them as "clever" people, with "good heads." The two terms for them, *naaTTaamee* and *talevan,* can both be translated as "head-person," but I have argued elsewhere that "head" in this context refers only to their cleverness, not leadership, for they totally lack authority (2000b:93). They may not punish or impose arbitration, and they certainly do not stand above other people, even temporarily. Their subtle, self-appointed task is to soothe or distract without violating the rights of the people in conflict (see fig. 5.1).

The Gods

Male and female gods also participate in problem solving (Gardner 1991). About once a week, the otherwise self-reliant Paliyans ask what I came to call their "protecting gods" to send them injured food animals, to send rain that would make yam digging easier, to ward off epidemics, to diagnose and heal illness, to help people explain or cope with unusual events including conflict, and to watch over their "grandchildren," particularly while they are walking in the forest. One or more individuals beat drums and, occasionally taking a deep breath, chant prayers of petition in long drawn-out phrases, asking the gods to possess them and speak through their human hosts. I have seen it take anywhere from a few minutes to an hour and a half for the gods to descend on people. If and when they do come, the gods may be addressed as "grandparents" instead of by name, and Paliyans in need, especially those who are ill, may curl up on the ground in front of the possessed, like distressed children pleading for protection. Interestingly, it is grannies who most often protect children from disrespectful mothers. Bearing in mind that in adult Paliyan society such a display of dependence would be disrespectful, it is notable that it is the height of propriety to turn to gods for nurturing care and authoritative knowledge. Gods, too, have their expectations, and they may be stern or demanding. Paliyans' inattentiveness is of concern to them; it is common, for example, for the gods to allege that Paliyans have made inadequate offerings. They also prescribe proper behavior and punish acts that offend them: One should refrain from sex the night before going into the forest, avoid excessive contact with outsiders, and abstain from eating wild bison or touching bovine leather.

Community Meetings

A final, but seldom used, technique for conflict management is a *kuTTam*, a community gathering with no outsiders present. Such an assembly may be called to diagnose a problem and discuss possible solutions. Only one took place during my study, it being carefully scheduled for a time when people knew I would be absent. Most people were reluctant to say much about it, but I learned enough to see there was evidence of uneasiness over its outcome—a gentle rebuke. It had been called to take up a dramatic case of a man who struck his very pregnant wife when he learned that she had deprived herself and her unborn child of food in order to feed other family members adequately. He then stood in his doorway, trembling, with a machete-like billhook in his hand, threatening all who came to his wife's aid. Asked by many anxious people to "do something," I had been the one to tell him gently that the blade was not needed, wrap my fingers around it, and lift it slowly from his hand. Examining peoples' reactions to the kuTTam, I concluded that there was incomplete consensus that assemblies of this sort have the authority to take any action.

Level of Disrespect

About once a week, I noted that, in two somewhat larger than average Paliyan groups, there would be a few minutes of tension due to interpersonal problems. I gave an inventory above of thirty-one cases of disrespect. These are all that came to my attention during the 202 days when I had twenty-four-hour contact with Paliyans. Because I slept in the midst of the communities, conversations at night commonly woke me, hence my claim to have a virtual twenty-four-hour record of audible or visual disturbances within the actual communities. Events that took place in scattered work parties constitute an obvious exception. Even so, I occasionally witnessed the aftermath of conflicts which arose in such settings and was able to reconstruct the events.

The rate of disrespectful acts can be expressed with greater precision. In the more forest-oriented band, I recorded a rate of 0.9 episodes per person per year and, in the settled community, the rate was 0.8 episodes per person per year (2000a:230).

Referring to these acts of disrespect as "disturbances" may be misleading. As we have seen, some, such as the theft, complaining, and malingering, appeared to have been totally ignored by those who might have felt injured. Fully twelve out of the thirty-one acts of disrespect took place without either the attacker or the victim raising a voice significantly. In another four cases, the victim made little noise, but the attacker raised a voice. A few episodes took the form of a mother scurrying after a child, usually a four-to seven-year-old, protesting its behavior in a relatively normal-level voice, and perhaps swatting toward it with her hand, a piece of grass, or a flaccid frond of greenery—very mild attacks by most cultural standards.

Victims' Responses to Disrespect

Although I have written before about how Paliyans handle conflict, I have never attempted to examine variations in what could be called the positive, neutral, and negative reactions of those who are the injured parties. It is informative to do so.

Three kinds of difficulty account for most of the episodes. Problems among adults over affairs and marital relations represent fully 35.5 percent (11) of the episodes; adults, usually mothers, being annoyed with frustrating children constitute another 35.5 percent (again, 11); and children squabbling among themselves make up 16 percent (5) of the episodes. The remaining 13 percent (or 4 episodes) consist of one event each of teasing, petty theft, complaining, and malingering—all among adults. For purposes of analysis, these last four cases will be folded in with other adult-adult difficulties, giving us a total of 11 adult-child, 15 adult-adult, and 5 child-child conflicts.

A set of three tables summarizes the reactions of the injured parties to these three kinds of disrespect situation. In column one of each table, lack of response and separation of the parties in conflict are both deemed to represent purely positive reactions to the disrespect. They are called positive because both involve the kind of self-restraint and pulling back that are valued by Paliyans. Moving to column two, soft sobs and cries are reactions of sorts. Due to the fact that they draw attention to conflict without being retaliative, such outbursts might be helpful when vulnerable individuals, such as children, are the victims. A case could be made, however, for viewing them as relatively neutral reactions, neither self-restrained nor inflammatory. Separation together with soft sobs or cries, in column three, constitutes an unproblematic mix of positive and neutral reactions, unproblematic in the sense that it should not lead to escalation of conflict. Separation coupled with a verbal retort or physical retaliation, in column four, represents a combination of the positive and the negative. Finally, in column five, there are wholly negative reactions, such as loud accusations, counteraccusations, angry retorts, actual or attempted physical blows, and combinations of these. These last responses all enlarge the original problem, for, as Paliyans put it, they result in there being two disrespectful parties rather than one. They represent the initial stage of escalation of conflict.

Comparison of the tables shows that conflict situations were the least serious when adults were disrespectful to children (table 5.1). All of the reactions to such disrespect were positive, neutral, or a combination of these. None were negative. Why so? It is possible that children were awed by the sight of an adult out of control and sensed that it would be dangerous to further aggravate the situation by doing anything other than fleeing—which some did. I surmise that a couple of children felt they were owed protective intervention by other adults and merely curled up on the ground, crying, to elicit

Table 5.1. Positive, Neutral, Mixed, and Negative Reactions to Adult Disrespect Toward Children (N = 11 cases)

NUMBER AND PERCENT OF CASES	NO RESPONSE OR SEPARATION	SOFT SOBS OR CRIES	SEPARATION AND SOFT SOBS OR CRIES	SEPARATION AND VERBAL OR PHYSICAL RESPONSE	VERBAL AND/OR PHYSICAL RESPONSE
Number	2	3	6	0	0
Percent	18	27	55	0	0

Table 5.2. Positive, Neutral, Mixed, and Negative Reactions to Adult Disrespect Toward Other Adults (N = 15 cases)

NUMBER AND PERCENT OF CASES	NO RESPONSE OR SEPARATION	SOFT SOBS OR CRIES	SEPARATION AND SOFT SOBS OR CRIES	SEPARATION AND VERBAL OR PHYSICAL RESPONSE	VERBAL AND/OR PHYSICAL RESPONSE
Number	7	1	1	4	2
Percent	47	7	7	27	13

it (after all, they would now and then have seen a grandmother, especially, stay an upset mother's hand or pluck a sobbing child out of harm's way). Or, they may have sensed that their own irritating behavior underlay the disturbance. All of these suggestions are speculative, though, the motives of the children being beyond definitive interpretation.

The cases of difficulty between adults were more problematic (table 5.2). Only 60 percent of the reactions in these cases were positive, neutral, or both. The remaining reactions were partially or wholly negative. In three of the four cases of mixed response, the negativity was not very pronounced; wives simply accused their husbands of having or wanting affairs as they, the wives, moved out. That is all. The other mixed case was quite another matter. It began when a publicly acknowledged affair took place between two married people, Potteyan and his wife's cousin, Paappa. It was previously described thus:

> Following a day-long tryst..., Paappa's brother, Kaamaacci, asked Potteyan where he had taken Paappa. Potteyan snapped back "Why do you ask?" Being told that his reply was rude, Potteyan struck Kaamaacci with a stick. Kaamaacci grabbed his neck and they fell, fighting. A neighbor tried clumsily to separate them. Then Kaamaacci's mother arrived in tears and asked "Why are you beating my son?" Potteyan turned on her rudely saying that, if her son stayed, he would kill him. Despite the turmoil, no physical injuries were in evidence, but Kaamaacci and his mother were shaken. On the old woman's urging, Kaamaacci, his wife, and daughter left the community temporarily. (Gardner 2000a:227)

This was by far the most violent incident between Paliyans that I recorded. The hitting was unrestrained, but, as I indicated, no cuts or bruises were to be seen afterwards. What is more, it was brief, and voluntary disengagement followed.

The two wholly negative responses to adult-adult disrespect involved the same elderly couple. Once he struck her in response to argumentative words. The other time she objected loudly to his having given their household food to his hungry granddaughters without asking her first.

Table 5.3. Positive, Neutral, Mixed, and Negative Reactions to Child Disrespect Toward Other Children (N = 5 cases)

NUMBER AND PERCENT OF CASES	NO RESPONSE OR SEPARATION	SOFT SOBS OR CRIES	SEPARATION AND SOFT SOBS OR CRIES	SEPARATION AND VERBAL OR PHYSICAL RESPONSE	VERBAL AND/OR PHYSICAL RESPONSE
Number	1	0	0	0	4
Percent	20	0	0	0	80

When children were at odds with each other (table 5.3), it was usual for there to be retaliation, and this tended to prolong the episodes. In no instances, however, were the hitting and retorts at all severe. Although some of the children were preadolescents, old enough to be free of parental guidance, a thirty-two-year-old woman told me after one of the quarrels that it was natural for such children to hit each other back. She recalled doing it herself at that age.

What are the most prominent responses to disrespect? Positive responses of some sort occurred in 74 percent (23/31) of the episodes. Separation of the parties to the conflict occurred immediately or eventually in 52 percent (16/31) of the cases. Retorts or counterviolence took place in only 32 percent (10/31) of them. The total is more than 100 percent because the types of responses are not mutually exclusive. These percentages make it clear that Paliyans do, indeed, qualify to be called an extremely peaceful people.

It is conspicuous that the two worst altercations took place in the settled Paliyan village, these being the husband hitting his pregnant wife for giving her own food to the rest of the family and a fight which ensued when a young man questioned his sister's lover about their tryst. While sedentary life had brought a slight decrease in the frequency of disputes, I noted a modest increase in the seriousness of settled Paliyans' responses to disrespect. Self-restraint had lessened slightly (see Gardner 2000a:232; 2000b:99–100).

Coping with New Challenges

During my 2000–2001 revisit, I found that culture contact had increased sharply for most Paliyan bands. Although the forest boundary itself was unchanged, irrigated fields, hamlets, and bus lines from the plains had crept up to its very edge. The formerly dry, desolate hinterland was disappearing. India, with its rapid change and hunger for resources, was pressing in on most Paliyan bands in consequential new ways. Given the traditional Paliyan reliance on flight from threats, reduction in their isolation is bound to be problematic. Several negative developments, which I will consider first, became apparent to me immediately, but, as I will also discuss a little later on, a relatively new nongovernmental organization was mitigating at least some of the difficult circumstances for a few Paliyan groups. There were indications that other positive developments also may be taking place. The Paliyans seem to be making greater use of their dispute resolution assembly, the kuTTam, and they seem to be becoming less timid in sticking up for themselves as they deal with the encroaching non-Paliyan world.

In one of the most dramatic cases of negative change, the Tamil Nadu State Forestry Department had just named a tribal hill region the Giant Grizzled Squirrel Wildlife Sanctuary. At the time I was there, the District Forest Officer in charge of the sanctuary had made no discernible provision for dealing with its displaced hunter-gatherers. Though they had been relatively undamaging denizens of that forest since ancient times, they had been given no new habitat, no training for an alternative livelihood, and no compensation of any kind. Instead, what I found was a stripping operation. Ten bands of Paliyans had not only been stripped of their traditional right to forage in the region for subsistence and trade, but they had also been told by men in khaki uniforms that, if they were found living in the deep forest, they would be shot on sight. That may not in fact be the official policy, but the threat has had the desired effect. In 2001 Indian colleagues and I ascertained that the threat had resulted in all of the deep-forest bands of the region edging closer to the margin of the forest. They, and other Paliyans who were already dwelling at the forest's edge, were languishing there with no obvious safe or legal way of making a living. I was told that there were plans for yet another game sanctuary in a range farther north. It promised to impact an even greater number of Paliyan groups.

Another dramatic case took place a few years earlier, in 1983, and it involved some of the same people who were to be displaced by the sanctuary. Suddenly Paliyans were in the national news. Eight families that I knew from my research in the 1960s had become indebted to a plantation manager who employed some of the adults as laborers. He charged them such exorbitant interest that, despite making payments, they found that their debts were growing rather than diminishing. It is illegal in modern India to exploit tribal people in this way. For a number of months, the manager and his wife imprisoned all eight indebted families together in a single crowded room each night, their children included, as soon as each day's work was finished. Even children were forced to stand while eating, with the penalty for noncompliance being a whipping. Ironically, the plantation was owned by the renowned Sri Andal Temple in Srivilliputtur, and its manager served as one of the temple trustees. When word reached New Delhi that tribal people were being kept as bonded servants, an immediate, on-site hearing was ordered by the Supreme Court of India. Thanks to a question raised in the hearing by a Paliyan child, the trustee was demonstrated to have not only kept many tribal people illegally confined, he was also shown to have tampered with the testimony of the Paliyan plaintiffs on the eve of the hearing. He was convicted for his abuses of the tribal people and imprisoned.

Also in the 1980s, other Paliyans, who again were among those who would later be displaced by the wildlife sanctuary, had been deprived of the right to officiate at worship services in two small but popular Hindu temples, Mahalingam Kovil and Sundaralingam Kovil, located on a forested mountainside. This tribal priesthood was an ongoing tradition that I had studied and photographed in 1963 (2000b:219, plates 23 and 24). A several-centuries-old copper plate, inscribed by an ancient ruler, granted a Paliyan and his descendants the right to conduct the worship services in perpetuity, this having been done in response to an earlier attempt to seize the temples and unseat the tribal priests. Paliyans had held the inherited priesthood since the initial construction of the two sacred edifices. Seizure of the temples was alleged to have been motivated by a simple desire to pocket revenue from temple services.

In 2000 Paliyan children in another range of hills, near Bodinayakanur, were reported to have been told by the local revenue officer that their special tribal rights to educational assistance would be unavailable unless the children produced their "family land deeds." It sounded like harassment, but, given the townspeoples' lack of knowledge of the forest, another interpretation is that the officer was simply ignorant of the nature of their tribal way of life. It is fairly clear that seminomadic hunter-gatherers possess nothing resembling land deeds, nor could anyone hold valid title to land which had long been government reserve forest.

These four cases illustrate that many Paliyan groups have recently been victims of thoughtless, predatory actions that deprive them of their freedom, rights, or traditional resources. In keeping with the Paliyans' preferred way of dealing with conflict—backing away—there appears to have been no tribal challenge to any of these actions. I learned about each problem from Tamil plains people of good will who approached me because they thought all friends of the Paliyans should be aware of the recent difficulties. I was able to get reliable, on-site corroboration of most of the events.

Another kind of problem arose a few years ago, this time with Paliyans contributing to it. In 1993 non-Paliyan illicit toddy makers began producing alcohol in the immediate vicinity of the Paliyan settlement where the Sri Andal trustee had detained his bonded servants. At a time when other employment opportunities for Paliyans were scarce, the bootleggers hired several tribal men to work in their operation and made alcohol accessible to them. Slowly, consumption of alcohol by the Paliyan employees began;

a few other incautious Paliyans also took part. Some eventually became habituated to drink. One Paliyan in his thirties told me that his father died from excessive drinking. He also claimed with great certainty that, as drinking had increased among his people, so had open conflict within their settlement. This accorded fully with the Paliyan theory about alcohol undermining one's self-control. Although I previously identified six factors that "may help us to understand the striking continuity of nonviolence" among Paliyans—one of them being the continuing belief of the people that alcohol begets violence—the recent experience of my former study community suggests that temperance might have been an especially important item in the list (2000a:232). It bears emphasis, though, that we are referring to a decline of order in only one community.

One direct and desirable outcome of the bonded servant case was that, in 1987, a modest nongovernmental organization (NGO), the Society for Tribal Development, had been founded to work with the affected band and other nearby Paliyan groups. The sensitively managed society had already done a health survey, seen to the treatment of the main infectious diseases, taught Paliyans how to obtain on their own the government benefits for which they were eligible, and helped to ensure that Paliyans establish community governance in accord with their own traditions and values. One result of the community members petitioning for government benefits was that all were well housed, and each family had acquired more than one set per person of what Tamils would deem to be respectable new clothes. Such respectability probably has subtle advantages in contact settings.

In view of the complexity of the situation facing present-day Paliyans, it is reasonable to ask precisely what impact the NGO is having on the day-to-day social life of the tribe. My revisit was just long enough for me to get a sense of the directions of two kinds of change. These were taking place in the areas of (1) general behavior of Paliyans when they are in contact settings, and (2) increased and more open use of community meetings, or kuTTams.

It was apparent in 1962–64 that Paliyans could become fairly self-confident, bold, and direct with outsiders they knew well and trusted. Males were this way with the priests in those Paliyan families which had lived for several generations on a Jesuit coffee estate. In a band which had moved a century earlier into agricultural labor, both sexes were comfortable with their Tamil neighbors and coworkers. In 2000–2001, I was seeing the same pattern in both sexes in the once-timid band I had studied during 1963. I stress that it was both sexes that had changed, because I had found earlier that many local employers' preferences for male workers meant that men were outpacing women at developing even the beginnings of such ease. The timid group's rate of change since the 1960s was especially surprising in light of the fact that I had documented a period during the 1970s when Paliyans retreated from abusive contact in that valley. Although self-confidence in contact settings had grown, I saw little evidence that it had been accompanied by much change in Paliyan-Paliyan relations.

An important factor in the pace of the change may have been the adroit style and actions of Sridhar, the director of the Society for Tribal Development. First, he had developed a remarkable grasp of, and appreciation for, Paliyan values. It was clear that he truly respected the people and was not attempting to impose on them the south Indian values with which he had grown up. Second, he worked on a daily basis with male and female, young and old. He told me that the young were the hope of the community and that women seemed to be emerging as some of the most effective workers for change. Third, he understood that the best long-term approach was teaching people ways to help themselves. Accordingly, he pulled back from personal involvement in new ventures as soon as he could. A case in point was his training of certain young adults to go by bus, in an unaccompanied group, to the district headquarters to arrange for or pick up government pension payments for all in the community who qualified. He had taught them to make repeated visits if that was what it took to succeed. There would be no more of the traditional Paliyan retreat from those who were loud and surly. I foresaw no danger in this change.

The NGO director had a yet grander plan. He regarded the members of the community he had helped transform as being the best possible agents for bringing about change in other Paliyan bands. He was already traveling with them to get this process started. While Sridhar uses more than a few Gandhian self-help principles here, he found ways to keep the content of the programs purely Paliyan. It was a brilliant scheme. I cannot refrain from saying that applied anthropology programs are seldom anywhere near this sensitive to the values of their subjects or even approximately this effective. The new self-confidence of the people was understandable. They had not just found a friend, they had been given a sense of their own worth and effectiveness.

Regarding the increased and more open use of kuTTams, this change was only just beginning. On the last day of my revisit, I found myself asked to attend the community's third-ever kuTTam. It had been called to deal with a dispute and to acknowledge the unexpected visit of their long-lost anthropologist and his twelve-year-old son. Three features of the meeting surprised me. For one thing, there were other outsiders in attendance besides my son and me. Present as well were a Tamil family from the plains, who were parties to the dispute, and the director of the Society for Tribal Development. This openness was wholly new. Secondly, the assembly had a new tone of authority. It seemed to be effective, and, even though the problem was resolved as the plains couple had hoped, I got a sense that no one walked away grumpily afterwards; no one behaved as if the kuTTam lacked legitimacy. And, finally, the dispute was resolved in a curiously Paliyan way.

The problem arose due to conflicting pregnancy practices of a Tamil bride and a Paliyan groom in a mixed marriage. The bride's parents expected her to follow their practice of spending the last months of her pregnancy in their home. The hitch was that they asked the groom to accompany her, because, as they put it, tribal people are known to be loose and inconstant in sexual matters. They expected that, if he was left alone in his home community, their son-in-law might stray. The groom's parents, particularly his father, were offended by the disrespectful tone of this expectation, and they were worried as well about the possibility of their son being lured away permanently into the outside world if he lived there for several months.

At the kuTTam, some twenty-five young and middle-aged Paliyan men and women, the bride and her parents, the NGO director, and my son and I sat in a large circle. A young Paliyan man called the meeting to order and spelled out the agenda. About half the Paliyan men, half the Paliyan women, and the bride's parents spoke, with Sridhar butting in twice to urge the bride's mother to subdue her most offensive outbursts. To my surprise, Paliyans spoke directly and firmly in the mixed forum, but they all honored their tradition of avoiding retaliatory remarks. What I called the "curiously Paliyan" resolution of the problem took place when, after a dozen or so people had spoken, the groom's father suddenly withdrew his objections to the Tamil family's requests. His was a classic Paliyan retreat from conflict. Though quiet for some minutes afterwards, he soon relaxed and became a participant in the subsequent celebration of my son's and my visit. Finally, a young man (different from the convener) brought the meeting to a close. They accomplished what they set out to do without a leader, without heavy-handedness, and without according special prominence or authority to males or elders. While the meeting had operated differently from anything I had seen or heard of previously in a Paliyan community, it functioned fully in accord with Paliyan values. The NGO director appears to have nudged the kuTTam into becoming an effective instrument for conflict management, while keeping it true to the culture.

My recent revisit was sufficiently brief that it would be a mistake to draw firm or detailed conclusions from it. It was encouraging though that the very Paliyans who have had to cope with (a) seemingly official death threats, (b) whippings while illegally imprisoned by an employer, and (c) heightened intracommunal conflict that they attribute to having drinkers in their midst were nonetheless doing well. News of the methods used to evict them from the deep forest had reached me before my revisit. They had not fled from the threats in disarray as I anticipated. Far from it. On my arrival I saw resilience and good humor where I expected to find demoralization. The

Paliyans' new sense of self-confidence, seen especially in their youths and young adults, their strengthened ways of conducting and using meetings to resolve conflicts, and their apparent retention of key traditional values gave me reason to predict that they might succeed in fashioning a workable new mode of living in this time of serious challenges. Even though they may prove unable to remain hunter-gatherers for long, their distinctive social life shows at least some signs of durability. Should their insistence on respect for others survive, and it has so far, Paliyans may well remain for a while longer on the roster of this planet's most peaceful inhabitants.

Study Questions

1. According to Gardner, why are peaceful societies more than just a "fascinating human oddity"? Do you agree with Gardner? Why or why not?
2. In what ways does *respect for all* form a Paliyan core value? How does respect operate within the society? How does Paliyan respect relate to peacefulness?
3. Do the cases of *disrespect* that Gardner carefully records and analyzes contradict the idea that the Paliyans are nonviolent? Why or why not?
4. How do the Paliyans maintain their peacefulness?
5. Explain what occurs during a *kuTTam*.
6. Gardner compares nomadic Paliyans with recently settled Paliyans—the latter being in closer contact with Indian society. Have settled Paliyans become less peaceful than their nomadic peers?

6
Multiple Paths to Peace: The "La Paz" Zapotec of Mexico

DOUGLAS P. FRY

Whereas not all Zapotec communities are peaceful, Douglas Fry draws on his own fieldwork and that of colleague Carl O'Nell to describe one Zapotec community that has created a peaceful social life. The "La Paz" Zapotec have established beliefs and cultural institutions that, in contrast to some neighboring communities, contribute to a peaceful social order. Fry examines beliefs about "respect," the presence of nonviolent role models during child rearing, La Pazian negative perceptions of aggression, and the manner in which conflict management mechanisms promote peace while assisting disputants to find resolutions. Fry's comparison of this community with neighboring San Andrés reveals that cultures of peace are about human choices.

—GK

This chapter draws on the research of two anthropologists, Carl W. O'Nell and the author, who have worked independently in the same community. In the 1960s, O'Nell arrived in the Valley of Oaxaca in southern Mexico and began fieldwork in a small Zapotec community. Since some of his research topics were of a sensitive nature—personal accounts of illnesses and dreams, for example—O'Nell thought it prudent not to use the community's real name in his publications. La Paz, or Peace, came to his mind as an apt label for a community that was, in his words, "relatively nonviolent" (O'Nell 1989:118).

Although animosities and quarrels exist, O'Nell explained, "Relatively few of these problems have led to physical violence" (1979:302). O'Nell estimated the La Paz homicide rate for a forty-year period, 1935 to 1975, to be about 5 per 100,000 persons per year, a tiny fraction of the homicide rate for the State of Oaxaca (1989:118–19). The homicide data in the district archives for an overlapping time period, 1920 to 1968, yields an even lower homicide rate for La Paz, equivalent to 3.4 homicides per 100,000 per year (Paddock 1982, Paddock pers. com. 1986; see Fry 1992a, 1994). Overall, O'Nell's research led him to the assessment that La Paz is a nonviolent place: "Reputationally, it has long enjoyed a distinction for tranquility and harmony. And, although interpersonal violence erupts occasionally, the overall control of physical violence appears to be a hallmark of community life" (1978:9).

In the early 1980s, benefiting from much kind advice offered by O'Nell, I began a comparative study of La Paz and a neighboring community referred to as San Andrés (Fry 1988, 1992a, 1992b, 1993, 1994, forthcoming). The study entailed conducting systematic behavioral observations of children, collecting tape-recorded structured interviews on child discipline and related topics, and recording in field notes ethnographic observations of community life. As of my last visit to La Paz in 1991, various lines of data suggest that La Paz has continued to live up to its pseudonym.

In this chapter, I will describe the nature of La Pazian peace. Following a brief ethnographic sketch of the community, I will explore conflict management in La Paz, beginning with an examination of the values, beliefs, and ideals that promote nonviolence and continuing with a consideration of the kinds of infrequent physical aggression observed in the community. Next, I will discuss some of the ways that the people of La Paz handle conflict without becoming physically aggressive. I will suggest, for instance, that the people of La Paz internalize a set of values, attitudes, and beliefs—such as *respect* for others—that are largely incompatible with physical aggression. Key values, attitudes, and beliefs like respect are learned early in life as part of the socialization process and continue to be reinforced in adult life. The main point is that the conflict management system in La Paz provides the community with multiple and complementary paths to peace.

Ethnographic Sketch of La Paz

La Paz is located in the Tlacolula wing of the Y-shaped Valley of Oaxaca, a semiarid region some 1,550 meters above sea level (Flannery, Kirkby, Kirkby, and Williams 1967). Ancient Zapotecs built their capital, Monte Albán, at the top of the hills in the center of the valley. The present-day state capital on the valley floor below, Oaxaca City, teems with urban bustle near the impressive hilltop ruins.

There are some thirty-four communities, most of them Zapotec-speaking, in the Tlacolula end of the valley (Paddock 1978). La Paz has existed in its present location since at least the 1500s, when, according to village legend, a carved wooden image of a Saint made a miraculous appearance, thus indicating the appropriate site for the new village (see O'Nell 1972). Deposits of clay suitable for pottery making exist on the outskirts of the community, and the women of La Paz use this resource to make ceramic pots, skillets, and pans to be sold in the nearby markets. Knowledge of pottery making has been passed from mothers to daughters over countless generations. The men view the women's special skill with some awe, explaining on occasion that "men don't know how to make pottery."

The people of La Paz converse in Zapotec on a daily basis, although most men and some women also speak Spanish. In the 1980s, the population of La Paz was almost 2,000. The longstanding subsistence activity in the community is the farming of maize, beans, and squash, and the harvest is totally dependent upon rainfall. Typically, a family owns three-to-five hectares of land. Men work the fields and periodically seek wage labor outside the community. There are no *haciendas*, other large landholdings, or political bosses (*caciques*) in La Paz.

Political and religious posts (*cargos*) in La Paz are filled for one-year terms. The name *cargo* reflects the burden of serving without pay in the civil-religious system; completing a term in office is generally viewed as a sacrifice that an individual makes for the good of the community. The highest-ranking civil authority is the mayor, officially called the *agente*, but sometimes referred to by La Pazians as the *presidente*. Another high-ranking official is the judge (*sindico*). Diverse duties of the mayor and the judge include listening to grievances and dealing with disputes that arise among the citizenry.

In preparing this chapter, I have drawn on O'Nell's publications, which are based on more than seven field trips to La Paz of variable length between 1965 and 1981 (see O'Nell 1969, 1972, 1978, 1979, 1981, 1989) as well as on my own research in La Paz, which consisted of initial fieldwork conducted from 1981 to 1983, followed by three short return visits between 1986 and 1991. Thus, the time period directly under consideration in this chapter begins in the mid-1960s and extends through 1991.

La Pazian Values, Attitudes, and Beliefs That Promote Peace

O'Nell (1981:354) suggests that "among the more prominent social ideals cherished by people in La Paz are values for respect, responsibility, and cooperation." In daily conversation, unprompted by the anthropologist, the

Figure 6.1. The Zapotec women of La Paz have a long-standing tradition of pottery-making that is passed from mothers to daughters. The men appreciate this special ability of the women and the income it produces. Overall, men and women get along well in La Paz. Men are not overly jealous and wife beatings are rare. D. P. Fry Photo Collection.

people of La Paz make regular reference to the importance of respect. Respect involves treating others as social equals and being courteous in speech and behavior. Acts of aggression are the antithesis of respectful behavior (O'Nell 1981:354).

The people of La Paz consistently portray a peaceful image of their community and compare themselves to other nearby residents, who are believed to be more aggressive. For example, during one of my first visits to La Paz, two villagers commented, "They fight a lot over there [in San Andrés, where I was living], but not us here in La Paz." Another person referred to La Pazians as peaceful or pacifists (*pacíficos*) by nature (Fry 1994:140). Drawing contrasts between themselves and residents of other nearby communities, such as San Andrés, is one way people in La Paz reinforce the importance of treating other people with respect.

La Pazians value domestic tranquillity and mutual respect between spouses. Jealousy is discouraged, and La Pazians do not consider themselves to be particularly jealous. The occasional husband, usually a young man, who expresses jealousy becomes the subject of disapproving gossip. The fact that for many generations La Paz women have produced pottery for trade or sale, and thus have made substantial contributions to household incomes, may also relate to the pattern of respect between men and women in the community (see Fry 1992a for further discussion). In any case, La Paz women have higher status than do the women in certain neighboring communities (see fig. 6.1).

Enacting the Beliefs: Low Levels of Physical Violence

Parents mention the possibility of administering corporal punishment to their children, but neither O'Nell nor I ever saw a child actually being beaten. Likewise, from time to time, the topic of wife beating comes up in conversation. However, neither O'Nell nor I have ever observed any wife beating during the course of our multiple fieldtrips to La Paz (Fry 1992a; O'Nell 1969). O'Nell writes:

> Commonly expectations are such that few men in a state of sobriety would feel comfortable in beating their wives frequently for alleged disobedience and misbehavior. For a wife to be so recalcitrant as to require such frequent punishment would lower her husband's position as one worthy of respect, reducing his esteem (and effectiveness) within the community. Furthermore, if all blame could be placed upon the wife, a man would be regarded as a fool not to divorce her. (O'Nell 1969:229)

La Pazians told me of situations in which wife beating might be expected but in actuality had *not* taken place. For example, in a case of infidelity that resulted in the birth of an illegitimate child while the husband was working in another city, the husband simply wept and demanded that his wife give the infant up for adoption in a neighboring town. In a similar case, after some arguing between the couple, the mother-in-law said to the young husband, "You both are young. Why didn't you come after six months or a year to visit your wife? . . . Probably you have a woman there. That's why you didn't come to visit your wife." Upon hearing this appeal, the husband ceased complaining, and that was the end of the matter. The teller of this story then drew a conclusion about the nature of men in the community, remarking, "Here in La Paz, they are calm—the men."

In La Paz, no instances of rape, attempted rape, or concern about rape perpetrated *by La Paz men* ever came to my attention. I was told, however, that a man from San Andrés attempted and perhaps succeeded in raping a woman from La Paz who had gone by herself to the fields close to the intercommunity boundary.

The concern for avoiding physical conflict is exemplified by the response of a thirty-two-year-old man from La Paz, who, when asked how he would respond if another person tried to harm him, gave me a multifaceted answer that included ignoring the other person, defending himself, fleeing, or responding verbally: "If it is not physical harm, just forget it. If the person tries to fight physically, then, one is able to defend oneself. . . . Or if one wants to avoid fighting, then run away and get away from the person. But, for example, if he is only saying infuriating things, then, say back what you want, but without stooping to his level."

Several points can be made about the infrequent physical fighting that does occur in La Paz. First, it tends to involve only men. Women were never observed fighting, although when I raised the issue with female informants, they did not treat the idea as a total absurdity. Second, it is highly likely that one or both persons who become physically aggressive have been drinking alcohol. Alcohol consumption preceded each of the three physical altercations I observed personally. A La Paz woman once expressed it simply: "They fight when they get drunk." Third, a rapid retreat by at least one participant is typical. In one instance, the recipient of two punches simply turned and ran away. In another case, I recorded in fieldnotes how two twenty-year-olds, after hours of celebrating at a wedding, "started fighting a little. One kicked the other very hard in the butt. The recipient of the kick (he was retreating when it was received) continued to retreat, thus ending the physical encounter." In the third fight witnessed, other men present attempted to break up the confrontation verbally and physically. Thus, the overall picture that emerges about physical aggression in La Paz is that it does occur, but not very often, and it usually ends quickly.

The perspective on La Paz is widened if we consider the rather different pattern of life in nearby San Andrés. The homicide rate calculated from district archive data is more than *five times higher* in San Andrés than in La Paz. The assault rate is also substantially higher. In San Andrés, I personally witnessed three instances of wife beating, repeated occurrences of children being physically punished, numerous fights between men—usually after they had been drinking alcohol—and several physical altercations between women (Fry 1990, 1992a, 1992b, 1993, 1994, forthcoming). Systematic observations of samples of three-to-eight-year-old children from the two communities also revealed that children from La Paz engaged in significantly less aggression and play aggression than did their age-mates from San Andrés (Fry 1988, 1992a). These findings are summarized in table 6.1.

Table 6.1. Peace-Related Differences Between San Andrés and La Paz

FEATURE	SAN ANDRÉS	LA PAZ
Respect	A valued ideal	A *highly* valued ideal
Physical fights	Periodic	Uncommon
Horseplay & swearing	Common	Rare
Jealousy	Pervasive	Rare
Wife-beatings	Observed	Never observed
Women	Subordinate to men	Nearly equal to men
Pottery-making or similar activity by women	No	Yes
Community image	Ambivalent	Pacifistic
Homicide rate	18.1 per 100,000	3.4 per 100,000
Favored response to child misconduct	Physical punishment	Positive verbal approach
Child-beatings	Periodically observed	Never observed
Children's play aggression	6.90 episodes per hour	3.71 episodes per hour
Children's aggression	0.78 episodes per hour	0.39 episodes per hour
Change in rate of children's aggression with age	Increases	Decreases
Obedience of children	Often *dis*obedient	Usually obedient

Note: See Fry 1988, 1992a, and 1994 for further data and discussion.

Conflict Management: Multiple Paths to Peace

Multiple factors contribute to the low level of physical aggression in the community. First, children are socialized into a belief system that emphasizes respect, responsibility, and cooperation, and which is largely incompatible with physical aggression. Second, a series of psychosocial mechanisms—also learned in the course of growing up in the community—favor avoidance and toleration over direct confrontation and self-redress. Third, community authorities provide a forum for the expression of grievances and the resolution of disputes without violence.

Socialization

In a large cross-cultural study, Ross (1993:99) found that warm, affectionate socialization techniques correlate with low levels of conflict within societies. In contrast, harsh treatment of children correlates with higher levels of conflict. The data from La Paz are in correspondence with this cross-cultural pattern. In La Paz, relations between parents and their children typically are affectionate. Socialization is rarely harsh.

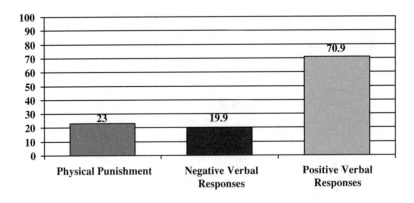

Figure 6.2. Disciplinary approaches advocated by parents in La Paz for various types of child misconduct such as lying, fighting, stealing, being disobedient, and not doing assigned chores based on an analysis of the verbs used by respondents. Physical Punishment verbs included to hit, punish physically, and strike with a stick. Negative Verbal Responses included to scold, compel, or threaten. Positive Verbal Responses included to say or tell, correct with words, educate, teach, show, talk to, and explain. Clearly, La Paz parents strongly favored Positive Verbal Responses over other approaches. Since the three categories of response are not mutually exclusive, the column percentages sum to over 100 percent. See Fry (1993) for additional details and discussion.

Correspondingly, La Paz parents do *not* favor the physical punishment of children (Fry 1993). As shown in fig. 6.2, a sample of La Paz fathers strongly favored positive verbal approaches to child misconduct over other approaches. Respondents advocated talking, telling, educating, showing, and teaching—all positively oriented nonphysical responses—more often than either corporal punishment or negative verbal responses such as scolding or lecturing. As one La Pazian expressed, "One must explain to the child with love, with patience, so that little by little the child understands you."

Psychologists Guerra, Eron, Huesmann, Tolan, and van Acker (1997:202) write:

> The specific conditions that have been shown empirically to be most conducive to the learning and maintenance of aggression are those in which the child is reinforced for his or her aggression, . . . is provided many opportunities to observe aggression, . . . is given few opportunities to develop positive affective social bonds with others, . . . and is the object of aggression.

Applying this empirically derived, four-part generalization to La Paz, I note that children are *not* rewarded for engaging in aggression; see *few* examples of physical aggression performed by their elders; have *ample opportunities* to develop affectionate bonds with their parents, grandparents, siblings, and others; and are *rarely* the recipients of aggression. It is as if La Paz parents have studied the psychological literature on how to prevent children from becoming aggressive.

As part of their socialization, La Paz children gradually internalize the beliefs, values, and attitudes that are regularly shared and expressed within their community learning environment. La Paz parents realize that they have an important role to fulfill in teaching their children how to respect other persons. One father stated: "That is the obligation of a father or a mother, to show very well to their children how to respect. That is the primary commandment that exists." Another man explained, "It is very important to teach respect—for the parents to show [the child] to have respect, because life goes better with respect for everyone else." Finally, an interviewee voiced his formula for preventing and correcting misconduct among children: "Teach them . . . so that they have respect. Educate them!"

In sum, socialization contributes to the maintenance of peace in La Paz as each new generation of children comes to imitate and adopt the key values and modes of interaction expressed, modeled, and appreciated by their parents. Children increasingly engage in behaviors that are accepted, expected, and rewarded by members of their community (Fry 1994). Specifically, the young La Pazians are rewarded for respectful, nonviolent behavior—the predominant type of interaction they have a chance to observe—and gradually internalize associated socially approved beliefs and behaviors. They also come to see their community as a tranquil, safe place to live.

Psychocultural Mechanisms That Prevent and Reduce Aggression

In other writings, O'Nell (1979, 1981, 1989) and I (Fry 1994, forthcoming) have elaborated on how certain processes—such as avoidance, denial, prevention of escalation, and prevention of envy—and psychocultural dynamics—such as fear of illness and fear of witchcraft—help to limit aggression in La Paz. Such processes and psychocultural mechanisms are listed in fig. 6.3.

Avoidance entails curtailing or ceasing interaction with another person and is a common approach to conflict in La Paz. In illustration, O'Nell (1981:360) recounts an occurrence shortly after his initial arrival in La Paz wherein an inebriated man began to make derogatory remarks to him at a community celebration. "But in order not to appear offensive myself, I made no effort to move. Also, . . . I did not want to appear as though I could be easily intimidated" (O'Nell 1981:360). However, a husband and wife from La Paz realized that avoidance on O'Nell's part would be wise and invited

Denial of anger
Denial that a dispute or problem even exists
Avoidance of conflict situations
Avoidance between disputants
Avoidance of angry, intoxicated persons
Beliefs that retreating from aggression is sensible, not cowardly
Internalization of key values such as *respect*, responsibility, and cooperation
Mutual respect between women and men
Relative equality between women and men
Beliefs that La Paz is a peaceful place (a community "self-image" as peaceful)
Concern about witchcraft
Concern about evoking-envy
Beliefs that anger, prolonged hostility, and aggression can cause illnesses
Attitudes that favor positive verbal approaches to child discipline
Attitudes that discourage the feeling and expression of jealousy

---

Figure 6.3. Psycho-cultural factors that likely contribute to conflict management in La Paz. The people of La Paz internalize a constellation of cultural values, attitudes and beliefs that help discourage aggression or that are incompatible with expressing aggression. See the chapter text for discussion (and also Fry 1994).

him to move over to where they were standing. A few minutes later, the intoxicated man had transferred his anger to another villager, who was also inebriated, hitting his new adversary with a piece of sugarcane. The people of La Paz view retreating in the face of potential or actual aggression as prudent, not cowardly.

Denial is another common approach to conflict. Once when I tried to engage one of my field assistants in a discussion, with the goal of resolving a work-related problem we were having, to my amazement, he repeatedly insisted that we had no problem (Fry forthcoming). At first I was very frustrated with his unwillingness to discuss the issue, but later I realized that his reluctance provided an important lesson about La Pazian approaches to conflict: If possible, problems should be denied and ignored. People from La Paz are also likely to deny that aggression stems from any feelings of hostility. The typical pattern is to blame acts of aggression on drunkenness or illness (O'Nell 1981, 1989:122–24).

In two of the three instances of physical aggression that I witnessed in La Paz, one of the participants retreated from the interaction. Retreating prevents the escalation of aggression. Escalation prevention also occurs when one party simply abandons the pursuit of a grievance (see Fry 1994).

The following example illustrates each of these forgoing psychocultural mechanisms. One night, when an angry intoxicated man came looking for one of his neighbors, the neighbor *avoided* the inebriated fellow by remaining in his house with the lights out and the door closed. The next day, the drunk of the night before *denied* that he had felt any hostility toward his neighbor on the previous night. His intoxicated condition made his denial more plausible than if he had been sober. Finally, in illustration of *escalation prevention*, both parties simply let the matter drop. In fact, the two men, to the best of my knowledge, did not talk about the event at all. Instead, women of the two families discussed the circumstances of the night before with some animosity but then let their anger fade (Fry 1994:141).

The people of La Paz are aware that others might become envious of them and believe that this is not good. A childless couple might become envious of other people's children, for instance, or persons with meager landholdings may become envious of neighbors with more land. In order to conduct a comparison of La Paz and San Andrés, it was necessary to set up residences in both places. My landlord in San Andrés, José, showed no concern whatsoever that I also rented a house in La Paz. By contrast, my landlord in La Paz, Marco, expressed concern about José becoming envious of him or harboring hard feelings. He insisted that I set up a meeting, because "it was good to avoid envy." Marco very seriously explained to José that I was living in both communities because my study required it—*not* due to the wishes of any La Paz person or persons. (It seemed to me that an implication of Marco's speech was: "If you are angry, José, then blame the anthropologist, not me.") "We must be in accord with each other," explained Marco. It seemed clear that José from San Andrés found this meeting a bit odd. He just listened to Marco's little speech and nodded a few times in agreement. I think Marco hoped for a reciprocal assurance of good will, but no reassuring response was forthcoming from José.

People of La Paz believe that witnessing or experiencing aggression can be frightening. In turn, fright can make a person seriously ill with a malady called fright sickness (*susto*). Beliefs that violence can cause susto in oneself or others provide another psychocultural check on aggression.

La Pazians also believe that certain folk illnesses—*coraje* and *bilis* for instance—can cause anger or aggression (O'Nell 1981, 1989). O'Nell (1989:123) explains that an afflicted person's internal organs are believed to malfunction, thus causing behavior beyond the individual's control. Consequently, the person is viewed "as a patient suffering an illness, not as a culprit meriting punishment" (O'Nell 1989:123). The key point is that by interpreting anger and aggression as resulting from an illness, La Pazians deny the existence of hostility. The "patient" can undergo a folk cure and resume social relations, as those concerned attribute the prior expressions of anger or outbursts of aggression to the person's illness rather than to malevolent intent.

Fear of witchcraft is also a factor to consider in the La Paz conflict management scheme. Other persons are believed to resort to witchcraft out of envy, or as a way to seek revenge for real or imagined misdeeds. Therefore, attacking someone physically might provoke the victim to retaliate by supernatural means. That witchcraft is taken very seriously in La Paz became apparent to my ex-wife and me after she became sick to her stomach while we where out and about the town. Upon returning to our rented house in Marco's compound, the women of the household observed with alarm that Kathy had not been wearing any earrings. The women explained that one of the two witches in town probably had cast an evil spell. The magic had entered Kathy's body through her pierced ears, which had been lacking the protection provided by wearing earrings, thus making her suddenly ill. The curer (*curandera*) arrived and proceeded to counteract the witch's spell by rolling raw chicken eggs on Kathy's stomach and massaging her abdomen forcefully. When presented with the next stage of the cure, drinking raw eggs, Kathy insisted that she was feeling much better already and that consuming the egg cocktail was unnecessary.

As Selby (1974) discusses, Zapotecs tend not to view their own relatives as witches. Witches are distant persons. Therefore, there is rarely absolute agreement in a small community as to who might be a witch. Conceivably, anyone outside a given person's immediate circle of relatives might be capable of witchcraft. Consequently, it is sensible to avoid harming others, creating envy, or prolonging disputes (Fry 1994). Handling conflict in ways that avoid creating hostility is not only in accordance with the positive ideals of respect, responsibility, and cooperation, but is also simultaneously pragmatic in terms of preventing the ever-present negative possibilities of envy, illness, and retaliation through witchcraft.

The Community Authorities

The agente and the sindico are available on an almost daily basis to listen to grievances and, when they deem it appropriate, to make judicial rulings. They can levy fines, order a person into the local jail cell, or refer the case to district or state authorities. The majority of disputes are minor matters and are dealt with effectively by the local authorities. In many cases, the authorities simply lend sympathetic ears to plaintiffs and never even summon the alleged defendants. For example, "A fairly common type of case is that of a mother (usually a widow) complaining that her son drinks too much with all that implies. Less commonly, a father levels a complaint against a young man whose attentions toward his daughter he wants to discourage" (O'Nell

1981:357). Being able to "blow off steam" in front of the agente, sindico, and other authorities seems to satisfy many such plaintiffs.

Getting into a drunken brawl is considered "disturbing the peace" and may land one or both antagonists in the local jail for a few hours. Word spreads through the village to an incarcerated person's family that he has been put in jail for "disturbing the peace." One woman explained how, "Later the man's wife goes to get him out, or perhaps the sons [go]. They must go to the municipal building and bring back their father." Sometimes the authorities order the family to pay a fine. In a taped interview, the same La Paz woman explicitly noted how physical aggression and respect are incompatible, saying, "A man no longer has respect. Therefore, he went to fight with others. And later they put him in the jail."

As an ideal, and also largely as a practice, the people of La Paz respect their authorities. There is a strong feeling that if a dispute cannot be avoided or tolerated, then the matter should be referred to the local authorities for resolution. O'Nell (1981) asked a sample of twenty-one men from La Paz what would justify the use of aggression. A majority, 57 percent, said that aggression could be justified as defense of one's person or property. Most other responses seemed to offer *explanations* for aggression, rather than *justifications* for aggression, mentioning drunkenness, jealousy, or other "nebulous circumstances." Ten percent of the men said there was no justification for aggression. O'Nell then asked a follow-up question about what one should do if harmed by another person. Twenty men offered unambiguous responses. The vast majority, 70 percent of the sample, said that they would take the matter to the local authorities; by contrast, only 10 percent said they would attempt to deal with the situation on their own. An additional 10 percent said they would refer the matter to other persons in the family. And the final 10 percent also said they would simply do nothing. These findings suggest that seeking the intervention of other persons, usually the local authorities, is felt to be the best way to handle a harmful attack in La Paz.

Nader (1969, 1990) has studied court procedures among the Sierra Zapotec in a more mountainous region of Oaxaca. Her conclusion, that a central goal of legal procedure among the Sierra Zapotec is to restore personal relations to equilibrium, also seems applicable to La Paz. The local authorities often attribute some blame to both parties appearing before them. Rulings often involve admonitions as to the correct way to behave. As in the Zapotec court studied by Nader (1964, 1969, 1990), adjudication is only one of several dispute settlement processes that take place in the courtroom. The La Paz agente may alternate between acting as a judge—making rulings and imposing sentences—and fulfilling the role of a therapist or family counselor as he listens sympathetically to grievances, offers personal

advice, or reminds individuals of appropriate social roles and expected behavior (see Nader 1969). Again, the goal seems to be to restore relationships
to normalcy rather than to declare one party the winner and the other the
loser. Black (1993) refers to this style of conflict management as *conciliatory*.

Summary and Conclusions

La Paz offers several insights about the construction and maintenance of
peace. Multiple interacting variables are involved. Beliefs, values, and attitudes that counter violence are important. On the one hand, the positive
value that La Pazians place on respect, responsibility, and cooperation is
incompatible with physical aggression. On the other hand, beliefs that expressing anger and aggression might result in illness or that aggressive acts
might be paid back through witchcraft constitute a different type of belief-
oriented disincentive toward aggression.

In their overall approach to dealing with conflict, the people of La Paz
favor avoidance, toleration, and referral to third-party authorities over direct
confrontation or self-redress. A range of complementary psychocultural
mechanisms are congruent with the La Pazian emphasis on avoidance and
toleration. People simply avoid problematic situations; for example, they
will leave the proximity of an angry drunk. Individuals also refrain from
the open expression of anger or jealousy, except perhaps while under the
influence of alcohol. The very existence of conflict is sometimes denied.
Steps are taken to prevent arousing the envy of others. If physically attacked,
a common response is to retreat rather than to fight back.

All of these dimensions of conflict management are part of the learning environment of La Paz children, who internalize the pacifistic beliefs of
their elders. Furthermore, given the low level of physical aggression in La Paz,
children are not provided many aggressive models to imitate, and given the
sparse use of corporal punishment, children are infrequently the recipients
of physical punishment. On the contrary, children enjoy regular affection
from their parents and other adults. As they mature, they learn the key values of respect, responsibility, and cooperation and realize that aggression
is incompatible with these social ideals. They also learn a constellation of
beliefs from their elders to the effect that conflict and aggression can lead to
envy, witchcraft, and illness. Children observe how their parents typically
deal with conflict: for instance, denying that a problem even exists, letting
disputes drop, physically removing themselves from risky situations, and referring matters to local authorities for resolution. As La Paz children become
adults, they take on the nonviolent conflict management paths typically utilized by others in their community.

Study Questions

1. What explanation comes to mind to account for the finding that three-to-eight-year-old children in La Paz engage in significantly less aggression and play aggression than do children of the same age in San Andrés?
2. What are the three broad types of conflict management techniques that Fry sees operating in La Paz?
3. What is the *conciliatory* style of conflict management? How is this approach practiced within the La Paz courtroom?
4. How does the La Paz court differ from courts in your society? In which setting is there more likely to be a clear *winner* and a clear *loser* of a case?

Resolving Conflict Within the Law: The Mardu Aborigines of Australia

ROBERT TONKINSON

Conflict is very much a part of Mardu society. As Robert Tonkinson shows, the Mardu can be verbally aggressive. Yet for the Mardu, consensual and peaceful outcomes to their conflicts are imperative to their long-term survival. Like the Hopi, they seek ways to counter potential violence that may arise in their conflicts. Tonkinson suggests that social organization and religion are the two pillars of their peaceful society. The Mardu inflict punishments on wrongdoers. Is it really violence (violation of the victim) if the "victim" accepts the punishment? Is the use of punishment an attribute of the overall peacefulness of the Mardu, or does it weaken their ideal to refrain from becoming aggressive? Of equal interest are the ways that the Mardu deal with potential conflicts with strangers. A stranger always represents an unknown quantity. Other societies discussed in this book use the fear of witchcraft and other supernatural beliefs to instill caution in dealing with strangers. The Mardu utilize the establishment of kinship ties with an outsider. This process is echoed in societies where interaction with strangers is common. One often finds a ritual wherein the two parties try to establish a kind of kinship tie—for example, fellow Freemason, "old school tie," common sporting interest, locality of origin, and so on—before they begin to deal with any conflict.

—GK

This account of conflict management among the Mardu is focused on their "traditional" society; in fact, their first contacts with Europeans occurred decades ago, and the last groups to abandon their nomadic hunting-gathering lifestyle did so in the 1960s. Much has changed since the Mardu began to leave their desert homelands in the early decades of the twentieth century and settle on cattle ranches and mission settlements. Today, many live back in these homelands in their own, self-managed communities. I witnessed the processes described in this account during anthropological fieldwork in a community called Jigalong beginning in 1963.

By the early 1970s, alcohol was more readily available to the Mardu, who had begun to acquire motor vehicles. It had the same devastating effect on their community life as elsewhere in Aboriginal Australia, where it remains the single most serious problem confronting Indigenous Australians—and, of course, many members of the dominant society (Tonkinson 1988a). Because no equivalent substance existed in the traditional society, no coping mechanisms had evolved to deal specifically with inebriation. Early on, especially, uncontrolled conflict involving drunken people led to a big escalation in levels of injury and death among the Mardu. Many people were killed in alcohol-related vehicle accidents and because of a failure to apply existing social control mechanisms that govern conflict to drunken people. The loss by drunks of their self-control was so deeply embarrassing—to be without shame is to be not human—that people would flee rather than confront disruptive inebriates. Aboriginal communities everywhere have resorted to a variety of different strategies aimed at minimizing the impact of alcohol, and at Jigalong, fatality levels appear to have fallen.

Today, the Mardu live in several self-managing communities, which have electricity, television, telephones, faxes, supermarkets, workshops, Western-style housing, and so on (Tonkinson 1974). These settlements are structured along Western-oriented administrative lines. They are controlled by elected Aboriginal councils, who are increasingly preoccupied with bureaucratic dealings with the outside world. Assistance is provided by non-Aboriginal staff in such positions as project officer, adviser, mechanic, or bookkeeper, and with government employees such as nurses and schoolteachers also resident. However, because the Mardu wear Western clothes, it is difficult for the casual observer to detect that important cultural continuities remain, continuities other than hearing people speak in their own language. Kinship remains the blueprint governing most social interaction, and the Mardu still appear to subscribe firmly to the truth and reality of the body of knowledge, activities, and prescriptions known as the Dreaming, or "the Law" as they call it in English (see below). For adults, certainly, it structures much of their worldview, and they continue to rate their religious life, with its strong focus on male initiation, as of greater cultural importance than what they term "whitefella business," which increasingly demands their attention. So, despite my focus on an imagined "precontact" Mardu society, the reader should keep in mind that many of the social control processes described below remain an important part of contemporary community life.

Are All Hunter-Gatherer People by Definition "Peaceful"?

In the anthropological scheme of things, the human mode of adaptation we label *hunting and gathering* or *foraging* describes small-scale, familistic societies with a way of life that with very few exceptions (such as the Pacific Northwest coast Indians of North America) involves low population densities and small, labile, usually highly mobile groups or *bands* of closely related people whose patterns of movement are dictated by both resource availability and a range of cultural factors. In small groups of very closely related people, serious conflict is a grave threat to orderly life that must be avoided or minimized, so most hunter-gatherer cultures place heavy emphasis on cooperation and interdependence. One virtue of nomadism is that it facilitates an effective strategy for conflict reduction and avoidance: A person who disturbs the peace can leave the group and join another, until tensions have eased and a peaceful return is judged possible. Hunter-gatherer societies typically lack centralized institutions for political control, such as chiefs, a judiciary, specialist peacekeepers, or other formal bodies that could deal with litigation and render judgments binding on all parties. They must therefore rely heavily on individual self-regulation, achieved largely through a combination of things, such as socialization processes that entail the internalization of inhibiting emotions, and the effective inculcation of values that reward amity and conformity while minimizing antisocial tendencies. Of course, individuals are allowed some variation from the norms of the society, but deviation, which constitutes a more serious threat to order, must be punished. This is achieved through a variety of informal (gossip, ridicule) and formal sanctions that are invoked to keep people in line. Hunter-gatherer societies, with their normally scattered bands and low population densities, are clearly not built for war making, since their members lack the organizing means, motivations, technology, and support apparatus to either wage protracted battles or engage in sustained feuding. Fighting over land and other property, a major source of much conflict in other kinds of society, is very rare, and cherished values and behaviors exist that stress the virtues of mutuality over competition and conflict. This mode of adaptation has served humanity very well for most of its history. Despite its limitations in terms of material living standards, the interdependence of men's and women's economic activities made for a generally harmonious, and—in terms of leisure time and the ability to satisfy wants—affluent society (Sahlins 1972).

There are, however, some anthropological critics whose view of human nature tends more toward Hobbes than Rousseau, which leads them to doubt that any society, no matter how low its levels of aggression, could accurately be characterized as "peaceful." They blame anthropologists' cultural relativism and their alleged desire to play down negative aspects of the societies they study, which leads these critics to claim that they pay insufficient attention to maladaptive behaviors (cf. Edgerton 1992, 1999). There is no doubt some truth in these claims, but, significantly for the argument just made in favor of a positive view of the hunting-gathering adaptation, it is no coincidence that the examples they cite in support of their contentions about maladaptations are drawn predominantly from settled societies.

The Australian Case

Prior to the European settler invasion, which dates from 1788, the entire continent was inhabited exclusively by hunter-gatherers, who shared a great deal in common economically, socially, and culturally (see Berndt and Berndt 1988). Nonetheless, there were important regional cultural variations (most obviously in material technologies) and some complexities of social forms and property relations that render the Aborigines somewhat anomalous in the hunter-gatherer literature (Tonkinson 1988b, 1991; see also Woodburn 1982). Many Australianist scholars would query the appropriateness of labeling Aboriginal societies as peaceful, since in some parts of the continent, serious conflict seems to have been a fairly common occurrence, both among males and, within families, against wives (see Malinowski 1913; Sutton 2001). For example, according to W. Lloyd Warner (1937), who did fieldwork among the Murngin of northeast Arnhem Land (a fertile area on the central north coast) in the 1920s, interclan feuding was one of the most important social activities, and significant numbers of men were killed while engaging in it. However, ecologically based explanations, which attempt to equate rich resources and boundary maintenance emphases with a propensity to conflict and boundary closure, would not work, since there are resource-rich regions, such as eastern Cape York, that are characterized by low levels of intergroup conflict (Chase 1984).

In the Western Desert, however, there *is* an important underlying ecological factor: the unreliability of rainfall and the irregularity of its spread in a region having no permanent waters. When considered together with a very high degree of regional social and cultural homogeneity, this climatological factor powerfully influences social outcomes favoring the dominance of cooperation at both intra- and intergroup levels. It necessitates a strong cultural stress on the permeability of boundaries and the maintenance of open and peaceful movement and intergroup communication within a huge area of desert. In these circumstances, to permit intergroup conflict or feuding to harden social and territorial boundaries would be literally suicidal, since no group can expect the existing water and food resources of its territory to tide it over until the next rains; peaceful intergroup relations are imperative for long-term survival (Tonkinson 1988c). It is not surprising, then, that the Mardu have no word for either "feud" or "warfare," and there is no evidence for the kinds of longstanding intergroup animosity one associates with feuding. The situation is one of small and scattered highly mobile groups moving freely within large territories rather than highly localized, solitary corporate groups contesting resources and maintaining boundaries.

Throughout Australia, social organization and religion traditionally formed the twin pillars of society. Aborigines lived their entire lives within a universe of kin, and the kinship system provided the fundamental blueprint for structuring interpersonal behavior. The continuum of conventional kin behaviors ranges from complete avoidance to compulsory joking and physical horseplay, with intermediate variations from severely restrained to raunchy and uninhibited. For every individual, then, there are certain categories of kin with whom severe restraint is observed and conflict is normally forbidden. In conflict management, as in all other aspects of society, it is thus impossible to adequately understand the dynamics of what follows during disputes without a firm grasp of the structures of kinship and concomitant system of obligations and responsibilities that define every kinship status. Once the kin relationships among the protagonists and the third parties who become participants in the event are known, the actions of most adults most (but not all) of the time are generally predictable and therefore explicable. Depending on specific kinship links to the combatants, there are those who should chastise, who restrain, who substitute for and defend, who inflame, who appeal to reason and calm, and so on. For example, if an enraged man persists in attempting violence and refuses to calm down, drastic action may be called for: A man related as *initiator* or a female *wife's mother* may enter the fray to confront and even touch him. This act, normally unthinkable because people so related practice avoidance, should so shame the man that he comes to his senses and calms down immediately. In the heat of passion, people do sometimes ignore kinship norms, in which case predicting their likely behavior will be based more on knowledge of their personalities and of how they react under aggravation and stress.

It should be noted here that, although Mardu children are constantly reminded of their kin relationships to all people with whom they come into contact, and about correct kin-based behaviors appropriate to every such relationship, they do not have to obey these strictures. They are rarely chastised and almost never physically punished by parents or other adults, and they rarely fight with one another. Sometimes, however, they can be seen, armed with toy spears and boomerangs, play-acting adult confrontations by hurling these missiles at one another. Without ever being commanded to do so, in their early teens, they will begin to experience intense feelings of self-consciousness and shame/embarrassment over their interaction with adults, prompting them to begin conforming to the behavioral dictates of the kinship system (see Tonkinson 1987).

In addition to a strong grasp of how kinship works, the observer needs to possess a thorough working knowledge of the Aboriginal worldview, which is profoundly spiritual. It is centered on a key cultural symbol, now commonly called the Dreaming, which both underpins and permeates the entire cultural fabric (cf. Tonkinson 1991: 19–25). To be human is to "follow the Dreaming," that is, to reproduce forms laid down in the beginning of time by the great ancestral creative beings. These superhuman powers not only left behind the first humans, but also gave them their language, culture, and the rules for living ("the Law"), which was to be obeyed unquestioningly lest society's continuance be threatened. In the volatile atmosphere of conflict among the Mardu, when kinship demands that many people become involved, spectators will sometimes loudly warn angry combatants to act *yulubirdingga,* "within the Law."

In traditional Aboriginal societies, there were crimes against the Law that carried severe penalties, up to and including being put to death. Elopement was not uncommon, but if the fleeing couple were, in kinship terms, wrong for each other and their union was regarded as incestuous, they could both expect grievous bodily harm or death at the hands of the eloping woman's husband and his kin. For Mardu men, for example, the theft of sacred objects was a capital offense, as was, for women, trespass (unwitting or not) into men's secret-sacred territory and/or the witnessing of men's secret-sacred activities or paraphernalia. Such grave offenses were said to be very uncommon, however.

The Individual in Mardu Society

If perfect socialization were possible, the ideal Mardu adult would, above all, be *gundawindi,* "having, knowing shame": what it means to be human and sensitive to others. He or she would be agreeable, unassuming, self-effacing, unselfish, and ever ready to share with kin and fulfill ritual and kinship obligations without complaint rather than being egotistical or boastful to excess. An active provider as parent, child of aged parents, and in-law, he or she would show strong compassion for others and respect for their individuality and integrity. The ideal person would also be deeply attached both to family and to homeland and a full and unquestioning participant in all aspects of the religious life. Individual status in Mardu society is very much a function of kinship, though there are both male and female ritual hierarchies that are very important markers of an adult's religious roles and responsibilities.

The measure of a person is divorced from material possessions or individual creativity; rather it has much to do with conformity to the dictates of the Law, particularly the fulfilling of kinship obligations in the style suggested by these ideal behaviors.

Despite marked inequalities in certain aspects of society (men enjoy stronger rights than women, for example, who remain permanently excluded from men's secret-sacred religious lore), the dominant ethos in everyday mundane life is strongly egalitarian in tone, and there is little tolerance for boastful or pushy people. The older vigorous man who successfully manages four wives, and/or whose religious knowledge is great, may be admired, but these are achieved statuses and have little effect on his everyday dealings with others. Mardu are typically gregarious, love animated discussion and repartee, and are very alert to what transpires in their social, natural, and spiritual surroundings. Most noticeable is their keen sense of humor and readiness to joke about themselves and others alike.

As in all societies, certain emotions and reactions if not kept under control are considered likely to lead people into trouble: active dislike, jealousy, covetousness, envy, promiscuity, malicious gossip and tale-carrying. However, there are socially acceptable ways of expressing emotion. For example, *yurndiri*, "aggressive sulking" is aimed at securing the attention of others so that one's grievances can be elicited, thus saving one the great embarrassment of broaching the matter first, among a people who find public oratory a painful ordeal. Appropriate verbal style in such situations is a quiet, self-effacing, and rather apologetic delivery, such that others will utter reassurances and words of encouragement. People are always heard out, and every effort is made to obtain consensus when decisions are being made at these ad hoc gatherings. However, what "consensus" really means is that those who have been arguing against the majority refrain from raising their objections publicly, so the matter may not be finally resolved at this point.

The marked reluctance of Mardu to shame themselves by public oratory probably explains why a popular time to debate and air disputes among band members is when people have retired to their family hearths after the evening meal. Under the secure cover of darkness, apart from the glow of campfires, each participant shouts from his or her camp, and these spirited exchanges can go on for hours. People seem to be less inhibited in the dark and more willing to be outspoken. Also, if tempers fray, it is most unlikely that anyone will throw weapons. In a society whose members are scattered in small groups most of the time, most public oratory is confined to such night sessions. Similarly, in terms of conflict minimization, it is against the Law of the Dreaming to engage in either verbal or physical conflict anywhere near ritual activities, and such behavior is forbidden outright in men's secret-sacred areas. This is partly because of the risk that such disruption will cause people emotional upset and ruin the mood of the occasion, but, more seriously, it will anger the spiritual powers whose cooperation is being enjoined through ritual performance, thus causing the rituals to fail in their objectives.

Managing Interpersonal Conflict

Despite the society's ideals, conflict is part of the Mardu social fabric, and physical violence sometimes occurs, because the society has not yet been invented wherein socialization processes produce total and continuous social conformity. Under normal circumstances, most Mardu adults are agreeable people of pleasant disposition. When aroused, however, they may become verbally aggressive very quickly, with much swearing and threatening behavior, creating the impression that physical violence is imminent and inevitable. This passionate arousal of emotions to a violent pitch occurs most often in anger or sorrow, and it can entail attempts at self-injury as a demonstration of anguish over the sickness or death of a relative or else the venting of anger on others. Intense anger can be engendered by seemingly minor upsets and can lead to intense confrontations. Yet such outbursts are not a defining characteristic of everyday life; what is most notable about them is how rapidly they subside and how very quickly the precipitating incidents seem to be forgotten. In the wake of such conflicts, people seem remarkably free of resentment and grudge carrying.

A ritualized conflict is expected among particular kin during certain stages of the male initiation process. For example, shortly after the sudden seizing of Janungu on the morning of his circumcision, and the initial laying of his prone body across the backs of those assembled, several members of the "mourners" moiety, related as *classificatory fathers* (that is, fathers and father's brothers) attacked the members of the other ritual category, the "activists." The mourners threw several boomerangs (all aimed to miss) and harangued the activists loudly for being in too much of a hurry to grab this initiate and for failing to consult first with all of the relevant categories of kin. No one was injured physically, but several of the accusers seemed genuinely incensed at what they regarded as the hasty action of the activist moiety.

In some cases, the person who provokes a confrontation may be held responsible by other adults who are present. In others, some nonhuman force is deemed to be at work, as when a pregnant woman is "pushed" by the spirit-child within; in still others, the knowledge that a person is commonly regarded as congenitally unstable or mad will modify people's assessment of his or her culpability. Typically, though, Law breakers must take full responsibility for their transgressions.

In the case of conflicts between males, the unstated aim of the many conventions surrounding such disputes is for them to be aired verbally rather than physically, allowing the protagonists to broadcast their grievances and accusations publicly and with maximum menace, thus achieving satisfaction from the drama of confrontation itself. The atmosphere is heavy with tension as the opponents draw closer to each other, shout louder, and shake their weapons. The pronounced ritualization of such conflicts is evidenced by the ability of both observer and actors on many occasions to predict the sequence of events. Once the combatants are face to face, both male and female kin will intercede to separate the fighters and prevent them from launching weapons, though women often play a more prominent role in physically restraining men, by dislodging spears from spear throwers, snatching and throwing away boomerangs and clubs, and clinging firmly onto the men. On the other hand, there will be some women and men whose kin relationship to one of the combatants directs them to an active encouragement of violence in certain disputes, especially when the guilt of one party is not in question.

Generally, though, should violence erupt, the thrust of events is toward its rapid extinguishment and the restoration of peace. If the rift has been serious (for example, a spear fight between two full brothers), the pair may be required to engage in a ritualized exchange of secret-sacred objects, after which further conflict is unthinkable. If one man is judged by the group to be clearly in the wrong, he must carve the object that is cut and shaped by the offended party. When a dispute arises from an obvious or admitted offense, the wronged person obtains satisfaction from the exposure of the offense to public notice and the punishment and group censure of the offender. In fact, very few transgressions can remain private in this society, where the ground can be read like a book and gossip is a common and acceptable practice. Although a Law breaker may flee from his group after wrongdoing, this solution is only temporary, and eventually he will have to face his accusers and accept the punishment meted out to him. Nonetheless, a prudent withdrawal may increase the chances that the ultimate clash will be less physical than it would otherwise have been.

Perhaps the fear of sorcery or of revenge expeditions prompts most Mardu to stay and confront the problem. People do not live in permanent fear of either of these institutions in desert society as long as they obey the Law; however, there are occasions when they may be alerted by signs or omens to the possible presence of killers in the vicinity, and the community's diviner-curers are on high alert to repel the threat magically.

Men judged to be guilty by their own local group will typically show their acceptance of this informal verdict by stepping forward into a public space to await their punishment, armed with only a single defensive weapon, a shield. Sometimes, the expiatory encounter will involve a group of people whose kin relationships to the offender designate them as punishing agents. They stand in a group at a distance and throw spears at the upper body of the offender, who parries them with his shield, until he is injured. A more common procedure, though, is that the offender offers himself submissively, head bowed and thigh held motionless, ready to receive the initial clubbing and jabs from stabbing spears carefully directed to avoid arteries. Shortly thereafter, some of his "brothers" and "grandfathers" will surround him to protect him from overzealous punishers. The multiple spear-wound scars, which every mature Mardu man and woman carries somewhat proudly as testaments to youthful rebellion, indicate the popularity of this form of punishment. This method is favored because the jabbing spear can be guided accurately to its target, whereas thrown missiles are far more unpredictable.

Jardi, a thirty-year-old bachelor, was frequently in trouble for persisting in affairs with "wrong" partners (those not marriageable in kinship terms), despite repeated warnings. After several public meetings in which he attempted, unsuccessfully, to justify his behavior, he armed himself with a wooden shield, and stood in an open area, inviting punishment from his eldest brother and several men who were potential husbands of the young women concerned. As they closed in, one by one, to club or wound him with stabbing spears, only his full elder sister and two other classificatory elder sisters attempted to intervene on his behalf, but they could not prevent him from receiving two spear wounds in the thigh and some severe club blows on his upper body. That Jardi picked up only a defensive weapon indicates his acceptance of guilt in the matter, as does his walking into the open to face his punishment. The punishment settled the dispute, and he ceased to pursue the women concerned.

When there is no clear offense or admission of guilt by either party to a dispute, each subsequently tends to express the conviction that he got the better of the other, or that group sentiment favored him. The purposes of social control in Mardu society are best served by a rapid and relatively bloodless defusing of tensions, which will restore a "good feeling" in the stomachs of the principals and an enduring sense of satisfaction and finality.

Within domestic groups, particularly, a quick-tempered outburst may lead to blows being struck, and sometimes women are severely beaten by their husbands. Verbal exchanges may prompt physical abuse when a woman swears at her husband and thus embarrasses him in front of other nearby families, who are certain to be paying close attention. The husband has the right to engage in such behavior, so others tend not to intervene, regardless of whether or not they judge the wife to be in the wrong. Close kin intercede to restrain a man only if he appears to be seriously injuring his wife, but women can and do arm themselves and fight back, though they should not initiate physical attacks on their husbands.

Figure 7.1. During a women's argument among the Mardu, two full sisters, both holding weapons and with arms upraised, exchange accusations while other women stand nearby, ready to intervene in the role of Friendly Peacemakers to drag them apart. Photograph by Robert Tonkinson.

Since Mardu society is polygynous, older men may have more than one wife, though more than three would be rare. Traditionally, older wives would welcome the economic contribution and assistance of younger wives, who were expected to heed their wishes; conflict among cowives was said to be uncommon. Yet when jealousy inflames passions, women may attack cowives, or more commonly, rivals for the affections of their lovers. When Mardu women fight each other, for whatever reason, the conflicts may be bloody and intense; they wield clubs or digging sticks to inflict bloody wounds to the scalp and upper body, or they use their hands and teeth as weapons. Women's fights (see fig. 7.1) within or between families are usually regarded by the local community as less serious than men's, and if short-lived, may be viewed as light entertainment by men (other than their husbands, usually). Sometimes, though, their ferocity may cause other women to intervene, and if the altercation persists, men may physically become involved if (as usually happens) their shouted warnings are ignored. Women very quickly put such altercations, even quite bloody ones, behind them.

Mala, married and in her late twenties, was camping with her father's sister Kalunu and several other women in a "single-women's camp" while their husbands were away on ritual business. After Kalunu accused Mala's six-year-old son of drinking all her tea, Mala denied it, whereupon Kalunu called her a liar. They exchanged blows before several nearby women quickly separated them. Mala accused Kalunu of fighting unfairly by using a steel crowbar and derided her for her unusual hair. This occasioned another attack with the crowbar before the pair were separated and disarmed by female relatives—but not before they had managed to exchange a few punches. Next morning the two women were seen sitting together, chatting amiably while Kalunu held Mala's infant son.

There are many fewer conventions covering female than male conflicts. The most notable is the requirement that a woman who is clearly at fault must bow her head and accept the first blow uncontested. She thus admits guilt and offers satisfaction to her opponent, regardless of who actually fares better in the club fight that ensues. Another convention dictates that clubs are the only men's weapons that women are permitted to use in fights. A young woman who commits the serious offense of having sexual intercourse deemed incestuous under the rules of classificatory kinship reckoning usually bears a much heavier burden of blame than does her male partner. Initially standing alone and unaided by senior female kin, she faces the savage attacks of women related to her lover as "mothers" and "sisters." The punishment meted out is severe and extremely humiliating but is understandable when the seriousness of such affronts to the rule of Law is considered. To behave without regard to kinship is to be like an animal, not a human, and persistence in such relationships in the face of social disapproval threatens the integrity of the social fabric itself and thus invites grievous injury or death. Casual affairs are frequent and widely tolerated, but passionate attachments that may threaten the marriage bond must be dealt with decisively.

The Context and Management of Intergroup Conflict

The fact that disputes between Western Desert groups occasionally occur suggests that strains involving the kind of local parochialism or suspicion that exaggerates differences do indeed exist in the region. Equally, though, the existence of so many dispute-minimization and -settlement measures shows how aware people are of the vital necessity to prevent the escalation or continuation of disruptions. The ideal is for honor to be satisfied without anyone getting killed for a less than capital offense; and I have no evidence to suggest that deaths were characteristic of such intergroup conflict or that it was chronic in nature. Instead of feud-inducing behaviors, then, strong cultural emphasis is placed on measures aimed at achieving as rapid, peaceful, and binding a settlement as possible. One of the most important of these expiatory measures is for people to defuse tensions by preemptively punishing an own-group member whom they judge guilty of an offense against a member of some other group; or, if the offender is a man, they will induce him to face the wronged group. Thanks to their open boundaries and the multiple linkages (shared values, religion, worldview, Law, kinship, friendship, and marriage alliances) joining every Mardu band to all others in their society, the arena of shared understandings is huge when groups need to resolve their differences. Everyone is mindful also of how much their survival rests on mutual hospitality and unfettered access to their neighbors' natural resources in both lean and bountiful times.

Disputes between groups tend to be more difficult to deal with than those between individuals, in part because kin relationships and friendships are typically more attenuated. Such breaches could stem from an actual event, as for example, when a member of one elopes with the wife of a member of the other. Breaches could also stem from an alleged offense, such as a sorcery attack; the theft of a sacred object; an ambush by a "revenge expedition" (a small group of men sent by an aggrieved party from a different group to punish someone who has allegedly wronged that person); or a failure in some way to reciprocate adequately or Lawfully. The attribution of most unexpected or suspicious deaths to sorcery, plus the belief that close relatives cannot resort to this practice, means that scapegoats tend to be sought among outsider groups, probably those with whom there has been some prior trouble.

Should matters come to a head and members of the two disputing groups up the ante from verbal insults to throwing missiles, women of the two groups, aided sometimes by older men who act as peacemakers, will soon intervene. They will persevere until the conflict deescalates into verbal abuse. Attempts may be made to shift the venue to men's territory as a way of stopping the violence. Uncontrolled exchanges are usually short-lived and frightening for combatants and spectators alike, thanks largely to the terrifying, wind-assisted trajectories of spinning boomerangs. Short of physical combat—or following it, if cool heads have not prevailed—there are other measures useful in effecting enduring settlements. Again, the most binding and permanent sanction is the cutting, exchange, and carving of secret-sacred objects by members of the two disputing groups.

If the guilt of an individual is beyond doubt, as in the case of most elopements, resolution of the problem can be attempted with the consent of members of both groups concerned. The threat to social order that is posed by such offenses is conceded by all, and few would stand in the way if the wronged man and his close relatives invoked self-redress to punish the pair. If the men of both groups cannot resolve the matter to the satisfaction of all, the only solution would be to delay adjudication until the next "big meeting." These periodic gatherings are the high point of the desert social calendar, when a number of groups from contiguous areas assemble at a prearranged venue to conduct the business of the society at large. The necessary rhythm of aggregation and dispersal that frames the nomadic adaptation of all hunter-gatherers heavily favors dispersal in the desert. The Mardu and their neighbors lived 95 percent of their time in small groups or bands of about fifteen to thirty people, but "society," as they imagined it, was and still is a much bigger entity, producing a "we-feeling" that extended to the limits of Western Desert culture.

At every big meeting, the first order of business following the host group's ceremonial welcome and the visitors' response is the airing and adjudication of outstanding disputes, with each group of litigants in turn putting its case to the large assembly, which is the closest physical approximation to "society" that the Western Desert people achieve. Everyone with a case to answer must come forward and face the accusers, then take whatever punishment is meted out, with the assembly acting as judge and jury. No serious ritual business—and there is always much to follow—can be conducted until the air is cleared and "stomachs are satisfied" (see fig. 7.2).

For example, at an intergroup gathering in 1965, dispute settlement was conducted as follows. The morning after the arrival of a large number of visitors from the south, they and the host group seated themselves about eighty yards apart. Then, in the area between them, seven separate disputes were aired and settled in the space of ninety minutes. For each, a small group of the visitors (men, or men and women) concerned in the particular dispute rose and moved into the open, then stood in a line facing the verbal, and sometimes physical, attacks expected from relevant members of the host community. Most clashes were verbal, apart from the tossing of a few boomerangs in the general direction of the alleged offenders, but in three of the more serious altercations, spearings were attempted. As it happened, the worst fracas involved a group of host men, but it was broken up by the combined efforts of people from both groups. The subjects of the disputes included elopement, wife stealing, allegations surrounding recent deaths, and allegations of sorcery. After the last of the disputes had been aired to the satisfaction of all, members from both groups came together in embraces, then sat in a single circle, grieving and wailing for the deceased over whom these accusations had arisen.

What also takes place is a series of formal introductions between those members of the various groups assembled who have never before met certain others from distant territories. The infinite reach of classificatory kinship means that every new person encountered must have his or her kin position

Figure 7.2. An outstanding dispute between members of two different Mardu communities is being settled at a Big Meeting. The participants wear decorations donned for the ceremonial welcome between hosts and visitors that precedes the airing and settlement of disputes. This phase of the Big Meeting is an essential prelude to the commencement of major ritual activities. Photograph by Robert Tonkinson.

vis-à-vis others established before interaction can proceed. Kinship is one of the most powerful integrating institutions in the desert, converting stranger to family and giving people a ready-made framework, not only for placing all others in relation to oneself, but for ascertaining appropriate behavioral patterns. These patterns bind people into obligations and responsibilities and, in turn, make for peaceable interaction and a sense of belonging.

Conclusion

The dominant ethos of Mardu society, in the sense of its emotional tone, is egalitarian and peaceful, but neither of these major strands that characterize its ambience is an uninterrupted condition. The egalitarian feel of the society is periodically overridden by hierarchy, most notably during domestic disputes, when men strongly assert their superior rights, to the detriment of women, and in the organization and execution of the complex, multifaceted religious life. In this major arena, both male and female ritual hierarchies structure much of what happens, but, once again, senior men are in firm control of the agenda and the secrets and mechanisms of power. Peaceful equilibrium, although underwritten by a battery of individual predispositions, inhibitions, and collective values and behaviors, is likewise punctuated regularly by short bursts of conflict and confrontation. These upsets result from individual volatility, which can rapidly generate and escalate tensions to a high and potentially violent pitch. Disequilibrium of this kind is sensed by the local agents of society at large as a perilous development, and it triggers instant reactions on the part of the noncombatants present. These actors are guided in their response most strongly by considerations of kinship and predominantly in ways directed toward a quick and lasting cessation of hostilities and the restoration of the peaceful status quo ante.

Study Questions

1. Explain the Mardu concept called *the Dreaming* or *the Law*. How does the Law relate to conflict management in Mardu society?
2. What does *permeability of boundaries* mean? Why is this important in Mardu society? How does it relate to the absence of feuding and warfare?
3. Tonkinson mentions the use of physical aggression in the context of ritualized conflict management. Do you think that the aggression in *expiatory encounters* undermines or strengthens Mardu peacefulness? Explain your reasoning. Is there a difference in meaning between ritual and nonritual violent actions?
4. What are some of the conflict management processes in Mardu society? How well do you think they succeed in keeping the peace? Explain your answer.

8

Putting a Stone in the Middle: The Nubians of Northern Africa

ROBERT FERNEA

There are many who argue that the way to peaceful coexistence is through economic interdependence. For example, they point to the European Union, which
has brought peace to its members. Here Robert Fernea shows, on a smaller
scale, how interdependence helps to create a peaceful society. It should be noted
that it is not through economic interdependence per se, but through social
structures and beliefs that Nubians create peace. Additionally, one may contrast
the duty of Nubian third parties to intervene during disputes with an opposing
tradition in many Western societies of "not getting involved." Finally, young
people in many societies nowadays temporarily or permanently migrate to find
work. Fernea explains how a pattern of migrant labor relates to Nubian peacefulness. There is something of value here for similar societies faced with the issue
of some members having to leave to find employment elsewhere.

—GK

Egyptian Nubians speak of Old Nubia as *balad el aman,* a land of safety
and security, a place where people and property were not at risk, where one
could live with total peace of mind. To those of us who lived in Nubia in
the 1960s, before the Nubians were resettled to "New Nubia" because of
the Aswan High Dam construction, these claims did not seem exaggerated.
The villages we lived in and visited seem to lack any form of violence. Nor
were the more subtle patterns of factionalism and hostility evident as they

sometimes are in rural areas elsewhere. Indeed, this quality of life is widely desired but unfortunately lacking in much of the world. How can we explain the peaceful nature of life in Old Nubia? In my view, understanding involves (1) the local economy and ecology of Egyptian Nubia, (2) kinship and social organization, (3) the values and attitudes associated with the basic conditions of everyday life, and (4) the relationship between these villages and the urban Middle East to which they were connected.

In Ballana, the district of Old Nubia where I lived, no officers or elected officials made executive decisions or judged conflicts. Patterns of association between individuals that sufficed to carry out agricultural work also managed to resolve the conflicts that occasionally arose in other areas of human interaction. Whatever political hierarchies existed in the past, during pre-Islamic times or during the days of Turkish rule, were gone long before our research in the 1960s, though many stories about the Kashif Mamluks were still told. Until the building of the High Dam and the resettlement of the Nubians to the north of Aswan, the 50,000 or so people of Old Nubia under Egyptian rule remained largely free of outside interference on the part of the central government in distant Cairo. There were forty named districts in Old Nubia, stretching along both banks of the Nile between Aswan and the Sudanese border. These districts consisted of small villages with clusters of mud-brick houses and their residents. In many villages that we visited, the residents could not remember when a stranger had ever been there before.

Features That Underlie Nubian Conflict Management: Economy and Ecology

By the 1960s, most Nubian villages were poor in resources, having lost most of their agricultural land to earlier Aswan dam projects, which began to be built at the end of the nineteenth century. Each time an old dam was heightened, more alluvial land in Old Nubia was flooded. Thousands of Nubian men were forced to look for jobs in the Cairo area during the first half of the twentieth century. After the Egyptian revolution in 1952, the new socialist government initiated a benevolent form of involvement in some of the more populated districts, where one-room schoolhouses, subsidized staple foods, fuel, and occasional medical services began to appear. There were also a few places where diesel pumps provided water for small irrigation projects. But these developments still had not touched the lives of many of the villages prior to the forced resettlement of the Nubians in the late 1960s.

Although the Nubian villages were tied to cities hundreds of miles away though labor migrancy, in terms of everyday life they were isolated far more than the thousands of other Egyptian villages north of Aswan. In most of these Egyptian communities, trips to weekly regional markets or nearby cities broke the daily and seasonal routines of village life. However, the desolate Sahara Desert behind the Nubian villages kept people close to the Nile. Movement from one village to the next was difficult by foot or donkey; it was sometimes impossible because of cliffs that blocked the shoreline and separated the communities. Travel by feluccas or other sailboats was tedious upwind and sometimes dangerous. A mail boat arrived in each district once a week with supplies and could be taken to Aswan or Sudan, but this was costly and time consuming. Many Nubians, particularly the women, had never been away from their own villages and spoke only a Nubian language. They were dependent on their husbands or male relatives for all contact with the outside world.

The number of adult Nubian men living in their villages was a direct consequence of the amount of arable land that remained to be cultivated. Irrigation was necessary, and in some areas far south of the Aswan dam the construction and use of waterwheels (*eskalay*), an invention introduced in Nubia during Roman times, was still common. These waterwheels could significantly increase cultivation by lifting the river water to land high above the river. The land irrigated and the waterwheel itself were *both* referred to as eskalay.

The district of Ballana where I lived was in the southernmost part of Egyptian Nubia, bordering Sudan. It had a number of waterwheels still in operation. The construction of these machines was expensive and required a financial outlay beyond the means of any one household. Wooden piles had to be driven into the muddy side of the river to support the structure. A horizontal wheel turned a vertical wheel that dipped a chain of buckets into the river and dumped the water into hollowed logs. A pair of cows turned the horizontal wheel around and around on a raised platform for hours at a time. Each part of the eskalay was individually valued, with different families taking responsibility for the construction and constant maintenance of these separate parts.

The people of Ballana point to the great expense of the eskalay to explain the connections between families in the villages. Any man who could share the investment necessary to build part of the waterwheel acquired the right to a share of the produce from the irrigated land. The shareholders of the eskalay often encouraged their sons or daughters to marry and settle near the wheel. Since the bride customarily brought to the marriage a certain number of shares in the eskalay, which the bridegroom added to his own shares, this provided a basic economic resource for the new household. Such marriages were the principal means of avoiding excessive division through inheritance of this means of production; they linked co-owners of the wheel and land through their offspring, reuniting shares that had been divided. And since Nubians prefer marriage between relatives, especially between paternal cousins, these unions rewove the strands of kinship with the shares of eskalay ownership from one generation to the next.

Nor was this pattern of kinship and economic interests limited to the eskalay. Palm trees constituted another form of the same phenomenon. The initial ownership of a palm tree was usually based on a three-way partnership between the landowner who had space for the tree, the owner of a palm shoot ready to be planted, and the person (usually a woman) who watered the planted shoot over the many months it look for its roots to sink deep enough in the ground to reach the water level. As a result of these investments of work, real estate, and capital, the ownership of the mature palm tree, along with rights to the dates, was divided three ways. Over time, as the shares in dates were divided between the heirs of the original owners, or were given to the owner's children as wedding gifts, rights to the dates and other useful parts of the tree became widely diffused. So every Nubian adult, male or female, was likely to be involved in many networks of date tree ownership, no one of which was exactly the same as the next. At the time of the annual date harvest, small groups of people would gather under different trees, watching and waiting while small piles of dates under each tree were divided and subdivided. Usually, these divisions took place under the supervision of older women, who best remembered the complicated rights of ownership involved. As the date trees usually ceased to be fruitful after thirty or so years, the rights to the dates of any one tree ended over time, but of course a person acquired rights in many trees of many different ages.

Cows were also corporately owned and were an essential source of wealth and energy in the Nubian economy, since they were the only creatures well suited to turning the waterwheels. Yet cows, subject to illness and death, were an investment which could rapidly depreciate, the possibility of calving notwithstanding. Following the same pattern of shared resource ownership described above, most farmers had interests in several cows, a "leg"—that is, one quarter of a cow—being the typical share. The person who sheltered and fed the cow when it was off the wheel was entitled to its milk and calves as compensation (though these arrangements varied); each of the other co-owners had to feed and water the cow during one of the twelve-hour shifts when it turned the eskalay. Each eskalay had a piece of land set aside for raising fodder for the eskalay cows, thus eliminating arguments among the various owners of the waterwheel over who was to provide food.

Buying shares in a cow was a high yielding if somewhat risky investment that often tempted Nubian men who had extra cash (perhaps upon return-ing from a period of migrant labor.) If he had no need for a share of their labor, a person could buy cow or calf shares, leave the animals in the stables of the other owners, and collect rent for their use in the form of a share of the crops produced. A study of cow ownership by El Zein (1966) revealed a complex stock market, with price fluctuations, marginal buying practices, and monopolistic potentials. For instance, some men became part owners of many cows and thus quite wealthy. On the other hand, hoof and mouth disease sometimes infected many cows, and one could lose the entire investment as a result. It was probably salutary for the general peace of the Nubian communities that eskalay and palm shares could only be inherited or given as marriage gifts to the young—and thus were never sold or traded like cow shares—because cows could become a source of discord among the share owners. Our studies also showed that in economic value livestock was the principal export from Egyptian Nubia to the Aswan market, and most of this was calves from waterwheel cows.

The Binding Ties of Kinship and Social Organization

The significance of the Nubian patterns of shared ownership went well beyond material considerations. An annual trip to a neighboring village to collect a few handfuls of dates maintained friendships between collateral branches of an extended family, for instance. "We know the family is still together," said one Ballana Nubian, "when it gathers to divide the produce from land or date trees owned by our great-grandfathers. When a shareholder says, 'I don't care, help yourself,' then we know the big family is starting to break up."

In the case of the eskalay, only two families at the most could live off its produce; these partners cultivated the land as shareholders and sharecroppers for the other often numerous and frequently absentee shareholders. Many of the shareholders were working in Lower Egypt or in foreign cities and were not in their villages for months or years at a time. The important social fact was that the absent villager was one of the eskalay owners, a member of this group, and that his ownership could be activated should he or other members of his immediate family return for a visit or settle down again in the village, as elderly men frequently did when they became too old for migrant labor. The agrarian resources of Nubia thus not only served to sustain the resident families, but also helped to maintain ties to the absent ones. An ethnographic survey showed that approximately 100,000 migrant Nubians maintained ties of some kind to their natal villages in Old Nubia (Fernea and Fernea with Rouchdy 1991). Thus, the resources of Nubia helped sustain ties with far more people than these resources could actually support.

The relationship between property and social life in Old Nubia was not just culturally implicit, present but not overtly recognized; rather, it was given explicit recognition, as witnessed by some of the above statements. Even more evidence of this awareness may be seen in the way in which the term for a kinship-based group—the *nog*—was also used for a network of people connected through the shared ownership of property. In both respects, the nog can be seen as helping to manage conflict by preventing factionalism in the Nubian communities.

In Ballana, a married man's first nog is his household, the group of people for whom he is economically and socially responsible, including his wife, or wives, and children, as well as any other relatives who live in his house(s) and are dependent on him for some degree of support. Few Nubians had more than one wife, but those who did felt it essential to have a separate house for each one of them. This was the only way a man's first nog could include more than one household. In fact, all of a man's dependents could be called his nog. It was through marriage that a man acquired a nog—women and children who obeyed, respected, and depended on him.

The second kind of nog is an egocentric network; it is composed of those relatives with whom one still divides the products of land and trees, no matter how materially inconsequential the shares might be. A man usually has two, largely overlapping nogs, the one from his father and the other from his mother. Given the practice of endogamous marriage, the two nogs—of kinship and ownership—were likely to be similar in composition, because the husband and wife could well share the same patrilineal ancestors. Yet such a wife is likely to have received some shares of property as an inheritance or gift at marriage from a kinsperson who was not related to her husband. When an exogamous marriage took place, the wife's nog involved herself and her children with a largely different set of people than those belonging to her husband's nog.

These bilateral nogs in a society of patrilineal descent are of more than economic importance to the child. Mother's relatives remain a separate and important category even when the parents were paternal cousins. As one Nubian friend explained to me, "My mother's relatives were those men [and women] I met while they were in the house with her; my father's relatives were the men I met outside the house with him." Although in Nubian communities social segregation of women is not rigorously practiced, men do not ordinarily venture into the women's quarters of a house unless they are close kin to the women of that household. Thus, even in these small villages, a child's world was divided between the loving and indulgent group around the mother, with whom relaxed behavior is permitted, and the father's friends outside the home, where respect for one's father must be shown as a matter of family honor and general good reputation.

The informality between members of a mother's nog sometimes continues outside the home. Many Nubians mentioned being taken by their mothers to attend a division of dates among her relatives and shareholders. Many Ballana men can recite the maternal lineage of their mother as readily as that of their father. Also, a number of my Nubian friends used their mother's name as a second, private term of address among close friends. There is a certain ambiguity about this; when I asked about this usage, it was laughed off and treated as a bit of a joke.

While the nogs are not exclusively patrilineal organizations and involve both kin and nonkin, when a Nubian boy moves to a more formal public setting, he is definitely his father's boy; the emphasis on paternal descent is asserted. In this context, a man's nog is understood to be the group of men who share the same family name. Unlike many naming practices in other parts of the Arab world, this nog is not named after a paternal ancestor. Rather, the name of the family nog often refers to a quality believed to be shared by all the men or an outstanding event marking the experience of the group.

One important nog of this type was the Fagirob, the members of which were settled in several districts and many villages near the Sudan-Egypt border. Some Fagirob can trace their ancestry back eleven generations to a man named Sherif. The group's name (Fagirob, from "Fagir," meaning "Fakir sect") came into use because, it was said, at one time the men of this group were Sufi teachers, and many Fagirob still avow a special interest in religion.

The use of an adjectivally derived name, rather than that of a specific ancestor, gives the formal family nog considerable latitude in its membership. For example, while men who never return after migration from Nubia are lost and forgotten, another man, who marries a Fagirob woman and settles with her people, can come to be regarded as a member of her nog. Certainly his children would be if they inherited property from their mother and gifts of property shares from her people.

This returns us to the relation between property ownership and nogs. Any man or woman formally belongs to their father's nog, more informally to their mother's nog, and also to other nogs made up of those with whom, as adults, they share property. This means that a person's nogs are overlapping and involve diverse, dispersed memberships. *This feature is very important, for the Nubian community does not easily split into opposing factions.* Nogs grow in number through birth and property ownership; they disappear through death, migration, and property loss, but this dynamic process never deprives an individual of overlapping networks involving numerous other persons. The Ballana Nubians knew about tribal feuds because of intermittent contact with Arabs traveling from Sudan to Egypt with their camels, and even more through contact with the Sayyidi society of Upper Egypt, among whom feuds were common. But they had no memory of feuds in Nubian society, neither in Ballana nor elsewhere. How could the divisions of interests and personal identities necessary for factions and feuds develop, given the nature of Nubian nogs?

Tribal systems depend on lineages and descent as the basis for member-ship, and while "the tribe" is often a far more flexible social organization than its formal description would lead us to believe, tribesmen can quite ef-fectively draw lines between "us" and "them" when disputes occur. The lines around nog membership cannot be so easily drawn, and so the nog seems well constructed for a society which was obliged to adjust to high levels of labor migration and the symbolic ownership of village property. The open-ended nature of the nogs, the fact that both descent and shared property were grounds for belonging, gave the absentee a basis for relationships with many other men who found themselves at work together in urban centers far from home. It also insured that those who returned to their villages, either temporarily or to retire, would have social ties to activate for marriages or for local subsistence. And the nogs made certain that dependents who stayed behind in Nubia would have recognized social positions in the households of their husbands or fathers as well as with other resident members of the community.

Conflict Management: "Putting A Stone in the Middle"
Peacemakers, Mediators, and Arbitrators

Nubians share with other Egyptians a traditional sense of responsibility for helping people around them resolve their differences. In Cairo, when a quar-rel between men or women breaks out in a public setting, voices will suddenly rise, and it will seem that all hell is about to break loose. Strangers will ap-pear to join in on either side of the argument, and physical violence seems sure to occur. Yet, in most cases, people are actually stepping in between the disputants, shouting, while at the same time pushing them apart and saving them from blows. This is very different from the American practice of either "staying out of other people's business" or, at the other extreme, "joining in the brawl"; someone who does not understand Arabic or the local scene might think the latter is common in Cairo, but it really isn't. In fact, an ad hoc process of conflict resolution is taking place, and the protagonists are being offered an honorable way of backing out of the conflict at the behest of others. It is almost a social duty to make this intervention. In this way, threats and accusations of the most dire sort can fly in both directions, and tempers can rise to the highest levels, with a shared understanding that the fight will be broken up and no one will have to lose face or suffer physical injury in public.

Traditionally, on a more private basis, when relatives quarrel in the Middle East, it is regarded by other members of the kin group as extremely dangerous. Every effort must be made to resolve such disputes as soon as possible. Why? Because such quarrels weaken and divide the one group of people upon whom an individual can depend for all his or her life—one's relatives, one's family. Quarrels among kinspeople divide the kin group, reduce the network of people mutually obligated to each other, and can leave the individual—and in the long run the kin group—too weak to maintain their proper position in the society, thus exposing them to the hostility of outsiders.

Of course, in urban and many rural contexts, the police are responsible for maintaining the peace. But even now, the police are generally more interested in securing law and order for the state than in resolving quarrels among citizens. Calling the police is widely regarded as a dangerous act that will lead to random beatings and imprisonment more often than peace among relatives. Furthermore, in the Middle East, it is kith and kin that the individual must depend on for marriage contracts, care in time of sickness, support during unemployment, housing when one cannot afford independent dwellings, and security in one's old age. It is on the family that any individual's reputation depends, just as the entire family depends on the reputation of the individual. Hence, most Middle Eastern societies—including the Nubians of Ballana—are misunderstood if they are thought of as composed of *individuals.* Societies are not best conceived as consisting of individual citizens and the State; rather, it is the *individual in the family,* one's kinspeople, and then the community which are best understood as the units comprising the whole.

This general cultural pattern in the Middle East is important to understand as the context in which Nubian peacemaking takes place. Keeping peace among members of the household nog is primary, but keeping peace within the community at large is also important, for nog membership extends well beyond the individual household. Obviously, the sharing of resources in the Nubian community could be a prime source of disagreements. The members of several households, who share resources in overlapping rights to eskalays and palm trees, must agree on ways in which these bases for subsistence are to be used. Who is to benefit, who is to work in the community, and who is to leave and work in the city?

Until the late 1960s, it was the father who formally decided which sons should leave for the city and which ones should remain behind and farm in Ballana. But traveling to the city was seen by most young men to be a source of adventure, a chance to make money for marriage, to acquire material possessions for himself and his kin, and perhaps to indulge in habits not approved of in the home village. Indeed, labor migration was a rite of passage marking adulthood, and the men who never migrated were small in number and were below average in intelligence, or so it seemed.

In the village, the eskalay was the central means of production. Marginal subsistence made any loss of its use a danger for those who remained in

Ballana. As we have seen, many people had shares of ownership and conceivably could have fallen into quarrels over its repairs (which were often necessary) or the division of work and the food it produced. But the eskalay was also a symbol of unity for those who owned it, a tie with long-dead grandfathers. An ample number of kinsmen and nog members would be linked to both sides in any quarrel among its users; they would therefore be ready to mediate differences and reconcile the adversaries. No matter what the exact relationship between the disputants might be, intermediaries, *wasta* or "go-betweens," would be there to come forward and carry messages between the antagonists, arrange a meeting, find a compromise, and, if necessary, shame the principals into overcoming their differences.

The fundamental Nubian conviction that each adult man or woman has a basic responsibility to intercede in quarrels is well illustrated by a Nubian anecdote of apparently recent origin, a combination of an old story and a new one which I was told several times while I lived in Ballana. The old story concerns two men who were constantly quarreling over the division of water provided by an eskalay they shared. To irrigate both pieces of land that the two men farmed, the water had to be channeled first into one ditch and then into the other. One of the men was always accusing the other of taking more than his share of water. An uncle overheard the shouting one day. He found a large, flat stone and put it on its side in the middle of the canal. This effectively divided the water into two streams, thus putting an end to the cause of the contention.

The new variation of the stream and the stone story involved the Egyptian nationalization of the Suez Canal in 1956. During the brief military conflict between British and Egyptian forces, Nubians were hurrying back and forth between their fields and their homes to listen to the latest news on battery-powered short-wave radios. An old man sat in the shade under a palm tree next to a path on which the men were running. He would struggle to his feet to ask what was going on, only to have the men go on by without stopping. Finally, in frustration and annoyance, he succeeded in grabbing the clothes of one of the younger men and demanded the attention that, as an older man, he deserved. "So what is the big commotion about?" he asked. "Grandfather," the young man said, "the British and the Egyptians are fighting over the Suez Canal!" The old man reflected on this for a moment and then said, "What's the matter with them? Couldn't anyone put a stone in the middle?"

The Nubians enjoyed telling this story, and it reflects a political art at which they are extremely skilled and that they take very seriously: making peace. Most frequently, arguments between kinfolk are resolved quickly by a third, usually older relative. If more kinsmen become involved in the dispute, or if the quarrel concerns a serious matter not amenable to small-scale diplomacy, the Ballana Nubians might call a family council involving the men from the larger, property-sharing nog. Then all the resident kinspeople gather—not only the men, but also the women and children, while an elder kinsman presides over the council.

Such a council had the objective of arriving at a consensus. Both sides of the argument were presented, and the case was discussed until a majority among those present—and better still, the whole group—decided who was right, who was wrong, and how the matter might best be rectified. One well-known elder liked to settle matters by relying on the fact that in most cases one disputant was going to be older than the other. He would make the younger man come forward and kiss the older person's head, asking his forgiveness because he had not respected him as an older person. Then the peacemaker would oblige the older man to embrace the younger, asking his forgiveness for having tempted the youth into disrespect by quarreling with him in the first place. All of this took place in front of the assembled family and neighbors, and once it happened, things usually settled down.

Devaluing and Sanctioning Violence

Conflict resolution takes a more serious tone in violent offenses, such as physical injury, rape, or homicide. The news of such offenses is kept from women and children (if possible), and the matter is not discussed publicly, for it is a disgrace to the families involved and to the community as a whole. Only the men most closely related to the offender would gather to hear about and discuss the case. The sanction might be social death for the criminal, who would be required to leave Ballana and Nubia forever, forsaking all his material rights in the community. If the culprit refused, then he would be ignored until complete social ostracism obliged him to leave. On the other hand, I was told that should a victim or the victim's family take his or her problem to the police, he or she would receive the same treatment as the offender: total ostracism.

Punishing the victim for going to the police was deemed appropriate because such action exposed the community to the perils of outside intervention. Crimes would be punished according to alien laws in ways that could be far more detrimental to the village than the consequences of the original violation. The Nubians firmly believed that the greatest protection for the weak is secrecy. So the few Egyptian police who were sent to Nubia complained of boredom; aside from investigating minor cases of smuggling goods in from Sudan, there was nothing to do. Indeed, I could not find out about any serious crimes committed by the Nubians in Ballana; as far as they were willing to say, no such crimes had ever happened.

No feuds, no fractious disputes, no pervasive factionalism, no violence: even if this picture of Nubian life is not entirely realistic, and is in part the result of my ignorance as an outsider, it was nonetheless the Nubians' image of their society and the one in which they took great pride. Within the closely woven fabric of kinship and economic life, ample numbers of peacemakers could be found to resolve a quarrel. And, of course, other factors also reduced sources of tension between individuals, migration to the cities being of particular importance in this regard.

The Exit Option: "Letting Off Steam" in the City

By the time of our research in the 1960s, almost every Nubian adult male had spent part of his life working in an Egyptian or Sudanese city, and sometimes in other Arab countries or Europe. Increasingly, wives and children were finding a place in these urban settings with their husbands and fathers. Unquestionably, the city provided greater privacy of action and freedom from the social constraints of the tightly knit villages in Nubia. The village was the conservative end of this bipolar world, a place to be revered in the conversations of the Cairo migrant and to be honored and idealized by the older absentee. It was, however, hardly the setting for a young man who wished to explore the forbidden pleasures of alcohol and sex outside of marriage, or even just to gamble and be rowdy with age mates in a favorite coffee shop. More than one dignified elder in Ballana, the paragons of respectability, had been the subject of stories about rakish behavior in the old urban days.

The young male schoolteachers were the most discontented village residents. They had lived outside their natal villages while going to teacher training school and had enjoyed their independence. Upon returning, they felt unduly constrained by the conservative elders in the villages where they worked. Older men were generally religiously conservative. They were the ones who attempted to put an end to dancing at weddings, something widely enjoyed by younger people. And of course it was also true that in Ballana no one could visit a friend's, much less a girlfriend's, house without everyone else knowing about it; even the mildest flirtations were instant sources of gossip. Exceptional events rarely happened without becoming common knowledge. Formality, respect, and constraint characterized the relations between generations, and a private life—if that means anything secret—was very hard to come by.

When a younger man on donkey back passed an older man, he was expected to dismount immediately to greet him properly. Nor should a young man smoke in front of his elders. The intergenerational tension was perhaps most intensely felt by the young men back from the cities who had recently married, for marriage was a primary mark of young adulthood. Such men were anxious to assume the new rights and duties of this status. Young boys and old grandfathers perhaps enjoyed the most relaxed forms of social intercourse, as expressed in a song by the Nubian musician Hamza el Din. He tells how the young and the old enjoy each others' company when both are largely ignored by the rest of the family. While affairs of general concern were commonly discussed after Friday prayers at the village mosque, it was usually the young men who proposed and the old who disposed. Migration to the city, therefore, helped relieve some of these generational tensions as well as provided for village economic needs.

Preventing Envy: The Evil Eye Paradox

Another factor contributing to the peacefulness of Nubian life was the definition of misfortune in these communities. As in other parts of the world where witches are found, human beings in Nubia were sometimes considered the agents of others' bad luck. However, in Ballana these were not willful agents, but rather the unfortunate possessors of the "evil eye." In every village, there were a few such people. When animals fell sick, children got fevers, men broke legs, water jars cracked, or house walls collapsed, it was surely the result of an envious or admiring glance from a person with the evil eye. Only by being inconspicuous—avoiding drawing favorable attention to oneself or one's possessions, and by wearing blue beads or other charms—could one ward off such disasters.

Yet a person with the eye was considered unable to help him- or herself. It was something missing in one's life, the lack of normal rewards and pleasures, that brought on the evil eye. A young widow, a childless couple, a mistreated child, these were the kind of people who had the evil eye. Nubian insistence on the impersonal nature of this force was very strong, and punishment of someone was not considered because that person had the eye. But such people were also expected to be very careful. Men sitting with a man with the eye would suddenly shout at him when he was noticed to be absentmindedly staring at something or someone to be admired. At the same time, a male baby—the most highly valued—was often dressed in ragged clothes, or even sometimes dressed as a girl, because he was then less likely to attract an envious glance. It was also bad form for anyone to exclaim over the beauty of a baby or the health of an animal, for this was bound to attract the attention of someone with the evil eye.

The danger of trying to use the eye willfully to harm someone was equal to the risk of inadvertently attracting it. A Nubian friend told me the story of a farmer who had quarreled with his neighbor and decided to punish him. He brought an old man who was known to have the eye to the edge of a dune overlooking the field where his neighbor's cows were pastured. "Look at those fine cows down there," he said. "Where?" asked the old man, whose sight was failing. "Down there, under that palm tree, off on the left," said the vengeful farmer. "My! What good eyes you have," said the old man.

Another more personal story on the same subject comes to mind. One winter day in Ballana, I took Abdulla, a good friend from the village, out in our motorboat in the early morning mists to hunt ducks on the Nile. He fired his shotgun at a number of them, but the ducks always flew off unharmed. Finally, I got cold enough and said it was time to give up and go back home. Abdulla was reluctant but finally agreed. As we headed to shore, another flock of ducks suddenly appeared on the water in front of us, and Abdulla excitedly stood up behind me and shot over my head so close that a few peashots went through my hat, and I was totally deafened by the loud explosion. When I got home, my head was still loudly ringing, but I was more worried about how Abdulla would feel about the incident. He was a good friend, and I didn't want a rupture in our relationship. In an hour or so, he came to my house to see how I was doing, a lot more cheerful than I had anticipated. "Remember that boy who wanted to go out hunting with us?" he said. I said I really didn't, but Abdulla passed this over. "He was down by the boat when we went out. Well, that kid had the bad eye!" The near accident was not Abdulla's fault, and the duck shooting fiasco was set aside.

The Nubians believed in the eye, but they also believed in modern medicine and would seek treatment for themselves or their children when it was needed. In this sense, there is nothing reactionary about their notion that some unfortunate people have the evil eye. But the idea does help smooth over misfortunes of many kinds, keeping them from becoming a source of rancor or dispute in a community where getting along together is basic to the common good.

An Open Question: How Has Peace Fared in "New Nubia"?

The Nubians of Egypt have been living in their settlements in "New Nubia" for almost forty years, and I have been able to visit my friends from Ballana there several times over these decades. Are they still "peaceful people?" Yes, as far as I can tell, they are. But life in the new settlement is far different from that of past centuries, and I cannot be sure how important this is or how widely peaceful attitudes prevail. There are almost three times as many people living together in less than one-fourth of the space that accommodated the old villages. New Nubia might best be described as a rural housing project. The hand of the central government is much more clearly present, in the form of police stations, schools, clinics, and other offices. Among more than 300,000 Nubians live many Sayyidis from Upper Egypt, who work on their land as sharecroppers in many cases, and who may rent homes from their Nubian neighbors. At the same time, many Nubian men are still migrant laborers, often working in the richer Arab countries, preferring to have their landholdings (issued by the Egyptian government) sharecropped by other Nubians or Sayyidis.

The economic situation in New Nubia has also radically changed. Some Nubians are much richer than others, and this is reflected in the way many homes are now fully remodeled and furnished with new electrical appliances and TV sets. Nubian women, even older ones, now speak Arabic as well as Nubian languages, and young people gather for dances and music making often out of their parents' overview. All of this, and more, makes it possible to say that the Nubians have become "modern," like us, so far as such changes make this so. At the same time, Old Nubia is a source of great nostalgia, the *balid el aman*—the place of safety and security—that was largely free of government authority and outsiders, an independence that is no longer part of Nubian life. I have not been aware of any violence while visiting New Nubia. Women and children walk and visit on the streets along with the men, enjoying the new stores and taking the buses into Kom Ombo and Aswan to shop. Yet I also know that they have installed modern locks on the doors and windows, and I heard many complaints about the fact that there are always too many strangers around. Not everyone knows everyone else as in the past. The waterwheels are gone. The stock market in cows no longer seems to exist. Certainly, the basis for the old nogs, the old property sharing of the past, is gone. It should be added, however, that the Egyptian government has never issued legal titles of ownership to the houses in New Nubia, so a lot of common claims now revolve around many of the Nubian homes.

What has replaced the peacemaking economic institutions of the past along with the common knowledge of everyone else's affairs is a new sense of identity. By this I mean that in the past being a Nubian was of far less significance than coming from a particular village and belonging to particular nogs. Now, the Nubians consider themselves a single people. They believe themselves to be superior to other Egyptians, and to some degree they look south to the Sudan for a common folk, a place where many have relatives and everyone is black, like Egyptian Nubians. This new sense of common identity is strong and has resulted in poetry and songs as well as novels and oral histories that are creating a much wider sense of commonality than was known in the past. Or more specifically, before the building of the Aswan High Dam, Nubians in the cities of Egypt were assumed by other Egyptians to be servants; this is no longer the case. They are fully part of the modern urban world, with a place of their own in Upper Egypt.

Conclusion

I have outlined the social and economic features of life in Ballana, Old Nubia, that helped the villagers maintain the described low levels of factionalism and high levels of accord. As I have shown, the local economy and ecology, the kinship and social organization (especially, the nog), the values and attitudes that were associated with these conditions, and the pattern of labor migration to cities all contributed to the ability of villagers to value a peaceful life very highly and to implement their attitudes with highly developed peacemaking skills. Of course, these conditions and attitudes varied in time and space in ways that could not be measured with any exactitude. However, I doubt we would have become so interested in peacemaking among the Nubians had they themselves not mentioned so often the peaceful nature of their lives together. In other words, this was their image of themselves, what they told outsiders about Nubia, and what their children grew up understanding about themselves. Could there be something of a self-fulfilling prophecy in this regard, that what they thought to be true was what they themselves made come true?

Even though there is reason to believe that centuries ago there were wars in Nubia, that dynasties of various origin rose and fell in Nubian lands, the only historical violence to which my Nubian friends would admit was against the Egyptians. Indeed, in New Nubia there is now widespread belief that modern Nubians are the descendents of the Kush, people of the south, who once ruled the Nile valley. So, it was only against outsiders that the Nubians of old are ever thought to have gone to war.

Shared ownership of resources, through symbolic as well as material divisions of the means of production, was clearly more and more necessary in Old Nubia as the first dams began to be built in Aswan at the turn of the last century. This gradual diminution of local resources could have led to the deterioration of village life, but in fact, it resulted in new ways of managing subsistence and promoting the continuity of Nubian society. For this the Nubians have to receive full credit, for in this regard they had little outside help. Will the Nubians today succeed as well? Biologically, they certainly have insured that they will continue as a minority in Egypt. Perhaps in defining themselves as an ethnicity in modern Egypt, they will also succeed in keeping peace among themselves. Perhaps they will replace the old economic ties with new cultural constructions based on real and imagined differences between themselves and their Egyptian neighbors. If so, one of these constructions will certainly be a common belief in their exceptional peace-loving nature.

Study Questions

1. How do the patterns of *eskalay* and palm tree ownership contribute to Nubian peacefulness? You may also wish to consider patterns of cow ownership.

2. What is a *nog?* How does the nog system contribute to Nubian peaceful-ness? Are there any comparable features, at least to some degree, in your own society?
3. Explain the meaning of "putting a stone in the middle."
4. What are the main characteristics of conflict management in Nubian society? To what degree might some of these conflict management mech-anisms be applied (probably with modification) to reduce violence in other societies, such as your own?

9
Keeping the Peace in an Island World: The Sama Dilaut of Southeast Asia

CLIFFORD SATHER

Clifford Sather shows how the Sama Dilaut have established a peaceful society in a climate of violence. Sather helps to dispel the myth that in the current world of violence, peace cannot be created. As Ximena Davies-Vengoechea points out, peace is a dynamic force, and violence does not completely negate a path to peace. Sather also portrays a society that has created and maintained peace through much social and economic change. The Sama Dilaut linguistic conceptualization of what they have done to create a peaceful society is particularly interesting. The term *addat*—very roughly, all the norms and rules that guide behavior and, when followed, result in smooth social relations—is similar to certain concepts, such as the Mardu's conception of the Law, that we have seen in other societies. In addition, Sather discusses the concept of *magkiparat,* which deals with ritual reconciliation. The Sama Dilaut recognize that not all conflicts can be resolved amicably. Some disputes, for whatever reason (due to disputant personalities, miscommunication, and so on), can result in deep enmity. For the Sama Dilaut, this poses a threat not only to the society and its addat, but also for individuals and their health (a kind of immanent justice). Thus friends and relatives can call for magkiparat—ritual reconciliation. Sather shows that this ritual is often conducted if someone does fall ill. There is a similar thought within Western holistic medical traditions, which also see psychological roots for human ill health. Magkiparat seems to be a powerful tool for those conflicts where mediation has failed.

—GK

For nearly two centuries, the region encompassing Sulu and the eastern Borneo coast was a byword for piracy in the Malayo-Indonesian archipelago. From the eighteenth through the mid-nineteenth century, slave raiders from this region, notably Ilanun and the Balangingi Sama, swept across the archipelago in large, coordinated fleets. Every year, slave raiders captured several thousand slaves—seized in raids carried out over virtually the whole of maritime Southeast Asia, from Riau and the Bay of Bengal to the Timor and Arafura Seas—and transported them to the Sulu Sultanate, the principal polity of the region. At the height of its power, slave raiding was an integral part of the maritime economy of the sultanate. Slaving fleets operated under the patronage of powerful Tausug *datus*, supplying slaves in exchange for trade goods, firearms, munitions, and cloth, although the raiders themselves were mainly outsiders, living in or sailing from the territorial margins of the state. Only with the introduction of steam-powered gunboats and increased cooperation between the Western colonial powers was large-scale slave raiding brought to an end in the second half of the nineteenth century. In the decades that followed, slavery itself was abolished, and in 1915, the Sulu Sultanate ceased to exist.

However, throughout the region, small-scale raiding continued as before. In the aftermath of World War II, organized forms of armed conflict revived, including feuding and armed vendettas (Kiefer 1969). Local leaders surrounded themselves with armed retinues, giving protection to those who offered fealty, and physical violence, or the threat of violence, became a central feature of politics and social life in Sulu, particularly among the politically dominant Tausug (Kiefer 1969, 1972a). By the beginning of the 1970s, fighting took on an increasingly political character, becoming linked to Islamic secessionist politics; and the Sulu Archipelago became, from the late 1970s to the present, the site of heavy fighting among Philippine government troops, rebels, and secessionist forces including, most recently, the now infamous Abu Sayyaf (Sather in press).

The Sama Dilaut

Given this history, the Sulu Archipelago-eastern Borneo region would seem to be an unlikely place to encounter communities of peaceable people. Yet, such communities did exist and continue even now to make their homes in the area. This is so, even though the way of life of many of these people has changed markedly over the last half century, and a few have been forced to flee from Sulu to refugee settlements in Sabah.

The members of these peaceable communities describe themselves as the Sama Dilaut, or, more simply, as the *a'a dilaut,* meaning, literally, the "sea people" (see fig. 9.1).

Figure 9.1. Sama Dilaut men haul in nets in 1965. Photograph by Clifford Sather.

To outsiders, they are generally known as Bajau Laut, while other Sama/Bajau speakers call them *Sama Pala'au* or *Pala'u* (Sather 1993:30, 1997:2–5). *Pala'au* is a pejorative term, and like the Tausug term for them, *Luwa'an,* which means, "to vomit out," its use reflects a view of these people as constituting a pariah community, excluded socially and religiously from the dominant society around them (see Sather 1997:43–44, 2002: 37–41).

The Sama Dilaut are better known in the anthropological literature as the Bajau Laut (Sather 1997). Although I have also described them as the Bajau Laut in the past, the name is open to confusion; I think it is preferable, for a number of reasons, to refer to them in the way in which they describe themselves, as the Sama Dilaut (see also Nimmo 2001:2).

Historically, what distinguished the Sama Dilaut from others was the fact that they lived permanently in boats, dividing themselves into small anchorage groups. Although tied to local fishing and marine gathering sites, these groups were characteristically mobile, and, by identifying themselves as sea people, the Sama Dilaut adopted a highly portable identity, one which they historically carried with them throughout the whole of the Sulu Archipelago, the eastern coast of Borneo, southern Sulawesi, and beyond. With this identity, they found hospitality, wherever they voyaged, among other sea people who were similarly situated in relation to the majority shore people living around them (Sather 1997:2–5).

Within the Sulu Archipelago-eastern Borneo region, the traditional political structure was organized territorially, in terms of a hierarchy of interlocking territorial units, with authority at each level delegated to leaders holding title rights over particular island or shoreline areas (Kiefer 1972b). Being boat dwellers and without claims to, or strong identification with, areas of land ashore, the Sama Dilaut were essentially "illegible" (cf. Scott 1998) to those holding power; thus, they lacked an acknowledged political status within this structure, except, very loosely, as the clients of local land-based leaders who had jurisdiction over the particular areas where they anchored. As a result, the Sama Dilaut, as outsiders, enjoyed considerable autonomy in arranging their own internal affairs, which they did along lines very different from those that defined political relations among their numerically dominant neighbors.

This paper discusses a single small community of Sama Dilaut living in the Semporna district of southeastern Sabah (Malaysia); it explores the social and cultural mechanisms by which the members of this community have been able to contain conflict and maintain conditions of relative peace among themselves in an island world otherwise characterized by a long and troubled history of endemic violence.

Sea and Shore People in The Semporna District

The Semporna district lies at the extreme southeastern corner of Sabah. Consisting of a narrow, mountainous peninsula bordered by scores of islands and rich coral reefs and terraces, the district has long been a focus of maritime trade, as well as a physical link between the island world of Sulu and the eastern Borneo coast (see Sather 1997:21–34).

Although a distinct community, the Sama Dilaut belong, culturally and linguistically, to a much larger congeries of Bajau/Sama speaking peoples. In Semporna, the Sama Dilaut speak a chain-related dialect readily intelligible to their neighbors, most of them Sama-speaking strand and island people. The Sama Dilaut describe the latter as the *a'a déa,* the inland or shore people. These people are fragmented into a number of groups, each distinguished by a toponymic name or names, referring to an individual island, island group, or smaller area of coastline. In Semporna, the largest and politically dominant of these groups is the Sama Sikubang, traditionally present on the central islands of the district—chiefly Omadal, Larapan, and BumBum— but, today, also in resettlement communities on the Semporna Peninsula (Sather 1997:31–32). In 1964 when I began fieldwork, the Sama Dilaut numbered 660 in the Semporna district. In 1995 their numbers had grown to more than 3,000, out of a total district population of 92,000.

Boats, Moorage Groups, Houses, and Villages

Until 1955 the Semporna Sama Dilaut lived entirely in boats, with each boat (*lepa*) serving as home to a single family, consisting in most cases of a married couple plus their dependent children, often with one or two additional kin (Sather 1997:56ff.). The family was the chief domestic and child-rearing group and the principal fishing unit. Each family identified itself with a local moorage site. Here, in the past, families returned between fishing voyages to anchor, collect stores of fresh water, and trade. Local communities consisted of those who regularly anchored together at the same moorage site. In the past, these communities ranged in size from two or three to as many as fifty families. Within an anchorage, related families typically moored their boats in tightly aggregated groups, often tying them in tandem to a common moorage post (*soang*). These groups, called *pagmunda',* were typically organized around a set of married siblings, both brothers and sisters, or, less often, a couple and their married sons and daughters. Larger pagmunda' groups were typically formed of two or more sibling sets related by marriage. Sometimes pagmunda' groups anchored separately, but more often they joined others to form larger, more heterogeneous moorage groups.

Families from different moorage groups living in the same region generally fished the same fishing grounds, with families from neighboring groups
often fishing together. Although each anchorage site gave a degree of territorial definition to family voyaging, families from different moorage groups
often encountered one another at sea, and when they did, they frequently
combined their nets and fished together, exploiting the same fishing sites,
mainly zones of reef, coral terraces, and intertidal beaches (Sather 1997:
56–60). In the past, the largest gatherings of Sama Dilaut families occurred,
in fact, not at moorage sites, but at sea, in the course of periodic large-
scale fish drives called *magambit* (Sather 1997:124–28; forthcoming). In the
Semporna district, the largest of these drives took place over the Legitan
Reefs and drew families not only from Semporna, but from Sitangkai and
the nearby Sibutu Island Group in what is now the Philippines (see fig. 9.2).
These drives ceased in the late 1970s.

In 1954 Semporna town, the administrative center of the district, was
attacked and looted by pirates. In the aftermath, the Sama Dilaut, many
of whom had by then come to anchor close to the town fish market, were
required to leave the town harbor, which was placed under nighttime curfew.
This curfew was still in effect in 1964–65, the period in which I started my
fieldwork. Most families moved beyond the eastern edge of town to a shallow
lagoon at the north entrance to the strait separating the tip of the Semporna
Peninsula from BumBum Island; here they established a moorage site called
Bangau-Bangau. A smaller group established a second moorage at Labuan
Haji, immediately across the strait, near the eastern tip of BumBum Island.
Piracy has not ceased. In 1996, one year after I left the field for the last time,
Semporna town was attacked twice, and eight pirates were killed by police
near Omadal Island while robbing fishermen.

In 1955 the first government-appointed leader and headman of Bangau-
Bangau, Panglima Atani, with a brother-in-law who later became his suc-
cessor, Panglima Tiring, built the first two Sama Dilaut pile-houses in the
district. Others soon followed, and by 1964, most families had given up boat
dwelling and were living in what had by then become two densely aggregated pile-house villages, one at Bangau-Bangau and the other at Labuan
Haji (cf. Sather 1997:63ff.). From these two villages, most families continued to embark by boat, singly or in small fleets, on extended fishing voyages
lasting from one or two days to several weeks at a time, except for a few
family heads who had, by 1964, abandoned fishing, mostly for casual wage
work in Semporna town. The house groups that took form in this process
of settling down were typically large, with half of them comprised of two or
more family fishing units. At the same time, the larger pagmunda' groups
gave rise to house group clusters, consisting of tightly aggregated groups
of neighboring houses occupied by closely related families. Called *ba'anan*,

Figure 9.2. A fish drive among the Sama Dilaut over the Legitan Reefs in 1965. Photograph by Clifford Sather.

these clusters were, and remain, the major focus of everyday social life in the village. Each house group, or *luma'*, is known by the name of its house owner, who acts as the group's spokesman or leader (*nakura*) in village affairs (Sather 1997:134ff.). The most senior or articulate nakura luma' within a ba'anan is generally acknowledged as the cluster's primary spokesman. Today, both house group and cluster leaders play a major role, as we shall see presently, in containing village conflict.

Changing Political Relations Within and Outside The Community

Colonial rule was gradually extended over the Semporna district in the last decades of the nineteenth century (Sather 1997:44ff.). Prior to this, individual moorage groups were considered the clients of local land-based leaders. In Sama, patrons were said to "own" (*taga*) their Sama Dilaut clients, with "ownership" in this context signifying that the patron was prepared to defend his clients and to protect his interests in them against rival leaders (Sather 1997:60). Each patron was thus expected to protect "his" sea people from harassment by other land-based groups. In return, the patron enjoyed a privileged trading relationship with the Sama Dilaut families under his protection. This relationship involved the exchange of both subsistence and locally produced artisan goods, and the provision by the patron's Sama Dilaut clients of maritime commodities of trade. In return for fish, usually dried, Sama Dilaut clients received cassava, the chief dietary staple, or, less often, rice, fruit, areca nuts, and other land-grown produce, as well as cloth and manufactured goods (Sather 1997:62–63). Each moorage group also traded with neighboring artisan settlements from which the sea people obtained iron goods such as fish tridents, cooking spatulas, and knife blades; plaited roofing for their boats; *pandanus* palm sleeping mats; tortoiseshell combs; earthenware hearths; water jars and other craft products; and even, at times, boats (Sather 2000:181–82; 2002:31–32). More importantly from the patron's perspective, Sama Dilaut families gathered marinè trade commodities, such as dried fish, pearl-shell, and *trepang,* thus supplying their patron with an important source of trading capital (Sather 2002:31).

Outside of trade, patrons interfered very little in the lives of the sea people. Living on boats, families could readily detach themselves from one anchorage site and reassemble at another. Living afloat prevented their close surveillance by outsiders, and for land people, enforcing clientage relations was impossible without some degree of willing compliance on the part of the Sama Dilaut themselves. Thus, if a patron interfered in the internal affairs of the clients, or placed too burdensome demands upon them, the latter might simply move away, join another moorage group, or establish themselves at a new anchorage site under the protection of a rival leader. Clientage relations, although couched in an idiom of "ownership," were thus typically fragile and, for the sea people, always reflected an uneasy balance between a need for protection in a political system of endemic violence and a desire for autonomy. Adapted to the political and economic realities of precolonial Sulu, the institution of clientage allowed the Sama Dilaut to maintain by choice a mobile, seminomadic way of life, which, at the same time, assured them a significant measure of independence.

In the late nineteenth century, all of this began to change. Semporna town was founded by the British North Borneo Chartered Company in 1887 with the intent to secure control over the lucrative east coast birds' nest trade. For the Sama Dilaut, the political and economic consequences were far-reaching. Chinese traders settling in Semporna at once diverted regional trade away from Sulu to the newly emerging colonial ports of Sandakan, Labuan, Singapore, and Hong Kong. Marine products, initially at least, formed a major component of this trade, and Chinese traders quickly supplanted local patrons, as Sama Dilaut families transferred their trade to the Semporna town market. Here, too, they found relative security. At the same time, the monetization of trade severed the former connection that existed between exchange and hierarchical differences in political status. Responding to these changes, the Sama Dilaut moved to erase those conditions that formerly marked them as a pariah group. Moorage groups gradually coalesced and, with the dissolution of patronage relations, gravitated closer and closer to Semporna town, thus setting the stage for the abandonment of boat dwelling and the construction of the present pile-house villages. As houses were constructed, the Sama Dilaut also began, over the initial opposition of local land people, to efface their former status as a people "without religion," by building mosques and adopting the ritual practices of Islam. By 1964 these practices were thoroughly a part of village life, and the social exclusion of the Sama Dilaut was beginning to fade (Sather 1997:19–20, 2002:39–43).

Since the 1970s, the population of Semporna town has grown rapidly, and today the former village of Bangau-Bangau has become largely enveloped within its urban boundaries. For administrative purposes, Bangau-Bangau is now divided into two villages, each with its own headman and community development committee. The economy has also become increasingly diversified, as most families have taken up market trading or wage work, leaving fishing largely to Sama Dilaut newcomers from the southern Philippines. Since the late 1970s, a new village has taken form close to the former Bangau-Bangau moorage site, settled chiefly by Sama Dilaut refugees (*pelarian*) from Sulu.

When they still lived on boats, the Sama Dilaut belonged to a series of leader-centered groups, ranging from the family, through pagmunda' groups, to the anchorage community as a whole. Leadership was (and still is) vested chiefly in the "elders" or *matto'a*, comprising the senior generation of active family heads. These elders include those who are still economically active and who continue to play a major role in managing the affairs of their households. The very old, although their advice is regularly sought, generally withdraw from this role of mediating conflict, hearing out grievances, and attempting to conciliate between those involved in disputes. Instead, they leave these matters to the headman and other middle-aged family heads, often to become religious figures, spirit mediums (*jin*), or, today, *imam*, village prayer leaders and ritual officiants.

In marked contrast to the dominant social and political structure around them, interpersonal relations within the community were notably egalitarian rather than hierarchical; there was no ascriptive ranking; and the matto'a, as community leaders, owed their influence not to titles or threats of coercion, but to their relative age, experience, kinship seniority, and ability to conciliate and resolve conflict among their followers (Sather 1997:62). House group and cluster spokesmen have now taken the place of family and pagmunda' leaders, but the significance of the matto'a is preeminent. As a group, they continue, as before, to be responsible for mediating disputes and looking after the interests of their followers. Respect for age was, and still is, a deeply held value in Sama Dilaut society and applies to unrelated villagers as well as to kin. In return for respect, community elders are expected to be generous and to look after the interests of their followers (*tendog*), out of, the villagers say, a sense of compassion (*ma'asé'*). Respect persists even after death, as the elders are believed to become, as ancestors (*mbo'*), a continuing source to the living of possible favors or reproach.

The Sama Dilaut are now incorporated in the larger political structure. Each village is represented by a headman or *ketua kampung*. The title is conferred by the state government, through the District Officer (*Pegawai Daerah*), and the incumbent is directly accountable to the native chief who has jurisdiction over the community. The headman represents the primary link between the village and the district government. Even so, the headman's position remains largely an external creation, and, within the village, such authority as he possesses is mainly an extension of his status as a senior cluster spokesman and the representative of an exceptionally large and extended kindred network. Panglima Tiring, the headman of Bangau-Bangau in 1964–65, was one of thirteen children. Five of his brothers and one sister each headed a village house group, while his wife had three brothers and one sister who headed another four house groups. They also had two sons who each headed a house group at the time, so that, in all, thirteen of the thirty-six house groups in the village were headed by the headman and his wife and their immediate kin. The headman was also the spokesman of the largest house group cluster in the village, and he and his wife had personal kin ties to individuals in virtually all of the remaining house groups. The chief task of the headman and other elders is to maintain the peace between members of the various house groups and clusters making up the community. Their ability to do so depends on their domestic status and the network of personal ties they are able to maintain with other house group and cluster elders. Like other leaders, the headman should be a person of good sense and judgment who, the Sama Dilaut say, is able to reason or think (*pikil*) for those who are less experienced, and so constrain their possibly more impulsive actions.

Mechanisms for Containing Violence

The Sama Dilaut have long seen themselves as a peaceable, comparatively nonviolent people, especially in contrast to their neighbors, particularly the Tausug (Sather 1997:208). In describing themselves, an expression one hears again and again is: "We [Sama Dilaut] fight only with our mouths" (Sather 1997:62).

At first, I understood this phrase to be—as indeed it is—the overt verbal expression of a conscious social aversion to physical violence, an aversion to taking up weapons other than words in situations of conflict. Only gradually did I come to understand that the phrase is also an admission that the Sama Dilaut, as a group, do indeed fight—frequently, and often with great passion—but that such fighting should be conducted by means of words, rather than by resort to physical confrontation.

Even by the end of my very first week in Bangau-Bangau, I realized that the Sama Dilaut were not a people who silently repressed their differences or hid them behind a veil of evasiveness. Instead, they did indeed fight with their mouths. Verbal quarrels and shouted harangues, the latter usually exchanged between village women standing at the edge of their house platforms or on neighboring boat-landing ladders, were a regular and dramatic feature of village life. Quarrels often centered on verbal insults and accusations of disrespectful speech; if serious enough, they might escalate into an exchange of curses (*sapa*). To exchange curses is a grave matter and may result, as we shall see, in a public declaration of formal enmity. Paradoxically, those who enter into such a relationship, called *magbanta,* sever all communication and, as a hallmark of this relationship, cease speaking to one another. This marks a dramatic rupture of normal social relations. Verbal courtesies are a significant feature of everyday social life, especially—for a seafaring people— in situations of welcome and leave taking. Food sharing, too, is a major form of sociality, and gifts of food, exchanged between kin and cluster allies, are regularly received with a verbal pledge of return; thus reciprocity is expressed simultaneously in words as well as in material transactions. Thus, the Sama Dilaut not only fight with words, but they also use words to express amity.

The villagers also, as we shall see, use speech as a way of resolving, or talking out, their differences. The principal way in which disputes are resolved is through the give-and-take of verbal mediation. It is only when mediation breaks down and speech is cut off that relations harden into formal enmities. Once this has occurred, a speaking relationship can only be renewed by ritual means, after a verbal rehearsal of past differences, a pledge to put these differences aside, and a spoken vow of future amity. With this, the copious flow of words, expressing both amity and contention, once again resumes.

Addat

A major responsibility of the headman and other village elders is to safeguard the socially binding rules, canons of behavior, and sanctions that the villagers describe as *addat*. The Sama Dilaut are not unique in this regard, as other Sama speakers also share this same concern with addat, and, indeed, cognate notions are found throughout the entire Malayo-Indonesian world. These notions, particularly ideas of "adat law," are the subject of a vast literature in which "adat" is sometimes defined in extremely broad terms as "a divine cosmic order and harmony" (Shärer 1963:74–75), such that infractions of its rules are said to disturb this order and so create a state of cosmic disequilibrium. However, in village life, the application of addat is very different. The villagers see this application in highly personalized terms. Each individual, in order to live in peace with other community members, must act according to the specific provisions of addat, as these relate, in different situations, to himself and others. In practical terms, the Sama Dilaut see disagreements as an inherent part of human affairs. Harmony is something to be strived for, not a pre-existent condition of social life. The significance of addat in this respect is that it is thought to make reconciliation and the containment of dissension possible. This is not to say that the Sama Dilaut do not also see addat as having far-reaching ramifications in terms, for example, of health or physical well-being. Those who repeatedly breach the rules of addat, or refuse to submit to conciliation, are thought to endanger the social fabric and are believed to invite calamity (*busung*), both upon themselves and others. While actions contrary to addat are felt to be imperiling, what absorbs the interest of the Sama Dilaut is not so much notions of cosmic equilibrium, but rather, more specific violations of addat. The Sama Dilaut pay particular attention to specific acts of wrongdoing, to the individuals who commit or are affected by these acts, and, even more, to the specific measures required to redress the effects of these acts and bring about a reconciliation that repairs the potentially damaged social fabric. These measures emphasize not so much harmony as reciprocity.

Very generally, addat covers all of the various norms, rules, and injunctions that guide an individual's conduct, as well as the sanctions and forms of redress by which these rules are upheld (cf. Sather 1997:204–5). Every sphere of human activity has its own particular addat. Thus, the villagers talk of marriage addat, the addat of greetings and leave-taking, mourning addat, and the addat of food sharing. The Sama Dilaut distinguish addat from religion (*ugama*). The rules of ritual and prayer are matters of ugama, not addat, and are the concern of the imam, elders, who lead public prayers and act as the custodians of community ugama. The rules of addat regulate interpersonal relationships and define the obligations that exist between persons standing in various relationships to one another. They also define property rights, rules of inheritance, and the manner in which tangible goods may be transferred from one person to another.

Like the English term "custom," addat may also be used to describe personal habits. Addat, however, has a strongly normative connotation, and its rules refer essentially to what an individual ought to do, not necessarily to what he or she does do. In this sense, the Sama Dilaut distinguish social and personal conventions that lack a moral or normative basis from addat. These are called *pantun*. The villagers often speak of individuals as possessing a personal addat. Reflecting its moral basis, such addat may be good (*ahap*) or bad (*alaat*). To have good addat implies that an individual's behavior not only accords with specific rules of addat, but, more importantly, that it exemplifies more abstract moral ideals, such as generosity, sensitivity to duty, compassion, or responsiveness to the needs of others.

The elders, and in particular the headman and other senior house group leaders, are expected to have a knowledge of addat and to use this knowledge in settling disputes involving their followers and other village members. The villagers say that most quarrels (*magsaghau*) arise between women. Certainly, these quarrels are the most visible, due perhaps to the fact that related women tend to predominate in house groups and clusters, with younger men typically marrying in. Hence, women manage most aspects of food sharing and kinship reciprocity, areas in which quarrels and grievances are most likely to arise. However, quarrels between men are thought to be more disruptive, in the sense that they are more likely to lead to the breakup of a house group or even a cluster unless they are resolved. In the case of serious quarrels, particularly those involving persons from different house groups, cluster spokesmen and other elders may be called in to help find a settlement. Should a dispute involve members of other groups, elders from the groups involved will normally try to work out an informal settlement, without referring the dispute to a higher level of leadership. Failing this, a quarrel may develop into a verbal challenge (*magsasa'*). This is viewed as a serious escalation of differences, so serious that the villagers describe it as only one step removed from physical confrontation (*magbono'*). If a dispute, having hardened into a challenge, cannot be dealt with informally, it is likely at this stage to be referred to the village headman.

Village Hearings

Unlike other elders, the headman has the power to convene an informal meeting of the parties involved in a quarrel or a breach of addat (*sa'*), or to call a more general village hearing in the event of a serious infraction of addat or a dispute, often involving a challenge, that threatens community peace. In a minor dispute, the headman invites the parties to his house for an informal face-to-face meeting, with each side usually represented by its house leader and other elders. Most meetings are held at the request of an individual nakura luma' who takes part in the discussions. The headman acts chiefly as a mediator and public witness (*saksi'*) to any agreement reached by the parties in the course of talking through their differences. If the two sides cannot find an informal solution, the matter is likely to be referred, at the headman's urging, to a formal village hearing.

The Sama Dilaut distinguish between two types of hearings. The first is called *magsalassai* and is generally considered to involve less serious matters, usually marital disputes, insults, acts of disrespect, or personal grievances. The emphasis is upon reconciliation, and fines are not levied. The second is called *maghukum* and generally involves more serious matters, often a violation of addat, a more explicit attribution of wrongdoing, and, frequently, the imposition of a fine or the award of compensation. The purpose of magsalassai is to work out a mutually acceptable settlement of differences. Magsalassai, from the root *sinalassai*, means "to settle a matter" or "to settle something by mutual agreement." It also has the sense of "to end," "wind up," or "dispose" (as of a business or debt). *Maghukum*, in contrast, refers to a formal settling of a dispute in terms of addat, although today the term is also used by the villagers when they refer a case beyond the village by taking it to an official court, or by using the process of modern state-administered law, either through the native or district court (*Mahkamah Session*) or the religious court (*Mahkamah Syariah*).

All village hearings take place in the evening in the house of the village headman, either inside the headman's house, or, in the case of formal hearings that typically involve a large gathering of participants, on his house platform. Anyone may attend, raise questions, and express an opinion, but the proceedings are normally dominated by house elders and other matto'a. Women as well as men are included. In 1965 three of the thirty-six house group leaders in Bangau-Bangau and one cluster spokesman were women. However, men greatly predominate, although their wives, including the headman's wife, frequently speak out during village hearings. While everyone who wishes to speak is generally heard out, the elders, particularly the headman, tend to take a leading role in summarizing, commenting on, and placing in perspective the words spoken by others.

The headman opens the proceedings by stating that its purpose is to settle a dispute, or to hear a complaint. He then outlines the nature of the complaint and stresses that those taking part should seek to restore good will between the litigants and their kin (see Sather 1997:206). In this way, the headman calls attention to the purpose of the hearing and the overriding responsibility of everyone present to reestablish amicable relations between the parties involved. Hearings are sometimes heated, and it may be necessary to remind those voicing opinions of their responsibility in this regard. The basic purpose of a hearing is to create *magsulut,* meaning, essentially, a state of mutual accord or reconciliation. To achieve magsulut, a settlement most often calls for concessions from both sides.

Magsulut is a basic ideal of village life. It refers to a state of accord, of going along or being in agreement with the opinions, wishes, or behavior of other village members. The root, *sulut,* means, literally, "to go along," "go parallel," or "to not act against one another's wishes." The term is used in daily conversation, for example, to advise others to "*magsulut kaam,*" meaning, "to be united," "be together," or "be of one mind" or "of one opinion." Ideally, a state of magsulut should prevail in relations between relatives and those living in the same house, cluster, or village. The opposite of magsulut is *embal magtalua,* meaning "not in accord," "at odds," "out of sorts," in which the views and actions of individuals are at cross-purposes. The ideal of magsulut is best achieved if the outcome of a hearing is one in which both parties emerge as more or less equal (*tabla'*).

Village hearings, as well as more informal mediation sessions, deal most often with marital disputes. Before a couple is granted a divorce, they are called to an informal meeting with the headman, who first attempts to bring about their reconciliation. A reconciliation that averts a divorce is called *amahilala'* "putting matters to right." If the headman finds either the husband or wife is at fault, he may pronounce a warning called *batang-batang.* If reconciliation proves impossible, the couple is referred to the District Imam to initiate a formal divorce. Further proceedings are likely only if there are difficult property issues to be resolved. These are generally brought before a village maghukum presided over by the headman, who, again, acts as mediator and witness. Other frequent subjects of maghukum hearings include sexual delicts and elopement, disputes over debts, property loss or damage, and personal insults, slander, or serious acts of discourtesy. Considering the importance given to words, it is not surprising that accusations of verbal discourtesy, insults, slander, and false accusations are frequent subjects of litigation. Hearings may be called to bring about a public retraction of an insult or an exchange of apologies. In the case of hearsay slander, or a charge that one person has secretly cursed (*anukna'*) another, the accused may clear himself by swearing a public oath (*magsapa*) while touching the Qur'an in the presence of witnesses (Sather 1997:207).

The headman has little authority over persons who are not members of his own house group, and he cannot, as a rule, impose a judgment that is not mutually acceptable to both sides. It is here that addat and the knowledge of the elders regarding past settlements becomes especially important. If a case can be linked to a specific rule of addat and to past settlements of a similar nature, it becomes increasingly difficult for either side to reject a proposed settlement out of hand. Today, if they do, the other party has a strong case to refer to the native court, where the outcome is likely to support the views of the headman. Litigation is frequent, and most families are involved at least once a year in some form of village hearing.

While the headman can intervene and call disputants together to discuss their differences, he cannot compel them to accept a judgment. He must rely instead on house and cluster elders to secure compliance with a decision reached through mediation or by the informal discussions that take place in his house. Here, the elders are expected to put to the fore the long-term interests of the community, and particularly relations between the groups they represent and others, as part of the larger fabric of reciprocal social relations. In addition, the concept of busung, referring to a state of calamity or misfortune, enters as an important inducement to settlement. Those who reject the verdict of a hearing, swear falsely, or break off proceedings before a settlement can be reached are believed to leave themselves open to busung, in the form of sickness or ill fortune.

Diat *and* Bangun

Even though the Sama Dilaut see themselves as a peaceable people, in cases of serious conflict, there is always a danger that the injured party may retaliate directly against the culprit or his family. Physical violence is not unknown among the Sama Dilaut. In the past, it was considered a legitimate form of redress in situations of adultery, sexual relations with an unmarried woman, physical injury, and homicide. Today, cases involving physical injury, including homicide, are usually dealt with by the police and state courts; while adultery and other sexual offenses are generally brought before a formal village hearing or are taken outside the village to the native or religious courts for settlement.

Traditionally, the threat of retaliation was limited by the right of the headman and other community leaders to provide sanctuary to those involved in a dispute or accused of wrongdoing. This was, and continues to be, especially important in cases of elopement, which, among the Sama Dilaut, is frequent, accounting for more than a third of all first marriages (Sather 1997:249–50). Young people, including children, may also seek sanctuary, usually with grandparents or the village headman, when threatened with punishment for alleged wrongdoing or when faced with the prospects of an unwanted marriage arranged by their kin. In the past, the person seeking sanctuary joined the boat of the elder, or fled to seek protection with relatives living in another moorage group. Today, they take sanctuary in the house of the headman, the grandparents, or a cluster leader. Formerly, for the Sama Dilaut, flight was an important means of averting retaliation or escaping contention among kin. In 1964-65 extended fishing voyages were still seen as an important avenue of escape to be taken by families during times of particularly intense verbal bickering between village kin and neighbors. While the parties were separated, passions often cooled, and after several weeks at sea, most people looked forward to resuming the intense verbal give-and-take of village life. Moorage groups characterized by constant quarreling were likely to dissolve.

The act of granting sanctuary automatically brought the matter under judicial review through mediation overseen by the elder providing sanctuary, and so the potential for retaliation or open feuding was forestalled, at least temporarily. Providing sanctuary was, and still is, an obligation of village leaders and has traditionally worked as an important curb against violence, including what the villagers consider the unfair or unduly harsh punishment of children by parents or adoptive kin. By the age of five or six, children are expected to make themselves useful, whether at sea or around the house, but discipline is extremely mild. Harsh punishment is strongly disapproved of, and, as in other situations, receiving sanctuary precipitates community intervention in the form of a hearing or face-to-face mediation. Here, parents may be called upon to explain their actions and may be criticized if these are thought to be excessive. One of the very few cases of suicide in the Sama Dilaut community—which took place in Sitangkai, not Semporna, some years before I began my research—involved a father who, in a moment of anger, struck his young son on the back. The boy went to the stern of the family boat, lay down, and apparently fell asleep. A short time later, the father tried to awaken him and discovered that he was dead. Grief-stricken, the man went berserk (*magsabil*) and killed himself (see Sather 1997:226). The story was still told with horror in Semporna many years later.

For an elder, providing sanctuary is a further expression of the compassion or love he is expected to show toward those in need of his protection. Granting sanctuary does not necessarily imply that the elder supports the accused's actions, and in the mediation he is expected to remain neutral, while insuring that the accused has an opportunity to reply to his accusers and express his views.

Another means of averting retaliation was, in the case of serious physical injury, for the accused to pledge an item of inherited property (*pusaka*), usually a gong (*agung*), to the injured person's family as a sign of good faith. The pledge was retained until the injured man or woman showed signs of recovery, and it was then returned to its owner. Like the granting of sanctuary, the pledge secured a temporary assurance against resort to physical retaliation and signaled the intent of both sides to avert bloodshed.

There are two forms of traditional indemnification in Sama Dilaut society: (1) *diat,* paid as a token of solicitude in the case of an unintentional or minor injury; and (2) *bangun,* blood-money, paid in the case of homicide, provided the dead person's kin are willing to accept it.

Any injury, however minor, that results in bloodshed is considered serious. A powerful cultural aversion operates, and if a member of the village causes, or is in some way responsible for, a bleeding injury to another, the situation is handled directly through a formal convention called *diniatan.* Most cases resolved in this way involve injuries caused by negligence or accident. Common examples are when a person falls from a house platform belonging to another family or is injured by the collapse of a poorly maintained catwalk. Diat is seen by the Sama Dilaut as a symbolic token of concern. It consists of a small monetary indemnity. Its actual value, however, is less important than its symbolic intent as a sign of apology. Payment is also thought to have a curative effect. Without it, it is said, the injury will not heal properly. The person responsible for causing the injury, or a parent or other house group elder in the case of a youngster, carries the diat to the house of the injured person, together with a large dish (*lai*) filled with water. The water is used by the person who performs diniatan to wash the wound. While doing so, he or she recites a brief blessing formula, asking for a speedy recovery. For example, the performer may recite: *Murah-murahan kapahap bo' ka diniatan,* "May you, by means of this diat, soon recover." The injured person must eat his meals from the dish for three consecutive evenings. If the injury is serious, the person responsible, and often others from his or her house group, show their concern by regularly visiting the injured person during recovery. On the fourth day, the dish is returned to its owner.

In a typical example, a young girl named Norija threw a bottle out of the window just as a young man, Binsali, passed by on the walkway outside. The bottle cut Binsali slightly on the side of his head. In response, Norija's mother at once took diat to Binsali's house, as a sign of apology and concern.

In most cases, the injury compensated by diat is minor, and its payment involves only the families immediately affected. However, diat may also be paid between families living in different villages, should a person from one village cause injury to someone from another. This can take place only after the intercession of the headmen representing the two villages. In giving and accepting diat, both sides signal their willingness to end the matter and resume normal relations. The primary purpose is thus the same as a village hearing, namely magsulut, meaning, again, "conciliation" or "putting an end to differences." It is concluded with another characteristically verbal action, a mutual exchange of vows pledging future good will.

Diat always involves nonfatal injuries. Traditionally, a deliberate homicide is said to have required the taking of a life in retaliation. Reprisal might also be taken against any member of the culprit's family who offered him support or shelter or aided his escape. However, a community leader might again intervene, particularly if there were extenuating circumstances, and offer sanctuary until blood-money could be negotiated. Blood-money is called bangun, and the act of paying it is known as *binangunan*. In the past, bangun was usually accepted only in the case of unintentional homicide, where there existed kinship relationships between those involved or when there were mitigating or justifiable circumstances. Today, all forms of homicide must be referred to the police. Even so, in the case of deliberate homicide, there remains—despite the general aversion to violence—a strong feeling in favor of retaliation. This feeling is partly an expression of the principle, also reflected in village litigation, that the resolution of serious conflict can only be achieved by reestablishing "equality" between the parties involved.

Sama Dilaut society is not violence-free, but the amount of violence is conspicuously less than among neighboring land people, particularly the Tausug, with whom feuding is endemic and armed vendettas are a regular result of insults and crimes of honor. One homicide occurred in Bangau-Bangau shortly after I left the field, in which a husband murdered his former wife, who had refused to remarry him. In the opinion of other villagers, the young husband showed an abnormal interest in the old ways of the ancestors. He studied esoteric forms of magic with a number of elderly men and used this knowledge, the villagers claim, to escape capture by making himself invisible. However, he was eventually apprehended by the police on BumBum Island, tried, and imprisoned. The case was handled entirely by the police and courts, and there was no attempt at retaliation as all of the persons involved were closely related.

An aborted attempt at blood-money payment occurred during my fieldwork in 1979. The case had begun more than a year earlier with the murder of six Sama Dilaut men by pirates near Sitangkai in the Philippines. After the murders, the pirates, who were not Sama, scattered and went into hiding. The father of one of the men killed lived in Bangau-Bangau. After the bodies were found floating in the sea, he traveled to Sitangkai to identify his son. Two of the pirates were eventually located and killed by brothers of the murdered men.

Magbanta, Or Formal Enmity

Not all dissension between villagers is successfully resolved: A breakdown in relations may occur. It is almost always the result not of a single incident, but of a long history of disagreements and accumulated grievances that is so irreconcilable that it is marked by a complete rupture of relations. The most notable feature of this breakdown is the total cessation of speech.

Those who sever a relationship in this way are almost always kin. Among the Sama Dilaut, a person has the right to expect aid from a kinsman. The only way in which an individual may repudiate a close kinsman's claims on his support is by declaring a relationship of formal enmity. Such a relationship is called magbanta, and those who stand in it refer to each other as *banta.* The relationship is dyadic and banta no longer exchange words. Nonkin, should they have serious grievances, may readily ignore one another or pursue their differences through village litigation, but these options are not available to close kin, particularly those who live together as village housemates or cluster neighbors. Such persons are in constant contact and never, by virtue of their relationship, initiate formal hearings against one another. By contrast, those who are banta are entitled to disclaim any obligations that might otherwise exist between them. Magbanta defines a relation of mutual antipathy and nonsupport, and it expresses the absence of the compassion or love that kin should feel toward one another.

Entering a magbanta relationship is typically formalized by pronouncing a verbal curse (*magsapa*), in this case a spoken declaration of intent to sever all connections. To make such a curse (*sapa*) more powerful or authoritative, the declaration is often strengthened by reference to the Qur'an or to the ancestors. For example,

> *Allum sajja embo'ku boho' aku amolé' ni luma' iti,*
> Only if my deceased grandfather/mother comes to life again, will I come back to this house.

Once spoken, such sworn words become a *suvali,* a kind of vow (*janji'*) that cannot be broken (see Sather 1997:240–42, 287–90).

A declaration of enmity affects not only a single person-to-person relationship, but it also has major ramifications for house group and cluster alignments. If enemies were formerly cluster allies or even housemates, as is often the case, the result is almost always the withdrawal of one party or the other from the group. The resulting rupture of ties may have a chain-reaction if others take sides. The cluster itself may fragment, with some house groups aligning themselves with one antagonist, others with the other. Oftentimes, declarations of enmity bring to a head fissures that have been growing for a number of years. In 1965 Umaldani, a prominent house group leader in Bangau-Bangau, broke off relations with his mother following years of bickering between his mother and his wife. However, this swearing of enmity also marked the end of relations that had become increasingly attenuated following the death of Panglima Atani, the original village headman, in whose cluster both Umaldani and his mother lived. With Atani's death, new leaders emerged within the group, including Umaldani, and in the years that followed, new house groups were founded by the children of this succeeding generation of house group leaders. As a result, the families comprising the cluster were already well along in the process of realigning themselves around new house group and cluster allies. After a particularly heated exchange between Umaldani's wife and his mother, shouted from facing house platforms, the final triggering event occurred several days later when Umaldani pointedly refused to press his mother's hands as a sign of leave-taking and affection, as she was about to embark with other family members on a dangerous journey to Sitangkai in the Philippines. This act brought about an instant swearing of enmity and the withdrawal of Umaldani and his family, the tearing down of the connecting catwalks that joined his house with the others, and in the weeks that followed, by the dismantlement of Umaldani's former house and its reconstruction among the recently built houses of his sons in a nearby part of the village.

Once two persons, such as Umaldani and his mother, have declared themselves banta, the former relationship that existed between them can no longer be restored by mediation and certainly not by talking out their differences, as the two are now sworn to silence. It can only be renewed by ritual means, and, for this, the two persons must voluntarily perform a ceremony called *magkiparat* (or *magtiparat*).

Magkiparat, Or Ritual Reconciliation

Enmity is believed to be a source of busung, or misfortune. Those who continue to harbor enmity and go on, year after year, refusing to restore the flow of words are thought to invite busung upon themselves as well as their enemies. Hence, others are likely to try to convince them to resolve their differences and undergo magkiparat. This is particularly true if one or both fall ill, or if one appears to be close to death or faces a situation of physical danger. For example, when Layang's wife, Tia, became pregnant, she and Layang's mother underwent a ritual reconciliation. The two women had earlier become *banta* because of the older woman's fervent opposition to the marriage. In this case, magkiparat was performed to avert medical complications arising from Tia's pregnancy. Reconciliation was also prompted by a desire to make it possible for Tia to deliver the child in Layang's parents' house. During the women's enmity, the couple had been forced to live in rented quarters in Semporna town.

It is not uncommon for village curers to ask that a patient seeking treatment reconcile with his or her banta as a precondition to full recovery. Under such circumstances, the banta are likely to agree. Otherwise, they may be held responsible should the patient die or fail to improve. Above all, the villagers say, an individual should not go to his grave unreconciled with his banta. Consequently, if a person appears to be near death, a determined effort is normally made to clear away, through magkiparat rituals, all outstanding relations of enmity (see Sather 1997:213). Another circumstance that may encourage reconciliation is the passage of time. After a number of years, kin of the banta are likely to meet and plan for the process of magkiparat. The initiator may come from one of the two families, or the planning may be mediated by persons who are related to both sides. Before the ceremony is arranged, the banta and their families must pledge their willingness to forgive past grievances and renew their family ties in front of an audience of village guests and elders.

In Bangau-Bangau, magkiparat is usually performed by the village headman. It takes place just after sunrise with the two persons sitting side-by-side, facing westward (kasaddopan) in the direction assumed in prayer, with the headman standing behind them. Other families, besides those of the two enemies, are required to provide a small number of coconuts. Holding one of these in his left hand, the headman splits it with a knife, opening the shell just enough for the water inside to run out. While joining with the imam in reciting a prayer, the headman allows the water to flow over the heads of the pair seated at his feet. The empty coconut is then placed on the house platform and split in two with a single sharp blow. The two halves of the coconut must turn the same way, either face upward or face downward, symbolic of renewed accord. Otherwise, the procedure is repeated using other coconuts until the required result is obtained. As soon as the rite is over, the two are bathed and then join their families and other guests in public prayers (doa salamat) recited by the imam and other elders. This is followed by a majamu or kenduri, a thanksgiving feast. Until the rite is concluded, the two are not permitted to speak to one another. The final act of resuming speech (mahilling pabalik) marks the resumption of normal relations, including all social obligations renounced during their enmity.

What makes magkiparat so effective as a form of reconciliation is that it must be organized and provisioned by community members, not by the banta themselves, so that the community's support for reconciliation becomes an active factor in the process. Everything necessary for the ritual, like rice, fish, coffee, and coconuts, must be donated by other families. Only after everything has been organized are the banta called to be present in a public and highly ritualized setting. If their enmity was preceded by a curse (sapa), both parties must recount the causes and history of their magsapa before they utter the formula that "undoes" their enmity during the ritual.

For settled inland Sama speakers in the Semporna district, if a curse is serious, undoing it requires blood (*laha'*) in the form of an animal sacrifice (*tumpah*). By contrast, the Sama Dilaut never combine reconciliation with animal sacrifice.

Conclusion

Throughout this paper, we have explored the role of words in keeping the peace. The Sama Dilaut use words both to express their disagreements and also to reconcile and settle their differences. They are not a people who hide their feelings, whether of good will or enmity; rather, they continually put these feelings into words. A memorable village sight is that of women standing at the edges of their house platforms, shouting out their complaints against each other for all to hear. Equally notable, however, is the fact that these complaints may be resolved and, as the villagers say, brought to an end by talking them out or, alternatively, by verbally withdrawing an insult or an accusation of wrongdoing, exchanging apologies, and pledging themselves—again by the use of words—to live in peace with one another. While quarrels between women may be the most visible and, the villagers say, the most common form contention takes, it is usually men who escalate these differences by formulating them in words as a challenge or by turning them into an act of verbal retaliation as a curse. When differences reach this stage, the persons involved usually renounce any further exchange of words and become, reciprocally, banta, persons who do not speak to each other. At this point, the flow of words can only be restored by outside intervention in the form of a community magkiparat ceremony.

It is worth speculating on how these social and cultural mechanisms work to contain conflict and what it is that makes the Sama Dilaut a comparatively peaceable community. A partial answer almost certainly has to do with the special position in the past of the Sama Dilaut as a pariah group. Excluded from direct participation in the dominant political order, the community was generally insulated from the often violent competition for power that went on around them. At the same time, in culturally rejecting the evaluation of themselves by those living ashore, the Sama Dilaut inverted to some degree the values of the dominant society by taking pride in, and making a source of identity, their own nonviolence. Instead, they placed, and continue to place, high value on keeping the peace by averting physical violence to promote among themselves conditions of magsulut, or mutual accord, reiterating its importance again and again in community gatherings and in public rhetoric.

Respect for the elders also reinforces this avoidance of violence. As community leaders, the elders are expected to constrain the anger and impulsiveness of their less-experienced followers and to place conflicts in the context of long-term reciprocal relations between village families and house groups. To this end, addat, too, plays a role. In addition to providing the normative basis on which individual actions may be judged and shortcomings redressed, addat also provides the basis for reconciling differences. Furthermore, the fact that children can expect to find refuge with grandparents and other elders acts as a check on expressions of violence within the family. Finally, cultural aversion to violence and respect for the elders are reinforced by the notion of busung, which holds that discourtesy, enmity, false swearing, and a refusal to put aside differences all invite misfortune.

In all of this, the question arises as to how the Sama Dilaut have been able to replace violence or the threat of violence with the use of words. One answer, I think, has to do with the importance that the Sama Dilaut attribute to words and, above all, the way in which they assign to words, in some contexts at least, a powerful binding force, committing those who utter them to some particular course of action. This granting to words the power to commit or bind persons can be seen in the ways that the villagers express and contain conflict, for example, in verbal challenges, acts of cursing and swearing, and the pledging and taking of vows.

Finally, this intensely verbal way of coping with conflict works for the Sama Dilaut because their society also presents its members with avenues of escape. One of these is an escape into the silence of person-to-person enmity. The significance of rupturing the flow of words should not be underestimated. Paradoxically, a declaration of enmity acts like a tripwire in situations of escalating contention, breaking off relations just when they threaten to dissolve into physical violence. Although defined as a person-to-person relationship, the act of declaring enmity oftentimes has a cascading effect, bringing about a more general realignment of family and house group relations. The consequences often alleviate tensions in the sense that these realignments generally follow along emerging fissures in the social fabric and so allow families to disengage from relations that have become attenuated or a source of friction and to refocus on relations with persons with whom they feel a greater affinity. At the same time, identifying enmity with single individuals prevents the rupturing of contacts from becoming generalized, confining it instead to those individuals and, at most, their immediate families. In the past, the other much more common way to escape was by going to sea on a fishing voyage or by joining a new moorage group. Today, such opportunities are limited chiefly to tearing down and relocating one's house. As the Sama Dilaut become more like their settled neighbors, it remains to be seen whether this system of keeping peace will continue to work as successfully as it did in the past, when they were still truly "sea people."

Study Questions

1. Review the different linguistic conceptions and methods that are involved in the creation and maintenance of peace among the Sama Dilaut. Compare these concepts and methods to those used in some of the other peaceful societies described in this book. How are Sama Dilaut conflict management conceptions and practices similar to and different from those in the other case study societies?
2. Are any of the Sama Dilaut conflict management concepts and practices similar to the ones used in your own society? Explain.
3. Explain what *magbanta* is and how (paradoxically) it can prevent violence.
4. Describe briefly the *magkiparat* reconciliation ritual. How does social pressure operate to bring about reconciliation? How do Sama Dilaut beliefs about illness and misfortune help to bring about reconciliation?
5. How do the political and kinship structures of Sama Dilaut society support the maintenance of peacefulness?

10
A Model of Peacefulness: Rethinking Peace and Conflict in Norway

KRISTIN DOBINSON

Most of the societies discussed in this volume are small in scale. This does not mean that lessons about creating and maintaining peace are less valuable in these contexts—people face similar conflicts in any society. However, industrial societies do have unique problems; there is, for example, greater scope for structural violence. In Norway, we have a population trying to maintain a highly peaceful society. In this chapter, Kristin Dobinson reveals the strengths and weaknesses of the Norwegians' attempts. It is interesting to compare the Norwegians and the other societies discussed in the book. There are weaknesses in Norwegian attempts to promote and maintain peace, such as the racist violence that occurs in Oslo, but this is a society that sees itself orientated toward peace. As other societies seek to follow a similar path, there will also be failures as well as successes. One cannot simply become a peaceful culture overnight—it is a process of evolution and adaptation. Here is a society further along that path than many other Western societies. We may learn as much from its failures as its successes in our own social evolution to a culture of peace.

—GK

Norway is often singled out as a comparatively peaceful society. Ross (1993a, 1993b), for instance, terms Norway a "low-conflict society" and a "peaceful nation." Norway ranked lowest out of seventy-five countries on *all six* forms of conflict behavior (both domestic and foreign) identified in a study conducted in the 1960s (see Galtung 1974). Such studies have contributed to Norway gaining a mythical status as a model of peacefulness—a society renowned for its low levels of overt violence and its well-adjusted population. Norway's recent peace activism on the world stage has further reinforced this image.

This chapter takes a new look at Norway's peacefulness and reexamines the glowing portrayals of the society in decades past, taking into account recent changes in the social fabric and normative structures of Norwegian society. Norwegian society is not inherently or unproblematically peaceful, although it can perhaps be described, using Ross' terminology, as a "constructive conflict society." Conflict is an endemic feature of human existence. However, the extent to which it is managed, contained, or resolved varies from one society to the next, as does the extent to which violence is tolerated. By providing a more nuanced picture of contemporary Norway—its tensions as well as its more cohesive traits—much can be learned. The Norwegian experience can provide insights into a range of issues connected to societal peacefulness, such as mechanisms for handling conflict as well as normative and discursive structures that sustain a self-image as a peaceful society. These mechanisms in turn contribute to the notion of peace being highly valued, and, by extension, violence being widely and vocally renounced.

By stripping Norway of its status as a model of peacefulness, it could be argued that the Norwegian case actually gains more relevance—as a society which is no "better" than others, but where levels of overt violence and aggression, for myriad reasons, remain comparatively low. Despite the fact that rising levels of violence are the cause of great public concern and debate in contemporary Norwegian society, empirical studies show that by international standards levels of overt conflict and aggression remain low. However, peace cannot simply be equated with a lack of overt violence. Aggression— or overt violence—represents only one manifestation of conflict; people can also be harmed through social isolation, stigmatization, discrimination, or through being denied a voice for expressing grievances. The first section of this chapter provides a brief description of the types and frequencies of violence and physical aggression in the society. Norway's external relations are then discussed, before turning to norms, cultural values, and attitudes that have a bearing on peacefulness. Mechanisms for handling conflict in Norwegian society are then considered.

The Domestic Realm

Norway's apparent internal peacefulness can be partly explained by structural features of the social setting—not least the fact that Norwegian society has traditionally been extremely homogeneous in terms of ethnicity, language, and religion; although there have been cleavages, these are minor, compared to the profound divisions in more complex societies.

Crime rates have been rising steadily over the last few decades, although Norway still fares well in comparison with other countries. The number of violent crimes investigated by the police in 1992 (10,205) was almost six times that recorded in 1956 (1,720) (Statistics Norway 2002). The intervening decades witnessed a steady, though fluctuating, upward trend: 1,958 violent crimes investigated by police in 1960; 3,257 in 1970; and 4,309 in 1980, with the steepest rise taking place during the 1980s. The general trend for murder rates, which of course are included in these totals, has also been upward, although with great fluctuation from year to year. The lowest number of investigated murders was recorded in 1965 (just 5) the highest in 1989, when there were more than twelve times as many (62).

When compared to other countries, however, Norway still appears to be extremely peaceful (nonviolent) in many respects. In a comparative survey of criminal justice statistics for twenty-nine countries in 1998, Norway still ranks lowest for recorded homicides (Barclay & Tavares 2000:11). Norway's score of 0.86 police-recorded homicides per 100,000 population in 1998 is in a totally different league from that of Russia (20.20 per 100,000— although this figure includes attempted homicides) or South Africa (57.52 per 100,000). The figure for the United States (6.26 per 100,000) though lower than that of Russia and South Africa, is still more than seven times that of Norway. On the other hand, Norway's rate of recorded homicide is fairly comparable to that of Austria (0.95 per 100,000), Denmark (0.93 per 100,000), and Luxembourg (0.94 per 100,000). It should be noted, however, that comparisons between countries may be affected by legal differences and statistical recording methods and that statistics for Norwegian crime rates also vary; according to the Yearbook of Nordic Statistics (1994), for instance, Norway's homicide rate was 1.4 per 100,000 per year.

Irrespective of international comparisons, the perception in Norwegian media and popular discourse is that crime rates, violence, and tensions in the society are on the increase and have already reached intolerable proportions. Foreigners are frequently portrayed as culpable in Norway's rising crime rates and as more violent than Norwegians. Violence (*vold*) has become a topic of heated debate, covering newspaper pages on an almost-daily basis. In the capital city, Oslo, this debate is most striking. Not surprisingly, it is here that the increasing rates of violence are most intensely felt. In fact, when homicide statistics for selected cities are compared, Oslo's rate of 1.93 per 100,000 per year (average, 1996–1998) is actually higher than that of Tokyo (1.07), Rome (1.51), Athens (1.32), and Edinburgh (1.78) (Barclay & Tavares 2000:4). Headlines report Oslo's schoolchildren's increasing violence against teachers (Johnsen 2001); how families move in order to escape violent gangs (Sætran 2002); street violence (*gatevold*); and above all a recent spate of killings outside nightclubs and other establishments. In the first half of 2002, Oslo witnessed a fatal shooting and a fatal stabbing outside public establishments. In Moss, a town about an hour's train ride from Oslo, two doormen were killed at a nightclub. These are only the latest in a series of shooting and stabbing incidents, which have contributed in recent years to a popular perception that Norway, and particularly Oslo, are becoming unsafe. Such killings have been met with public outcry, and several times torch-lit processions have been held following murders—in memory of victims and also as protests against violence. The Norwegian Red Cross initiated the program *Stop the Violence* (*Stopp volden*) in 1995, in response to the shooting of a boy on the streets of Oslo. The first torch-lit procession, arranged by friends of the boy, was followed by a series of articles on violence and its victims in the national newspaper *Dagbladet*. *Stopp volden*, with its striking handprint logo, continued the awareness-raising work started by *Dagbladet*.

By far the largest public demonstration was held after the racially motivated killing of a fifteen-year-old boy in Oslo on January 26, 2001. The boy, whose father was Ghanaian, was stabbed by teenagers from a neo-Nazi group calling itself the BootBoys. Around 40,000 people participated in the torch-lit procession following the murder, including the prime minister and members of the royal family. *Stopp volden* was also prominent. It was reported in the Norwegian press that the killing had made the *New York Times*, with an article examining "the perfect country's" self-doubt following the murder, which was seen as a watershed—the first racially motivated killing in Norway.

What is interesting is not so much the rising rates of violence in Norwegian society (since by international standards these remain low), but the powerful reactions against violence that have resulted, both in popular discourse and in action, exemplified most visibly by the torch-lit peace marches. The level of public outcry in the face of violent crime suggests that peace, in the sense of nonviolence, is widely valued in Norwegian society and that there are norms for nonviolent behavior that are being broken. In many other societies, violent murders would not occupy the same newspaper column space, nor mobilize such powerful reactions from members of the society. Partly, of course, this reflects the fact that where violent crime is more commonplace, people become resigned to its occurrence, but it can also be argued that many other social settings do not share the particular normative and attitudinal features of Norwegian society, which would appear to encourage an aversion to interpersonal violence.

The International Realm

Turning now to the foreign realm, Norway's external relations are remarkably free of belligerent or aggressive posturing. In fact, since its birth as a nation-state in 1905, it can be argued that Norway has exhibited a consistent preoccupation with the peaceful settlement of international disputes (Dobinson 2000). Even the union with Sweden, which commenced with a brief war, was dissolved peaceably; this has been described as "the first Nordic *non*-war" (Wiberg 1990:15; Archer 1996:453). There have been a number of conflicts over fishing rights, but none of these have amounted to much, certainly not to warfare. Norwegians' Viking heritage, in contrast, testifies to a rather different attitude toward conflict than that which prevails today, and most modern Norwegians seem to view their glorious and gory Viking past with considerable pride. It has been claimed that although Viking warriors were feared throughout Europe, the domestic society was relatively peaceful (Eckstein 1966:115; Ross 1993a:57).

The long-standing preoccupation with the peaceful settlement of international conflicts can be seen at various junctures in Norway's recent history. To an extent, it can be traced to feelings of vulnerability on the world stage, but it also runs deeper than this. It has been claimed, for example, that a pacifist streak unique to Norway emerged during the period of union with Sweden (Burgess 1968:19–20). Alfred Nobel's choice to give Norway the honor of awarding the Peace Prize can also be seen in this context—as largely due to the Norwegian pacifist orientation and to the fact that far back into the nineteenth century the Norwegian parliament was interested in mediation, arbitration, and the peaceful settlement of disputes.

During World War I, Norway maintained a stance of neutrality, and an intra-Scandinavian "peace entente" developed, with all three states keeping out of the hostilities. According to Burgess, the experience of World War I confirmed to Norwegians that their peace traditions "were extraordinarily deep-rooted and were of such a nature that they would surely be respected by other nations" (Burgess 1968:34). However, World War II threw such assumptions aside.

The German occupation during World War II was a crucial experience, which heightened the Norwegian concern for peace and security. Galtung has spoken of the "9th of April complex" (the date of the Nazi invasion in 1940) as something that all Norwegians relate to (Galtung and Ikeda 1995; Dobinson 2000). After the Nazi occupation, Norway was forced to reassess its neutrality and chose to join NATO in 1949. The deteriorating Soviet-American relationship was of great concern to Norwegians, as they shared a border with the USSR, and they also feared the repercussions the conflict would have for the United Nations as a security organization. At the onset of the Cold War, taking an active role as bridge-builder between the major powers was discussed for a brief time (Egeland 1988:35–37).

It can generally be said that a nonbelligerent, peace-promoting stance has continued to characterize Norwegian foreign policy in the post-war period. Independent Norwegian foreign political activism was limited during the

Cold War, primarily due to the country's exposed strategic position. Instead, Norwegian foreign policy was mainly carried out under the auspices of the United Nations, where Norway has always been one of the most active members, particularly in peacekeeping operations.

During the Cold War, the Nordic region as a whole was widely considered to be an area of exceptional peace and stability. In order to explain this, the "Nordic Balance" theory has often been invoked (see Knutsen 1995:16–18). Archer speaks in a broader sense of a Nordic "Zone of Peace" (Archer 1996:454). He points to the absence of interstate war among the Nordic neighbors from 1814 onward, to the paucity of civil war and armed uprisings, and to the lack of military intervention by armed forces from the region in other parts of the world. In general, Archer (1996:456) maintains, "While disputes do occur between Nordic and other states, these are resolved through diplomacy, by methods short of violence and far from warfare." He also notes that the Nordic region has remained a "haven of calm" in an age of terrorism. Although the Nordic states have very small ethnic minorities and unusually homogeneous populations, "The region has had some potential for division but choices have been made by governments and groups not to push these to armed conflict . . . " (Archer 1996:460).

Since the end of the Cold War, with the removal of constraints on Norway's maneuverability, there has been a new burgeoning of foreign political activism, particularly in the sphere of human rights, promotion of democracy, and conflict resolution work. In 1993 Norway gained international recognition for its Middle East "Oslo Channel." This much-publicized mediation initiative is just the tip of the iceberg. Since 1990, Norwegian participants have contributed to peace negotiations in more than fourteen conflicts, with thirteen of these involving Norwegian mediation in some sense (Dobinson 2000). Details of still other mediation attempts may never be made public knowledge. Norway's lack of a direct stake in these conflicts has contributed to its image as an honest broker. For a population of just 4.5 million, this level of peace activism is noteworthy. For such an active peacemaking role to emerge in this relatively small sociocultural setting, with a significant number of Norwegians waging peace during international conflicts, it can be argued that the particular norms and "social stocks of knowledge" of this shared setting are somehow implicated in their decisions to mediate and to support a peace orientation (Dobinson 2000).

Cultural Beliefs, Attitudes, Norms, and Values

A consideration of cultural beliefs, attitudes, norms, and values is of central importance for understanding why a given social group generally chooses methods of resolving conflict that stop short of violence. Individuals, as social actors, are in part constituted by the history, traditions, and cultural heritage of their social group. In most everyday action, individuals act in a state of "practical consciousness" (Giddens 1984) or in "the natural attitude" (Schutz 1966). That is, people draw on the socially derived stocks of knowledge, which provide them with "recipes" for how to behave. This enables patterns of behavior and customary practices—for instance, socially approved practices for dealing with conflict—to emerge and endure over time. It is only when a problematic situation is encountered, such as the entrance of an outsider not sharing the same cultural background, that these taken-for-granted beliefs, attitudes, and values become visible, and thereby open to question (Habermas 1987:122).

Contemporary Norwegian society is rapidly becoming more pluralistic. With the comparatively recent entrance of immigrants (immigration first exceeded emigration in 1971), the societal make-up has changed quite noticeably over recent decades. "Difference" is now encountered more frequently in everyday life, and traditional norms and patterns of interaction are increasingly being challenged by new members of the society. The recent debates on violence are a case in point. Norms and values relating to peace and conflict, and to Norway's peacefulness, which were previously largely hidden, are now becoming apparent and being openly discussed. This all makes the Norwegian case particularly interesting at the present time.

Social Democracy and Lutheranism

Norwegian society has strong Social Democratic and Lutheran traditions, from which many of the society's norms and values are derived. The Labor Party (*Arbeiderpartiet*) traditionally dominated the political sphere, and although the party's position today is altogether different, "Socialism as a humanistic, egalitarian ideal has long had a strong position. Capitalism has few positive connotations in Norwegian culture." (Knudsen 1990:104). To a large extent there is broad consensus across the political spectrum on social democratic values (Østerud 1986:29).

Christianity is practiced widely in Norway, and there is a powerful lay tradition. Norwegian missionaries have been active from the middle of the nineteenth century to the present. In fact, Norway has sent out more missionaries per capita than any other country (Tvedt 1995:239). Today, membership of the Church of Norway lies at around 93 percent of the population, although only a small proportion of this number are active churchgoers (Holbek 1995).

Children and young people in Norway are socialized into the core Social Democratic and Lutheran values of the society, not least through the education system. The egalitarian emphasis of Norwegian society means that children receive a more uniform socialization than may be the case elsewhere (Vormeland 1993:207–11).

Social Democratic and Lutheran values are therefore prominent in Norwegian society and are often deeply rooted in people's self-understandings. There is a striking use of religious concepts in official political discourses—such as "fellow-human-beingness" (*medmenneskelighet*) and "love-of-one's-neighbor" (*nestekjærlighet*). This suggests that these values and concepts resonate with a majority of the population in some way. The normative underpinnings of much of Norway's recent peace work are clearly based on these traditions, as well as on the humanitarian tradition stemming from such national figures as Fridtjof Nansen and Bjørnstjerne Bjørnson. Together, the Social Democratic notion of equal rights for all and the Christian idea of a universal humanity provide the basis for Norway's egalitarianism, which for various reasons is central to the society's comparative peacefulness.

Egalitarianism, Conformity, and Equality-as-Sameness

Norwegian society is renowned for its egalitarianism, its highly developed welfare state, and relative lack of class divisions. Clearly, where a society has a comparatively equitable division of wealth and opportunities, this will limit the level of conflict between individuals and groups. In addition, it is suggested here that norms and attitudes deriving from Norway's egalitarian tradition encourage forms of behavior that limit the emergence of overt conflict.

Social relations in Norway are characterized by a marked informality and an aversion to pomposity and rank; for instance, the late King Olav V was regularly spotted riding around Oslo on his bicycle or using a public tram. It should be noted, however, that the practice of Norwegian egalitarianism often falls short of its ambitions or ideals. Despite Norway's reputation for gender equality, for instance, there remains room for improvement. Although there is a large number of women in the Norwegian workforce (by 1991 more than 70 percent of women had paid employment outside the home), few have reached the upper echelons of the private or public sector, and there remains a high degree of gender division in the labor market, with a majority of women in lower-paid caring and service professions.

Norwegians themselves often invoke a poem by the Danish-Norwegian author Aksel Sandemose, the so-called "Law of Jante" (*Janteloven*), when criticizing their egalitarian tradition. Its dictates (for instance, "Thou shalt not think highly of thyself") are seen as encouraging modesty and sameness, while repressing people of distinction or ambition. "The Law of Jante … expresses … an ideology of equality which deprecates the original and the unusual. It is widely held that the Law of Jante is a deeply embedded aspect of Norwegian culture, and that it discourages brilliance and high achievements" (Eriksen 1993a:17).

Of relevance here is the phrase "equality as sameness," formulated by Marianne Gullestad (1992:ix) to capture the essence of the Norwegian word for equality. Gullestad points out that the Norwegian word for equality (*likhet*) has this dual meaning—it implies *similarity* or *sameness* as much as it does *equality*. Gullestad argues that Norwegian society is not as homogeneous as some people claim, but that "similarities are stressed over differences and cleavages" (1992:104). She expands:

> Norwegians have...adopted an interactional style whereby sameness between the participants of an encounter is emphasized, and differences are, as much as possible, tactfully concealed. The Norwegian egalitarian tradition is therefore not necessarily actual sameness, but a way of *emphasizing* sameness and under-communicating difference. (Gullestad 1992:104)

Gullestad argues further that when people in Norway perceive the differences between themselves and someone else to be too profound, they tend to avoid each other. This means that by applying the value of equality-as-sameness to those who are perceived as roughly similar to oneself, "subtle social barriers" are created "against those who are, in one way or another, not perceived as being the same" (Gullestad 1992:7). This is, of course, a mechanism of conflict avoidance.

If indeed the concept of equality in Norwegian society is as bound up with emphasizing similarities (or sameness) between people as Gullestad suggests, this may have serious implications for the degree to which difference and plurality are accommodated in the society (see also Dahl 1986:108). Knudsen (1990:104) writes of Norwegian society: "Social values are strongly egalitarian and leveling. There are consequent tendencies to exclude those who seem different and toward group introversion. Many reject immigrant groups and strangers generally. Racist attitudes are more frequent than the predominant ethos of the nation would lead one to expect."

Although Gullestad suggests that the norm of equality-as-sameness does not necessarily cause problems for those who are perceived (or perceive themselves) to be different, there are indications to the contrary. To mention just one example, a recent survey revealed that one in four gay Norwegians under the age of twenty-five had attempted suicide, and that more than 20 percent of gays experienced harassment at their workplace (Hafstad and Leander 1999). Could it be that by emphasizing similarities between people and avoiding those who are too different, Norwegian society is kept comparatively peaceful, but that damage is being done to those who fail to fit in with the dominant norms of the social group?

Handling Difference

It can be conjectured, then, that the particular norms of Norwegian society render difference a difficult concept to deal with. "It is difficult...for

Norwegians to see people as being both different and equal" (Gullestad 1992:105). "The Norwegian equality-society...often regards difference as dangerous and damaging" (Monsen 1998, author's translation). Despite the prevailing Social Democratic, Christian, and humanistic values of the society, a failure to accommodate difference has at times been a severe black mark on the Norwegian copybook. This was perhaps most evident in Nordic policies mandating the forced sterilization of Gypsies and the mentally ill from the 1930s until the 1970s, by some accounts uncomfortably reminiscent of those of Nazi Germany (Norvik 1997). Norway's treatment of its indigenous Sami population is a second case in point. There is a long history of repression, and even in the 1970s, Sami children were forced to speak only Norwegian at school, and their traditional music, the *joik*, was forbidden.

The transition toward a more pluralistic society has been difficult for many Norwegians. The perceived disintegration of traditional norms and values has been lamented in popular discourse, and immigrants are often portrayed as culpable in the supposed loss of community. This partly explains the renewed preoccupation with "Norwegianness," as a quest to return to what is often depicted as Paradise Lost. A right-wing upturn has been visible in recent years, with the far-right political party, *Fremskrittspartiet*, coming in second in the 1997 election, and first in that of 2001. In 2002 opinion polls show it to be Norway's most popular political party, although it is not a partner in the coalition government.

The increased visibility of foreigners—difference—in a social setting that was previously so homogeneous means that immigrants have become a prominent topic in Norwegian domestic discourse, despite the fact that, in relative terms, the numbers remain small. The current debates surrounding immigrants appear to conflict with Norwegians' self-understandings and the values of their collectivity, making the topic an uncomfortable one. Long Litt Woon (1993:186) writes: "Accusations of racism in particular seem to cause Norwegians much discomfort and embarrassment. These accusations are at odds with their self image of being tolerant, moral and righteous members of the international community."

The Value Attached to Peace: Discourses on Violence

The recent debates on violence not only suggest that peace is highly valued in Norwegian society, but also that it is a concept central to Norwegians' self-image. Similar points have been made before. Ross (1993b:161), for example, claims that "avoiding conflict is a deeply held cultural value inculcated through a range of practices in all phases of life," and identifies a "norm against expressing aggression," internalized through early socialization which is, he maintains, high in affection, low in aggression, and relatively lacking in gender-based conflict (Ross 1993b:161). Norway is one of the few countries to have a law against smacking children.

According to Gullestad, the notion of peace (*fred*) together with that of quiet (*ro*) form a central category in Norwegian culture, "intrinsic to social identity and action in the world" (1992:140). She notes the regularity with which the word *peace* enters common Norwegian expressions and sayings, and the fact that during fieldwork it struck her "that very often people explained that they had both undertaken definite actions or refrained from action, by referring to peace or quiet or both together" (1992:140). Expressions such as "for the sake of peace in the house" and "the most important thing is to keep the peace" are "used as justifications for avoiding open conflicts" (Gullestad 1992:144). An emphasis is put on self-control, for instance, "to keep the peace one ought not to say things directly, but rather indirectly" (Gullestad 1992:144). Gullestad also argues that the notion of peace, in keeping with the strength of Lutheranism in Norway, takes on religious connotations at times and is valued for that reason.

The association of peace with quiet is interesting. If peace for Norwegians does indeed connote quiet, this could tie in with the society's norms for conflict avoidance. Peace as quiet is not necessarily a condition of justice, or a situation in which individuals are able to realize their potential in an unhampered way; it refers merely to the absence of overt, noisy conflict. In other words, such an understanding of peace could imply a state of *negative peace*—not necessarily devoid of *structural violence*—rather than *positive peace* (Davies-Vengoechea, this volume; Curle 1971; Galtung 1969).

The topic of violence and how it can be combated fills Norwegian newspaper discussion pages regularly and is prominent in official political discourse. The portrayal of foreigners as more violent than Norwegians is a recurrent theme. For instance, when an Oslo nightclub bouncer was interviewed regarding the constant threats he was experiencing, he commented: "But it is foreigners who come with death threats. It seems as though they often have a different, more aggressive culture than ours" (Eriksen 1998, author's translation). The perpetrators of the recent shootings and stabbings have mainly been of foreign origin, and this has intensified the debate. The compound noun *innvandrevold*, meaning "immigrant-violence," has been coined and frequently appears in newspaper articles, along with other nouns such as *voldsproblemet*, "the violence problem." Other discrepancies between the norms and values of native Norwegians and new members of the society have recently come to the fore in heated debates in the media: notably questions of forced marriage (*tvangsekteskap*) and the treatment of women in certain groups of non-Western immigrants. Norway's justice minister recently called for an open two-way dialogue on the questions of violence and equality between immigrants and native Norwegians, but he also stated that immigration inevitably means "importing violence" (Nygaard 2002:3). His comments came in the aftermath of a remark made by the head of police intelligence in Oslo that "the price of integrating foreigners in Norway is becoming high indeed" (Nygaard 2002:3, author's translation). If these discourses are analyzed, it is interesting how *others* (or *they*) are portrayed as violent and threatening, while Norwegians (or *we*) are peaceful, egalitarian, respecting of human rights, and so on. A notion of the Other is usually central in constructions of identity. "A notion of who/what 'we' are is intertwined with an understanding of who/what 'we' are not and who/what 'we' fear . . . " (Campbell 1993:26).

Similar constructions of self and others are also visible in foreign policy narratives that link Norwegian identity to peace and peacefulness (Dobinson 2000). This is no doubt partly the result of Norway's historical experiences in the international arena: the society's collective memories, which politicians are able to draw upon, do not involve military victory, but rather vulnerability, subjugation to foreign rule, and suffering at the hands of occupying forces. The notion of war as positive is definitely *not* prominent in discursive representations of Norway and narratives on Norwegian identity. The prime minister, in his New Year address to the nation in 2000, drew upon a famous poem by Norwegian writer Nordahl Grieg—in other words a cultural resource known to many Norwegians. "Norway must be a nation of peace—an actor for conflict resolution and peace-creating activity. [It must be] a nation which follows Nordahl Grieg's strategy: 'If you create human worth, you create peace'." (Bondevik 2002, author's translation).

The point is not only that peace is highly valued in Norwegian society and a central element in Norwegians' self-understandings, but also that dominant discourses reinforce this self-image of Norwegians as essentially peace loving. It can be argued that a dominant discourse of this kind also perpetuates societal peacefulness. Other representations of the society could have been chosen (for instance emphasizing its economic prosperity) but have not been. For a dominant discourse on national identity to catch on, it must not only be persuasive, but it must also represent a society in a way that accords with the group's deeply embedded notions of what constitutes its identity and culture. The fact that these discursive representations of Norway as peaceful are so widespread suggests that this image *does* resonate with a majority of the population (see also Weldes 1996, 1999).

Conflict Management Processes

Just as every familial household develops its own problem-solving behavior, so each social group has developed its own strategies of conflict resolution over time, uniquely rooted in local culture and passed on from generation to generation . . . (Boulding 1996:36)

Conflict Circumvention and Avoidance

A common observation about Norwegian society is the way in which Norwegians attempt to avoid conflict if at all possible; this has already been touched on in relation to Gullestad's idea of equality-as-sameness. An old Norwegian proverb, "Love thy neighbor but keep the gate," reflects this need for maintaining a certain distance in possibly conflictual social relations (Gullestad 1992:165). In many ways, this traditional conflict-avoiding mode of behavior remains important in modern Norway. A large proportion of the population still lives in remote, rural communities. Hollos (1974) studied one such community in the early 1970s and described a highly structured designation of family roles that served to avoid possible tensions.

Even Norway's larger urban centers are small compared to most European cities. One of my interviewees commented that you could not avoid meeting people with whom you disagreed. In his view, there was a double tendency—on the one hand, Norwegians strive for agreement; on the other hand, they want to isolate people who disagree very much. Another interviewee thought that Norwegians run away from conflicts, in contrast to more adversarial societies, such as Britain, where there is a belief that conflict *can* be a good thing (Dobinson 2000). Although conflict avoidance can result in an apparently peaceful social setting, such retreat is not always positive. In a study of the everyday lives of Norwegians, as articulated by the participants themselves, Gullestad (1996) notes the breakdown of relationships that occurs when differences become too great to conceal.

Compromise and Consensus

Even if conflict cannot be obliterated or avoided, it can be managed or defused before it reaches violent proportions. In Norwegian society, great emphasis is placed on consensus. Elder, Thomas, and Arter (1982) describe the Scandinavian states collectively as "consensual democracies," in which, for instance, conflict is obviated by maximizing agreement before decisions are made. Norway's multiparty system and the tradition of proportional representation mean that politicians in Norway cannot usually afford to view conflicts in zero-sum terms. Coalitions are frequent, and consensus through compromise is needed to avoid political stalemate. There is already much consensus between the elites of the major political parties in Norway, partly due to the fact that they are used to collaborating, and partly because cleavages over issues such as EU or NATO membership cross-cut the Left-Right political divide. The experience of World War II is also a factor in the Norwegian emphasis on consensus: "The war...fostered a deep understanding of the value of cooperation and 'staying togetherness' which produced a deep and lasting consensus in the post-war years" (Ugelvik Larsen and Ugelvik 1997:220).

Archetti (1984) claims that Norwegians are also consensus-oriented in their interpersonal relationships, again, in order to avoid overt conflict. Eriksen (1993b:17–18) summarizes Archetti's assessment that Norwegians "prefer a poor compromise to a violent quarrel—even if they were eventually to emerge victorious from the latter: They strongly wish to *agree*." There are many words and phrases relating to compromise in the Norwegian language, which indicates the centrality of the concept. One particularly colorful expression, meaning "to accept uncomfortable compromises," is "to swallow camels" (*å svelge kameler*). When a new coalition government was formed in the autumn of 1997, consisting of ministers with widely divergent views on such issues as the EU, there were so many references to "camel swallowing" in the press that a reader wrote a letter to the newspaper *Aftenposten* complaining about the "camel epidemic." This shows how the linguistic resources that Norwegians draw upon encourage particular perceptions of, and approaches to, conflict.

Conflict Delimitation and Pragmatism

Archetti has observed that conflicts are often delimited in Norwegian society. "There is a strong tendency to set clear boundaries for the conflicts and define certain problems as irrelevant" (Archetti 1984:50, author's translation.) By contrast, in Archetti's native Argentina, one actively seeks out the history of a conflict. "We find out who the father, mother and relatives of the parties are, in order to identify self-interests . . . " (1984:51, author's translation). In Norway, however, a conflict must always be "relevant to the issues and observable" (Archetti 1984:51, author's translation). Archetti has also observed that Norwegian conflicts are delimited in the sense that they are not usually allowed to reach a climax. He suggests that explosions are rare in Norwegian culture.

Conflict Management Institutions and Initiatives

When conflicts do arise that are not obviated as described above, they are frequently managed, contained, or resolved through methods that are often of a remarkably early vintage. Conflicts are solved outside the court system if at all possible (Nergård 1993; Shaughnessy 1992:50). Compulsory mediation of interpersonal conflict was established in all Norwegian towns by royal decree in 1795, when Norway was under Danish rule. In the same year, commissions on conciliation (*forligelses commissionen*) were also established by the Danish King Christian V (Shaughnessy 1992:17–18).

In modern Norwegian vernacular, these commissions (of which there are some 455 throughout Norway) are now known as the *Forliksråd*. Most civil disputes require mediation by one of these boards of conciliation before they can be brought to court. The emphasis is on facilitating constructive communication between the disputants. If a settlement is reached, it is recorded and becomes legally binding. In 2000 the *Forliksråd* handled some 166,000 civil disputes; their peak year was 1988 with 323,000. In addition to the Forliksråd, conflict resolution boards (*Konfliktråd*) have been established throughout Norway over the last decades. As with the Forliksråd, the mediators are lay people. The first such Konfliktråd was set up in the town of Lier in 1981, focusing on young offenders and aiming to secure voluntary solutions to conflicts that would otherwise have been handled as penal cases (Shaughnessy 1992; Nergård 1993). In 1991 the Law on Mediation in Conflict Councils went into effect and specified that all Norwegian municipalities should have such councils. The primary aim of the Konfliktråd is to mediate disputes between persons (involving injury, loss, or other violation) and thereby enable local communities to deal with minor breaches of the law at a local level, circumventing a punitive, court-based approach. In 2001 the conflict councils received 6,134 cases, of which 3,212 were civil disputes and 2,922 criminal cases. Eighty-nine percent of the mediations resulted in an agreement; 79 percent of the agreements were honored (Statistics Norway 2002).

Mediation is also used in divorce cases. Only 4 to 5 percent of such cases reach the courts (Tjersland 1995). Usually a separation will be granted after the submission of an application form, but Norwegian law also stipulates that a mediation certificate must be submitted together with this form. New, stricter legislation was introduced in 1993, stating that any separating couple with children must seek mediation before they can apply for separation, which must result in a written agreement concerning custody, parental responsibility, and visitation rights.

There are also mechanisms for the containment of industrial strife in Norwegian society. Some date from the late nineteenth century and are sophisticated (Elder, Thomas, and Arter 1982:26). In any case, industrial conflict is not particularly rife in Norway; a 1984 report by the International Labor Office stated that "the number of labor disputes leading to strikes or lock-outs has been far less in Norway than elsewhere" (ILO 1984:12). When labor disputes do occur, state mediation is used extensively, apparently with good results; according to the ILO report, failure was reported in only 5 to 10 percent of cases (ILO 1984:58). The authors praise the Norwegian government for avoiding conflict by involving representatives of employers, workers, and other social groups directly in policy making. In general, they note: "The country's social history reveals, and present practice confirms, a strong belief, held by trade unions and employers' associations ever since a very early stage, that permanent dialogue... provides the best answer to most problems" (ILO 1984:13). They particularly praise the way in which "neither freedom of association nor the right to conclude collective labor agreements has ever seriously been questioned in Norway" (ILO 1984:65, 11), and they conclude:

> Such a situation, quite exceptional at a certain stage in the history of social development, clearly reflects a remarkable degree of open-mindedness, a deep-seated sense of dialogue among equals—at least in the field of industrial relations ... — and a firm belief in seeking solutions to the problems which are bound to arise. (ILO 1984:65)

In recent decades, new mechanisms for dealing with conflicts have emerged on the Norwegian social scene, suggesting that defusing conflicts peacefully remains a priority. The *Stop the Violence* program has already been discussed (Norwegian Red Cross 2002). A few other initiatives can be mentioned briefly.

In 1995 the Norwegian Ministry for Justice initiated a pilot school mediation project in cooperation with the Ministry for the Church, Education and Research. Thirteen conflict councils, 45 schools and 3,500 pupils took part; the project was subsequently extended to a nationwide initiative from 1998 to 2000. School mediation was introduced as a democratic and pupil-centered method of conflict resolution to be used as a voluntary supplement to schools' ordinary systems of sanctions. Selected pupils were trained as mediators, with a teacher having responsibility for following up. In a report following the pilot project, it was noted that school mediation had not only led to increased awareness of conflicts, but also to greater tolerance for each others' differences, and to an experience and belief that conflicts could be solved constructively (see, for example, Norsk Senter for Barneforskning 1998). With mediation established in a large number of primary and lower secondary schools, a national school mediation project was initiated at the upper secondary level in 2001.

Another conflict prevention initiative is Swedish-born researcher Dan Olweus's work, which has spanned more than three decades, on bullying in Norwegian schools and kindergartens. The *Olweus Program against Bullying and Antisocial Behavior* was introduced in Norwegian schools across the country in autumn 2001, again with state funding (Jakobsen 2001).

As part of the *Stop the Violence* program, the Norwegian Red Cross has introduced "night wanderers" (*nattevandrer*): adults who walk the streets of towns at night in clearly visible tunics and who can be approached by young people who feel threatened. They do not intervene in conflicts but can contact the police should the need arise. In addition, the Center for Conflict Management-Norway, the Norwegian Red Cross, and the Norwegian Peace Center (in collaboration with the Nansen School) are among the places where courses in conflict resolution, prevention, or mediation are provided (see Center for Conflict Management 2002; Norwegian Peace Center 2002; Norwegian Red Cross 2002).

Conclusions

Norwegian society is not inherently or unproblematically peaceful. However, peace is highly valued within Norwegian society, and members of the society have exhibited a consistent preoccupation with the peaceful settlement of conflict, both nationally and internationally. Levels of overt conflict and aggression remain comparatively low, although increasing rates of violence are a cause of great concern in Norway. Political leaders and other privileged speakers who shape the society's dominant discourse have in turn reinforced popular notions of Norway as a peaceful place and Norwegians as a peace-loving and peacemaking people. Such representations contribute to perpetuating societal peacefulness. The recent debates on violence in the media and popular discourse, and the public outcry and torch-lit peace processions in the wake of violent murders, highlight the degree to which peace is valued by members of the society.

Norway's relative peacefulness can be partly explained by its traditional lack of profound cleavages. In addition, emerging over time are norms, attitudes, and modes of behavior that contribute to keeping the level of overt conflict in Norwegian society low. In encounters between people, emphasis is placed on similarities and commonalities rather than differences. Consensus is sought in a range of social contexts, and methods of conflict avoidance are generally prominent.

Each social group has unique historical experiences, norms, and attitudes that determine its "hidden peace-building strengths" (Boulding 1996:37), and the extent to which these can be transferred to other social settings is perhaps a moot point. Not all aspects of Norwegian conflict avoidance behavior are equally laudable, but it might be possible for some of the more beneficial norms and patterns of behavior in the face of conflict to be emulated in other social settings; over time they might gain ground. In any case, much can be learned from the Norwegian experience. The decisions taken by political elites to invest in mechanisms for conflict resolution and prevention—both nationally and internationally—are of particular relevance, together with their decisions to emphasize the society's more peaceful aspects in official discourses. Although Norwegian mechanisms for managing and preventing conflict date back to the late nineteenth century, such mechanisms continue to be prioritized in contemporary Norwegian society, with initiatives being launched—and provided with funding (at least for limited periods)—as new challenges arise. It is in this sense, as a "constructive conflict society," that Norway can best serve as a model.

Study Questions

1. What do you assess are some strengths and weaknesses of Norwegians' aim to maintain a peaceful culture? Mention some specific examples to illustrate your points.
2. What do you think are some key lessons from the Norwegian experience for other societies that seek to become more peaceful?
3. How does Norway typically approach international conflicts?
4. How does avoidance in Norwegian society compare with the types of avoidance described in various other peaceful societies?

II
Cautious, Alert, Polite, and Elusive: The Semai of Central Peninsular Malaysia

ROBERT KNOX DENTAN

The real test of peace occurs not in social isolation, but in the face of violence. There are many who assume that violence can only be countered by violence. This creates mutual pain, and that in itself can perpetuate the violence. Colombia, once the most democratic of Latin American countries, is now in a cycle of violence and counterviolence, ravaged for more than five decades by civil war. However, in the past decade or so, peace communities have been set up in Colombia, to try to address the violence in a different way. In this chapter, Robert Dentan reveals how the Semai of Malaysia have used nonviolence in the face of violence as a successful long-term survival strategy. Dentan emphasizes that peace is a practical solution, not a utopian myth. Those campaigning for nonviolence in other societies may find much to encourage them in this chapter.

—GK

Introduction

Who Are "Semai"?

"Semai" is the official name of the largest linguistic group of Orang Asli. Orang Asli are the indigenous people of peninsular Malaysia in Southeast Asia. Like most indigenous peoples Semai call themselves simply "people" (*Seng'oi* or *Sen'oi*). As of 2003, there are about 30,000 Semai. Traditionally, they lived by agroforestry, dry rice farming, and trading forest produce.

They were also subject to a particularly brutal form of slaving, which, I will argue, played a salient role in the development of their peaceable lifestyle. Increasingly nowadays, they are becoming small-scale commodity producers and unskilled occasional laborers (Gomes 1988, 1990, 1999). Although globalization, the end of British colonialism, and Malaysian economic development have changed many aspects of the Semai way of life, and although some Semai have successfully made it into the globalized mainstream, they (and Orang Asli in general) are worse off than ever; by almost any measure, they are the poorest people in the country. Their standard of living has not improved in the half century I have worked with them (Dentan 2000a, 2001c; Nicholas 1990, 1994, 2000, 2001). The shift of political control from British colonialism to domination by Malays, the ethnic group which now controls the government, has created fewer beneficial changes than first appearances might suggest (Dentan 1997).

Why Call Semai Nonviolent?

Characterizing a whole society as globally nonviolent is inaccurate and silly if you take the label to mean there is no individual or circumstantial variation (Endicott 1997; Heelas 1989).

> There are three major justifications for calling the Semai "nonviolent" in the face of their own indifference on the matter.... [1] They do not brawl...or feud like many other...peoples.... [2] [T]hey openly and often express fear that outsiders will attack them. They...teach their children to fear and shun strangers, especially non-Semai.... [3] [T]he Semai concept of violence is very broad.... (Dentan 1978:97)

Their notion of impermissible violence includes acts which increase personal (psychological) stress, as well as acts in which the physical harm is immediate and palpable (Dentan 2000b).

I spent more than four years actually living with Semai (in 1961–1963, 1975–1976, 1991–1992, 1993) with permission from the Department of Orang Asli Affairs, the local equivalent of the U.S. Bureau of Indian Affairs. I keep up with developments in Malaysia and stay in contact with friends and colleagues there. My last research visit, in the 1990s, involved a strenuous effort to uncover as many fights, murders, and suicides as I could. Semai are close-mouthed about violence, fearing that they will get in trouble. But I don't think I'm off by more than an order of magnitude (cf. Leyton 1997: 21–22). I found one murder in the 1970s, two in the 1990s, and have heard of one since 2000. The last victim had claimed to have killed someone by using Malay black magic and was then killed by the victim's son. One of the other three may have been accidental (Dentan and Williams-Hunt 1999). The other two were by young men of Semai origin who had rejected Semai identity. Since I wrote the foregoing part of this paragraph in 2001, there have been two or three murders by Orang Asli who seem to have been Semai: one involved a teenage boy trying to protect his mother from his drunken and abusive father. There were far more suicides, although Semai seem almost equally reluctant to discuss suicide (Dentan 2000c).

I have never observed serious physical fighting among Semai adults. Interviews uncovered only a handful of cases. Most involved young men briefly fighting with non-Semai. These young men blamed non-Semai who assaulted them without provocation, who called them insulting names, or who harassed Semai women. The rest involved alcohol, either drunken brawling between spouses or between young men whose friends easily subdued them after *ki-kawboy*, "he was acting like a cowboy [in the movies]." Increasing contact with Malay Muslim and Chinese patriarchal values seems to be encouraging aggression by young men (Thambiah 1999; Tijah, Thambiah, and Leong 2000): for example, in the 1990s, I first heard the phrase "be a man-child," a gloss I believe of Malay usage, to describe cocky bellicosity (Dentan and Williams-Hunt 1999). Some fragments of a conversation I had with two young men on 6 June 1992 illustrate this complicated change:

Yahyah, 24 years old, from the Cameron Highlands: There wouldn't be any fights at our *ronggeng* [Malay-style dance parties, with lots of flirting and drinking] if it wasn't for outsiders [*maay*]. Everybody comes to our *ronggeng*—Malays, Chinese, Tamils, everybody.

Sarip, 28, his covillager: We fight with Malays because they molest our women. The Police Field Force [Malay parapolice] kidnapped a woman from near our place and kept her naked for days and days while they gang-raped her. . . . The case was "settled" [using the English word.] Nobody went to jail. Not for raping a Semai woman. Just paid a few dollars. The usual. You know.

Yahyah: Listen, we're not *maay manah ntum*, old-time people. If somebody knocks us down, what're we supposed to do? Just lie there and smile? [laughs].

Sarip: Hey, if we had weapons, we'd drive the Malays off our land [aims an imaginary rifle, squinting and grinning]. We're not *maay manah ntum*.

But, youthful male boasting aside, acts of masculine *kawboy* aggression remain rare.

East Semai, those from northeast Pahang state, said in 1962 that sometimes an angry person might burn down the house of a person he or she was angry at, but I never uncovered an actual case of arson. More recently, fear of witchcraft seems to be on the rise, as a result of contact with Malay and Methodist Christian notions of witchcraft. But witches are not a salient part of traditional Semai cosmology. Mutual trust and dependence is easier in the absence of the belief that one's neighbor may be a witch; for traditional Semai, ghosts and outsiders (especially Malays) fill the role that witches or other deviants play elsewhere (Dentan 1992:219, 2001a; Robarchek 1988). But Semai ghosts are motivated by love, yearning to rejoin the people they loved in life. And Semai suicide seems to be just an escape from the pain of bereavement: loss of love, not an expression of anger (Dentan 2000c).

Semai still teach their children to be afraid/cautious, *-sng≫h* (Dentan 1978, 2001a). This word *-sng≫h* refers both to an emotion, which people find unpleasant, and to an attitude, which they say is desirable. Despite young men's posturing, traditional Semai say it is much smarter and safer to be cautious than to be brave. Children do squabble sometimes, but I have never seen anything like the violence that I see among American middle-class kids in my neighborhood. The highest incidence of squabbling occurs among Waar River Semai, who say that "children are like dogs, always snapping at each other." Elsewhere, where Semai adults do not expect children to be violent, the kids do not get hurt in even the most apparently violent games (Dentan 1978); and adults will intervene, especially in the latter communities, whenever childish quarrels seem to be getting out of hand.

But Semai do get angry, though they may sometimes deny it. Then they may deliver an angry harangue, or-*lees*, not necessarily to the offender but to the community at large, detailing how they have been wronged. They are likely then to launch into a campaign to win support by spreading malicious gossip, a tactic at which Semai excel. They also usually break off contact with the person at whom they are angry, a tactic called "withdrawal" (*kra'dii'*). This response is not always instrumental. Sometimes Semai are just so depressed by how badly another person has treated them that they avoid social contact with anyone as much as they can (Dentan 2000c). When they can not avoid the offenders entirely, angry people will simply not speak to them and will avoid meeting their eyes. The loss of love, of warm social ties, is acutely painful for both parties and threatens the mutual aid and comfort on which traditional Semai society depends.

Still, the rarity of violence within the community also results in people having little experience with handling their own violent impulses. Semai think of violence as abnormal, unlike antiviolence campaigns in the United States, which normalize violence (cf. Devine 1997:30–31). Thus, my mentor, Ngah Hari, said in 1992 that macaques go around in gangs (*geng*) like people, "but they fight," not like people. Terror and rage, emotions which are two sides of the same dark coin, could produce what Semai call "blood intoxication" and psychologists call a "dissociative state." This sort of dissociation, which Bah Tony Williams-Hunt, a Semai anthropologist, told me is "like spirit possession" (using the English phrase), is characteristic of long-suffering, peaceable people anywhere (Katz 1988:48–51).Then, when opportunity arose, Semai could kill mindlessly, compulsively, "like doves" as they say (Dentan 1995, 1999; Leary 1995).

In short, Semai values and normal behavior are nonviolent. But their nonviolence is not a lack, some sort of deficiency of essence. It is not an incapacity, but an unwillingness. It is a continuing choice, and, like people anywhere, Semai are capable of changing their minds. As Nudy's-Father, a shaman on the Waar River, said on 13 March 1991:

> At present violence isn't a problem here. By 2020 [when the Malaysian government plans to have industrialized the whole country] the Humans [Semai] will probably be violent. We're not violent now because we're still *primitif* [using the Dutch-Indonesian word]. We still have places to flee to now, but by then we'll be shut out of all those places [by dispossession and "development"]. We don't want to fight, but when we have no alternative, no place to flee to, we'll be forced to. (Dentan 2001c:5)

Conjectural History

Slaving

Beginning almost a thousand years ago and lasting, in Malaysia, well into the twentieth-century, slaving underlay the political economy of the indigenous states of Southeast Asia, which were frankly terroristic (Endicott 1983; Hoskins 1996). When I first talked with Semai in 1962, everyone knew about the slaving. They, like many other Southeast Asian hill peoples, had long been targets. The terrorism worked. In 1962 even adults fled the approach of strangers the way young children still did thirty years later. Many Semai women are still afraid to travel except in groups, for fear of kidnapping or rape.

The Hinduized coastal states of medieval Malaysia were mostly oriented toward trade, toward the ocean, and India. Even the Malay word for "west" comes from the Sanskrit word for "India." But when the states turned toward their hinterlands, they manifested themselves as phallocratic agents of the thunder god Indra or Siva the Destroyer, after whom the founders of dynasties named themselves, whose lingams (phallic megaliths) dotted the landscape, whose destructive power brought fear and death to those who resisted state power (Coedes 1968:23–24, 58, 64–69, 85, 110–29, 174, 187–88, 212, 249, 275n3).

Buddhist rulers as well as Hindu princes frequently identified themselves as agents or reincarnations of the ancient storm god... representing kingly authority and power (Cady 1964:37–38). For a thousand years these petty despots showed off their power by killing and slaving (Coedes 1968:58;

Dentan 2002b; Maxwell 1996), creating a "culture of state terror" (Hoskins 1996:3).

Slave raids and other incursions prompted the outnumbered and outgunned Semai to respond by scattering and fleeing invaders and raiders, to regroup later. They might ambush invaders bent on genocide, but there was no way to resist raiders' sporadic and temporary incursions (Dentan 1999). The jargon phrase for the resulting pattern of settlement is *fission-fusion*. To pursue this tactic, children had to learn that adulthood involved being willing and able to move around freely, to make decisions on their own: freedom. The constant movement undermined local hierarchies and left people dependent on their neighbors for security and love. This dependence required peaceability and made the threat of disapproval a powerful sanction.

The slaver state rested on a notion of power unfamiliar to Westerners. In that conception, power exists independently of the people who wield it; it is like electricity or gravity (Anderson 1990:22; McWilliam 1996). Without power of one's own, the intelligent thing to do, confronted with a person who has power, is to submit or flee (Anderson 1990:74), a combination I call "surrender." The resulting social relations work like patriarchy or protection rackets, in which subordinates "often feel bound to those they serve through misplaced gratitude for a 'protection' that is mostly only a withholding of abuse" (Card 1996:7, 10). The Semai response to the slaver state, their general deference to Malay culture, for example, makes sense in these terms. Unable to flee, Semai adopted a response rather like the Stockholm syndrome (in which hostages come to support their kidnappers) or "identification with the aggressor" (or "oppressor"), in which battered children take on some of the attitudes of their abusers (Freud 1966).

As long as state penetration involving slave raids and kidnapping was only sporadic a pervasive nonviolence was adaptive: Semai response was flight, not confrontation; and, when flight was impossible, submission (Adas 1992:89–90; Dentan 1992, 2002b; Trankell and Ovesen 1998:12–13). Overwhelming power of this sort is not subject to control by the governed, any more than a child can control its abuse by a parent. The question of legitimacy does not arise. Resistance is futile, like "hitting a stone with an egg," as Khmers say (Fisher-Nguyen 1994:99).

Here I need to interject a caveat. The analogy between slaver state-Semai relationships on the one hand and abusive parent-abused child relationships on the other does not mean that Semai, on their own, are like children. That equation would not only be foolish but, in a Western context, disrespectful. Western tradition does not respect children; on the contrary, it regards them as not fully human (Aronowitz 2001; Dentan 2001a, 2001b). The question in this essay is not of content but of structure: in most contexts, the disjunction between Semai power and the power of their Malay compatriots is as stark as the disjunction between children's power and the power of adults, the disjunction which may underlie the covert Western contempt for kids. By analogy, it is possible, indeed necessary, to say that 16 is to 8 as 4 is to 2, 16:8 = 4:2; the relationships (":" and ":") are identical. But that does not mean that 8 = 2. The same holds for the power relationship "slaver state:Semai = abusive parent:abused child." The relationship is at issue, not its content.

Learning Helplessness

> A person need not actually experience repeated [uncontrollable] events in order for them to produce [learned] helplessness. All that is needed is for the person to expect that events will be uncontrollable. . . . This expectation may come from a variety of sources besides induction: for instance, observation of others, cultural stereotypes, specific information. . . . (Peterson, Maier, and Seligman 1993: 147)

The feeling basis of Semai nonviolence rests on what Bateson (1958) would call an *eidos* of caution. An eidos is a sort of emotional background (cf. Robarchek 1980). The emotional background against which Semai make choices is one of what psychologists call *learned helplessness*. This eidos seems to arise from the people's historical inability to resist slaving. Traditional Semai history involves intermittent merciless raids by bands of slavers who raped the women, slaughtered adults, and took children and young women to sell to Malay aristocrats, who tortured and sexually abused them (e.g., Bird 1883:14–16, 330; Dentan 1992, 1997, 2002b; Endicott 1983; Robarchek 1979, 1986).

Semai have learned that in most cases counterviolence is useless; one just gets hurt again, they say. That does not mean that people like the young men I have already quoted never fantasize about fighting against Malay incursions, dispossessions, and abuse (Robarchek 1977). In fact, in the past, when conditions were favorable, they have actually mounted violent resistance against people who tried to kill them (Dentan 1995, 1999; Leary 1995). Most of the time, though, they just do not think physical violence will work. Why get hurt for nothing? This learned helplessness is similar in many ways to that which abused women and children endure. The oppressor is always present in the mind in what W. E. B. Du Bois called "double consciousness" (Dentan 1976). But accepting one's helplessness brings a kind of peace: one no longer needs to struggle, and, since the oppressor is not always present in fact, one can get on with the business of living life (Dentan 1992, 1994).

In some ways, learned helplessness overlaps with clinical depression, and there is some evidence that Semai are susceptible to depression. But, as a Buddhist anthropologist (Obeyesekere 1985) remarks, the difference between the description of Buddhist serenity and the description of depression is not clear. Similarly, the surrender in Semai eidos resembles the surrender central to the beliefs and practices of some therapeutic groups like Alcoholics Anonymous and of some deviant Christian communities like Mennonites or Amish (Dentan 1994). In other words, it can provide a serenity not otherwise available.

Learned Helplessness as a Successful Evolutionary Adaptation

In evolutionary terms, violence and peace seem to have evolved as flexible, facultative adaptations to particular situations (Fry in preparation). Here and below, I use the word "adaptation" in this specifically Darwinian sense. Adaptation results from differential reproduction over many generations, wherein organisms manifesting a particular trait leave relatively more off-spring than do organisms lacking the trait. Individual human responses to stress reflect evolutionary strategies successful in the past: fight, flight, caring for children, and making alliances (Dentan 2001d, 2002a).

Capitalist cost-benefit analysis suggests that games are a useful metaphor for situations in which individuals have to make such choices. People will be violent when they can gain something by doing so without getting badly hurt: bullies, generals, and abusers of children know that. Similarly, they will shun violence when they would lose by it and/or risk getting hurt. The Semai assessment of their political environment is a realistic one, and the response—surrender or flight—has been far more adaptive in a personal *and* evolutionary sense than futile painful resistance would have been. Like any beneficial behavior, the resulting underlying eidos has consequences in other areas of Semai life, which this chapter will discuss.

Also, like any adaptive behavior, surrender is adaptive only under partic-ular conditions. When those conditions change, people begin, by fits and starts and individual by individual, to change their behavior. Semai culture does not incapacitate Semai for violence (Dentan 1995, 1999; Robarchek and Dentan 1987): it foregrounds other ways of handling stress, such as flight, caring for children, or making friends and allies ("networking"). But all four possibilities, what the social psychologists call *fight, flight, tend, and befriend* (Dentan 2002a), are always available to all people at all times. When condi-tions change, so that violence has benefits and the associated risks dwindle, even peaceable people like Semai may find it more attractive. No human choice is final. Flight, the dominant Semai adaptation to predation by out-siders, at least from about 1800 to about 1950, requires what ecologists call a *refugium,* a place to which people can safely flee and in which they can focus on protecting their children and strengthening their social ties. Oc-casional incursions into the refugium by outsiders, slavers in this case, only strengthen the traditional response. But increasing penetration by outsiders in the 1950s made flight less successful as a reaction to violence. Evasive neutrality became difficult. Alliances with powerful invaders, like the occasional self-enslavement of half a century earlier, offers some promise of safety, although at the cost of becoming dependent and involved in their violence.

I repeat these platitudes at some length because Western values celebrate violence, whether or not they oppose it (e.g., Kappeler 1995:252). Even some anthropologists seem to think violence is always more adaptive than surrender or flight, although it seems plausible that organisms that avoid violence entirely are less likely to get hurt and thus more likely to produce fertile offspring than glorious fighters are: "Natural selection designs different kinds of animals and plants that *avoid* competition. A fit animal is not one that fights well, but one that avoids fighting all together" (Colinvaux 1978:144; see also Sommer, Denham, and Little 2002). Winning a fight and differential reproductive success are entirely distinct phenomena. To repeat: successful violence involves a calculation of risks and benefits. That is why domestic violence, by men against women or adults against children, is the most common form violence takes cross-culturally: it is the safest for the violent (Leyton 1997:43). We must not confuse violence with bravery; when violence is not safe, as in the Semai case, it is stupid, just as Semai say it is. The Semai people's reluctance to celebrate or engage in "stupid violence" is the reason it seems appropriate to call Semai nonviolent—under normal circumstances.

Responding To Slaving as an Environmental Stress

I theorize that the historical experience of slaving lies at the roots of Semai peaceability. Slaving generated fears—for one's life, for one's children—and led to a sense that outsiders in general and Malays in particular always threatened the peace and safety in which Semai, like most people most of the time, wanted to live. The fear probably did not reflect how often attacks happened. A single raid or kidnapping would demonstrate a whole river basin community's vulnerability (cf. Colvard 1997:21). Their territories, which they could until recently defend against organized invasion, were open to raiders (cf. Taylor, Gottfredson, and Bower 1984). Criminologists (e.g., McGarrell, Giacomazzi, and Thurman 1997) say that people's fear of being hurt reflects how vulnerable people feel. Semai felt, and feel, vulnerable.

Moreover, outsiders, who always represented the power that Semai in general lacked, tended to hold Semai customs and the people themselves in contempt. Meetings with outsiders threatened to produce the kind of social disorder that traditional Semai found particularly scary. Peace is the normal state of humankind; violence is unusual and frightening, even in wartime (Dentan 2001d; Fry in preparation; Nordstrom 1997; Sponsel

1996). The contrast between fearsome slavers and fearful prey made Semai think of themselves as helpless and nonviolent (Dentan 1979:61–64; Robarchek 1980) and of nonviolence as not merely a moral good, but a practical one.

Raising Cautious Children

> If the kids don't go to school, if [my husband] doesn't take them [to school on his motorbike, as it's a mile to the...terminus of Malay settlement and bus service], if he doesn't chew them out, I'll -*lees* [harangue] him. They get in trouble if they don't go to school. If the kids pick fights with their friends, I tell them, "Don't mess with your friends, be good to your friends, [if you aren't] you'll be sorry. If you're a bad friend, people won't want you around.

> I -*lees* about the Malay school kids. . . . They bully Semai kids all the time. They hit them, they take their books and papers. "Malay kids are bad," I say. "They'll pick fights with you. Don't you hit them back, you'll just get in trouble." (Kyah Grcaang's-Mother, R'eiis River, 1992 [Dentan 2001c:13])

Social psychologists say that looking after children is one of the ways people (especially women) deal with stress: the "tend" in fight, flight, tend, or befriend. Baboon studies (Maggioncalda and Sapolsky 2002: 64) suggest that demonstrating "strong male-female affiliation and parental behavior rather than male-male competition" is at least as likely to result in a male leaving viable offspring as is striving for dominance. Indeed, prolonged, stressful agonistic behavior seems to impair health and reduce fertility even if an individual is not harmed. The glucocorticoid stress results in impaired growth and tissue repair. Too much testosterone can be bad for one's health.

In evolutionary terms, this tending of offspring feeds into the generally successful human *K-reproductive strategy* of having few offspring but seeing them through to maturity (Taylor 2002). Preserving one's children from kidnapping by slavers is a reflection of this strategy.

Semai taught children to find refuge among their own kind, among Semai whom they knew (Dentan 2001a). In the Semai eidos, warning children about the dangers they face is one of the few tactics of resistance to Malay power that is available (see fig. 11.1). Semai children develop learned helplessness and nonviolence in part because (1) Semai adults expect and encourage children to be fearful, for example, by telling terrifying stories about outsiders (Dentan 2001a); and (2) Semai adults do not expect, model, or condone violence, for example, by beating, hitting, or spanking children (Dentan 1978, 2001b). Traditionally, Semai avoided disrespecting or abusing children, whose love they needed, thus offering the children no model for committing violence. Unlike Americans, they expected kids to be "soft" and timid (Dentan 1978). They said that hurting children risked killing

Figure 11.1. Semai girls at *'Icek* along the *Teiw R'eiis,* in 1992, try to control their giggling, having learned that self-restraint is a good thing. The two smaller girls are watching the tallest, to the back of whose head a pet macaque is clinging, to see if she is going to manage the task—the sort of social surveillance which helps keep Semai society peaceful. Photograph by Robert K. Dentan.

them, and that abused or neglected children made particularly fearsome ghosts.

This reluctance to coerce children fosters autonomy (see fig. 11.2). Children who grow up free of coercion tend, as adults, to value independence more than children who have learned to obey do. Like most egalitarian

Figure 11.2. This *'Icek* boy has been hunting for proteinaceous snack food, as Semai children routinely do to supplement their diet, which is becoming increasingly monotonous as more powerful peoples destroy their forest resources. This sort of self-reliance is characteristic of Semai children's activities. He carries a boy's blowpipe of inferior bamboo and is displaying a flying lizard (*Draco volans*), or *halvv'n* in Semai. Photograph by Robert K. Dentan.

peoples (see, for example, Boehm 2000; Clastres 2000; Wilson 1998:72–142), adult Semai value individual freedom and resist the obedience and discipline that hierarchy seeks to impose. The best way for a Semai to destroy any chance of becoming influential is by seeming to desire influence, which suggests a desire for power to coerce others. Children and adults need to be independent within their mutually supportive community. Still, the power involved in frightening helpless and dependent people, even one's own children, may also provide an ambivalent pleasure, kept secret most of the time even from oneself, as I believe it does in America. And like Americans, Semai seem unaware of that possibility (Dentan 2001a, 2001b).

On the other hand, most adults in a Semai settlement will look after all the children in that settlement (Dentan 1978; cf. Skeat and Blagden 1906, II:81). This *allomothering* seems to be basic to human evolutionary success; for men, looking after the children with the love Semai men show may also correlate with lower testosterone levels (Hrdy 2001) and thus with less striving for dominance (Kemper 1990). Among Semai, as among Orang Asli in general, gender inequalities are traditionally minimal, despite signs that patriarchy may be increasing (Dentan 2000c; Endicott and Endicott n.d.; Thambiah 1999; Tijah, Thambiah, and Leong 2000). Human communities in which all the adults look after all the children usually show a much lower rate of violence than matched communities where the adults mind their own business (Sampson, Raudenbush, and Earls 1997).

Making and Keeping Friends

Nudy's-Father: Let me give one answer to your question [about why Semai commit so little violence]. When someone does something wrong, like stealing, we don't beat them up badly or kill them. We bring them to judgment under our laws. We are one family, one people. Maybe we fine them, but only a little. And we bawl them out, urge them to change their ways, not to set a bad example for the children. We don't want to kill or beat people. We would be ashamed. And, number two, we would be like the beasts that kill/harm people.

Puk's-Grandfather: Right. What we think is, if we harm them, we lose out, we lose a friend. So, we withdraw and suffer in private [*kra'dii*]. We feel bad. But we need help in clearing swiddens, in feeding ourselves. We realize, if we harm our friends, we lose out. (fieldnotes from Waar River, 1991)

An evolutionary biologist (Bingham 2000) suggests that violence begets cooperation. The development of hunting tools made it possible for people working in groups to kill or threaten other people from a distance, lowering the costs of violence, that is, the risk of getting hurt or killed themselves. Both killers and their victims needed to form coalitions to protect themselves and their offspring. These coalitions, unlike those of other animals, are with nonkin. From the cost-benefit viewpoint of evolutionary biology, the alliance only works if nobody cheats. There has to be a way of raising the cost of cheating, not necessarily Bingham's "remote killing" but some added cost to cheaters. Semai social arrangements embody a number of such sanctions, social and ideological.

First, one reason traditional Semai are comfortable with each other is that they fear outsiders. To some extent, this statement is a tautology. One could say that fear of outsiders causes or facilitates love of insiders. But, to say that people fear outsiders, one has to make a distinction between insiders and outsiders. And when one says people fear outsiders, the implication is that they *do not* fear insiders. Why make the distinction otherwise? Instead of fear of outsiders *causing* love of insiders, the one is simply the flip side of the other or, in fancier language, it logically *implies* the other, at least to the extent that love is the opposite of fear. So instead of a causal one-way relationship, in empirical reality there is a two-way logical overlap in the analyst's head. It is just a matter of whether the analyst emphasizes negative peace, due to fear of violence, or positive peace, due to love of the placid and contented way of life that Semai call *slamaad*. The word *slamaad* comes from the Arabic word for peace (*salaam*) that comes from surrender (*Islam*). Anything that makes outsiders seem more fearsome makes insiders seem safer; anything that makes insiders more comfortable to be with makes outsiders more alien. There's a two-bit term for this process, *complementary schizmogenesis* (Bateson 1958:175–77). The phrase may be an unfamiliar jawbreaker, but the process is almost universal.

A second technique for keeping social relations peaceable, one that mirrors the way Semai deal with outsiders, is avoidance. The avoidance may be overt, as when people, especially women and children, flee at the approach of strangers. Or it may be ritual, as in east Semai *respect relationships*. There is always a potential conflict in a marriage between one's in-laws, who may expect to maintain their old relationships, and oneself, if one wants a bit of a monopoly. Therefore, for example, an east Semai man will avoid addressing, looking at, getting close to, or naming his wife's mother. Greater intimacy, for Semai, would be an incestuous violation of the natural order, which could bring on the violent dissolution of whole the settlement (Dentan 2000b, 2002b). The same restrictions apply to all one's spouse's elder siblings and, reciprocally, one's younger siblings' spouses. An alternative way to reduce the tensions that surround marriage is to make a joke of all the misbehavior that might happen, to create what anthropologists call a *joking relationship*. Insulting or making overt sexual propositions to a spouse's younger siblings and, reciprocally, to an older sibling's spouse produces a kind of familiarity that means a widow or widower can find solace with the dead spouse's kid brother or sister. Both the avoidance and the joking are ways of relieving interpersonal tension.

The third way of controlling violence involves what, for want of a better word, could be called *taboos* (Kroes 2002). Among Semai, these quite extensive taboos involve the realization that subjecting someone else to stress, for example, by treating them with disrespect, can make them more susceptible to disease or accident. For instance, when someone demands a share in one's meal, one should share what one can afford; otherwise the hungry person will be in *punan*, likely to fall sick or to trip and fall. Not showing up for an appointment can have similar ill effects. However annoying it may be for Semai to fulfill their social obligations, they are aware of the practical and moral consequences of hurting someone else's feelings, of causing a "spiritual wound," (*lukaa' sngii'*.) Recent studies of stress in Western and non-Western societies indicate that the Semai assessment of the physical effects of disrespect is correct (Dentan 2000b; McDade 2001).

Fourth, if a person has been frustrated, suffered a lukaa' sngii' as a result of someone else's action or inaction, the injured person can go to the offender's house and demand a gift, to restore normal serenity and to repair the damage done to the relationship. Semai use a Sanskrit-Malay word meaning "a fine" to describe this gift. There may be some haggling about what it will take to make everything all right again, but everyone understands that the slamaad—the peace—which allows people to cooperate is at stake (cf. Peterson 1993; Robarchek 1997). If the offender refuses the gift, then the hurt person may simply "steal" something he feels will restore his "spiritual" health. (I put "steal" in quote marks, because Semai use a different verb for this process than for theft; and "spiritual" in quote marks because the distinction between spiritual and physical is far less clear among Semai than in the Cartesian West.)

Alternatively, the offender may hold a ritual to restore the victim to health. The ritual will usually involve bathing with fragrant flowers and leaves, to attract back the patient's souls or spiritual powers, which the insult or slight has driven off or weakened: aroma and massage therapy, an observer might say. This healing costs the offender time and also usually a gift to the presiding shaman.

Finally, besides these decentralized and informal techniques of conflict resolution, some communities in Perak state have further institutionalized what Semai call "the law of fines" into a trial or town meeting (*bicaraa'*) (Robarchek 1979, 1990, 1997). Usually, the headman and his assistant have informally polled the settlement(s) involved—household by household—before the actual meeting, so that they have an idea of what the settlement consensus is going to be. Their job is basically to voice that consensus at the end of the meeting. At the meeting, usually held in the evening, elders lecture the quarrelling parties along the lines of the epigraph for this section: the need for cooperation and mutual love, the importance of behaving in a rational rather than a disorderly way, the duty to set a good example for the children and grandchildren. Everyone gets to speak, until everyone's verbal resources are exhausted, and the disputants are ready to yield to the consensus as expressed by the elders. The yielding usually takes the form of agreeing to pay fines for the various offenses involved. (Elders in this area can cite an elaborate ritualized schedule of fines.) In many cases, however, the participants reach no conclusion, "or a decision is made but later ignored and seemingly forgotten" (Brison 1989:97).

Whether or not the parties actually pay the fines is far less important than the acceptance of shame (*slniil*) in order to reconnect with the community. Slniil is "the feeling state that accompanies emotional disconnection" (Pollack 1999:32) or fear of such rejection. The bicaraa' institution, which has no other coercive ability, fails without slniil. It works, when it works, because people value social ties so highly—the same reason that similar conflict resolution programs in American schools sometimes fail. Now that the outside world both claims coercive authority over disputes and is at least potentially open as an alternative to the local community, the failures may become more frequent. Semai peaceability is resilient enough, however, that the failures rarely lead to violence. Learned helplessness and deference to individual autonomy may make it easier for Semai to accept such failures.

Winning and Losing, Failing and Succeeding

> Semai are indeed touched with nobility and have succeeded admirably in finding ways of handling human violence. They do have something important to say to the rest of us about good and evil. . . . Their utopian solution, however, is a poor competitor in the open market. And as all ideas, all mutations, in the end all species, must be judged on their success in competing with others of their kind, the Semai experiment has to be judged a noble failure. (Watson 1995:156–57)

> . . . but love's the only engine of survival. (Cohen 1997:6)

I have argued above and elsewhere that, in evolutionary terms, Semai are as much a success as, say, French people, and are more successful than a number of warlike peoples who have disappeared from the face of the earth. Semai are doing better than the Nazis are, for example. Even sympathetic assessments, like Watson's, confuse poverty and lack of military prowess with biological failure. That makes sense in terms of U.S. values, but not in terms of differential reproduction, the sole evolutionary criterion of success. Biologically, Semai are a success (Dentan 2002a).

But I do not want to repeat that old argument here. I want to point out that there is another kind of success that Semai amply demonstrate: the ability to live in harmony, without fear of each other. The fact that Semai history plays a role in their peaceability has a curious effect on people who would otherwise be enthusiastic about the Semai way of life. Their sympathy immediately wanes. They want what philosophers call positive peace, based on social justice and mutual love, which Semai do manifest; but they want it untainted by negative peace, which stems from the fear of violence. This odd feeling, that peace should stem from higher motives than violence, reflects the normalization of violence in Western society: peace should be impractical and should require a level of virtue abnormal to humankind.

In the U.S., helping professionals have pathologized learned helplessness and the associated mild depression, for example, in the diagnosis "battered woman syndrome" (Walker 1979). The reasons for doing so are good and sufficient: battered women are at risk. But the insistence that learned helplessness is pathological regardless of the conditions under which it occurs is as scientifically sterile as the insistence on normalizing aggression. Just as the value-laden assumption that violence is more natural than peace limits investigation into the circumstances which favor one or the other (Dentan 2002a; Dentan and Otterbein 1996), so the denigration of learned helplessness limits investigation into whether it is ever appropriate or positively adaptive (Prosser 2000).

Such judgments reflect the contempt for "sissies" that patriarchal values entail among peoples like traditional Malays or macho Americans. The judgments support the capitalist dismissal of uncompetitive and uncommodifiable goods like contentment or slamaad. And they reflect the value judgment, almost universal in hierarchical societies, that people in the lower socioeconomic strata are incomplete or damaged humans. Social workers have to insist that their clients are not mere passive victims, because they know the society as a whole sees being passive or victimized as being of an inferior essence. Societies that create victims despise them. Solutions to their plight must involve resistance or empowerment. In this welter of proviolence and propower assumptions, Semai nonresistance and their rejection of power as a culturally legitimate desideratum may elicit sympathy or endearment, but must also produce pity, condescension, and contempt.

But the traditional Semai response to violence is far more radical than the palliatives pushed by less sophisticated but more "advanced" peoples (Dentan 2000b). The Semai eidos rejects the whole complex of power-victim-resistance-heroism. Accepting the Semai eidos as legitimate would be as subversive of the world-conquering, Western, capitalist social order as actually practicing Buddhism, Taoism, Sufism, or any other peaceable egalitarian eidos (Dentan 1992, 1994; Wilson 1998). Semai ethnic identity may not survive the onslaught of globalized seduction and coercion. It may perish before scholars come to understand its complexity. Still, their sense of how the world works, and the way they live in it, may remain a possible and practical alternative in people's memories, like the ancient Chinese praised by Lao Tzu (Le Guin 1997:20–21).

> Once upon a time
> people who knew the Way
> were subtle, spiritual, mysterious, penetrating,
> unfathomable.
>
> Since they're inexplicable
> I can only say what they seemed like:
> Cautious, oh yes, as if wading through a winter river.
> Alert, as if afraid of the neighbors.
> Polite and quiet, like houseguests.
> Elusive, like melting ice. . . .
> To follow the Way
> is not to need fulfillment.
> Unfulfilled, one may live on
> needing no renewal.

Study Questions

1. Is Semai nonviolence adaptive? Explain why or why not.
2. Dentan writes, "Peace is the normal state of humankind." Explain the basis for his statement.
3. Does Dentan see Semai peace as *positive peace* or as *negative peace*, or as some combination of the two concepts?
4. What historical feature does Dentan see as lying at the root of Semai peacefulness? What do you think of this argument?
5. What is the *bicaraa*'? Are there clear winners and losers following a bicaraa'? How is it similar to the Paliyan *kuTTam*?

12

Conclusion: Learning from Peaceful Societies

DOUGLAS P. FRY

There are those who feel science is above politics, but nothing is above politics. Science is influenced by politics as much as is art, the media, religion, or any other aspect of human activity. It is not being aware of those influences that can undermine the value of the scientific enterprise. There has been much resistance to the concept of peaceful societies. In the first part of this chapter, Douglas Fry looks at that resistance and attempts to redress an imbalance and promote scientific debate. In the second part, Fry reviews conflict management in the peaceful societies discussed in this book, examining common themes in the creation and maintenance of peace. He finishes by exploring some lessons that peaceful societies might offer for developing and maintaining peace.

—GK

This chapter has two major sections. In the first, I will consider how the very existence of peaceful societies continues to be disputed and denied, the evidence of their existence notwithstanding. In the second section, I will highlight some common threads in conflict management that cross-cut the cultural case studies in this volume. In turn, this discussion will lead to an exploration of the practical question: What might we learn from peaceful societies about how to promote peace and reduce violence?

Having been interested in peaceful societies for a number of years, I have repeatedly observed what seems like a puzzling phenomenon: A substantial number of people do not like the idea that peaceful societies exist. It is interesting to ponder why this is the case. Undoubtedly, different persons have different reasons, but in any event, Hobbesian beliefs remain a prominent feature in Western thinking (Adams and Bosch 1987; Fry forthcoming). Shortly, responding with tongue in cheek to the challenge of how to get rid of a "nuisance," I will consider several ways to make peaceful societies disappear. First, however, a few introductory comments are in order.

As discussed by Kemp (this volume) and Davies-Vengoechea (this volume), it is unproductive to view peace and war as opposite, mutually exclusive concepts (see also Nordstrom 1997a, 1997b). From a cross-cultural perspective, it makes sense to envision a continuum of variation from nonviolence to violence (Fry 1999, forthcoming). At one end of the continuum, in a few societies such as the Semai (Dentan this volume) and the Paliyan (Gardner this volume), internal and external forms of physical aggression are virtually absent. Whether or not such societies will maintain this high degree of peacefulness in the face of ever-increasing intrusions and disruptions from the outside remains an open question. Moving along the cross-cultural continuum, physical aggression gradually increases. For example, still near the peaceful end, the Mardu lack warfare and feuding, but they do inflict spear wounds to a person's thigh as a form of punishment for breaking social norms (Tonkinson this volume). Also relatively near the peaceful end of a cross-cultural spectrum, the Hopi historically engaged in warfare to defend themselves from their more violent neighbors, but Hopi culture devalued violence, experienced a very low level of physical aggression, and did not glorify war (Schlegel this volume). A main value in conceptualizing societies as existing along a peaceful-to-violent continuum is that this perspective highlights the relativity of peacefulness and aggressiveness rather than rigidly dichotomizing peaceful societies and violent societies.

Furthermore, peace and violence are not static phenomena (Dentan 1992; Fry 1999). Dentan (2001: 11140) points out that nonviolence and peace refer to societal adjustments that "are often transitory rather than essential natures which persist indefinitely." Lawrence Keeley (1996:147) reaches a similar conclusion, noting that "peaceable societies can become belligerent, and vice versa." As Kemp (this volume) emphasizes, peace must be promoted, and this is an active, ongoing process.

In this book, the contributors have provided case studies on societies that currently lie near the peaceful end of the cross-cultural continuum; but nobody claims that these societies are violence free. As Robert Dentan (pers. comm.) points out, to think in terms of a violence-free society makes about as little sense as envisioning a peace-free society: "You'd never find a society in which the bulk of the people don't spend most of their time in peaceful pursuits." Furthermore, no contributor is claiming that societies are conflict free. Social conflict is expected in any social group with a membership greater than one. No two individuals are expected to have the same interests, needs, or desires all of the time. However, conflict is not the same as violence (see Dobinson this volume; Boulding 2000:89; Fry and Fry 1997).

In the case studies in this book, the focus is on how conflicts are managed almost all of the time without physical aggression. In the second part of this chapter, we will review recurring themes in conflict management and explore some broader implications for creating a more peaceful world. First, if I may use a little poetic license, I'd like to facetiously explore some ways to "deep-six" peaceful societies as a way to call attention to certain fallacious arguments.

Seven Ways to Make Peaceful Societies Disappear

Peaceful societies can be a nuisance. They contradict widespread Hobbesian cultural beliefs that human beings are basically nasty by nature, and this makes some people uncomfortable. In other words, the existence of peaceful societies creates problems for the view that humans are naturally violent and warlike. As Johan van der Dennen (1995:497) observes, "Peaceable preindustrial peoples constitute a nuisance to most theories of warfare and they are thus either 'explained away,' denied, or negated...." Peaceful societies also might make us feel inferior—or even guilty—by raising some uncomfortable questions. How is it possible that some societies have achieved more tranquil and secure ways of life than we have? Could we, too, be handling our conflicts with less reliance on aggression and force?

Before discussing ways to make bothersome peaceful societies disappear, it might be wise to assess the extent of the problem. First, regarding external conflict, some societies do not engage in either warfare or feuding, and others engage in feuding but not warfare. Following Otterbein (1968, 1970:3), war can be defined as "armed combat between political communities," whereas feuding is blood revenge that follows a homicide (see Otterbein and Otterbein 1965:1470; see also Boehm 1987). Feuding has its roots in personal disputes and does not involve political objectives associated with a community at large. After searching ethnographic accounts for several months, I was able to locate more than sixty nonwarring societies (Fry forthcoming). The vast majority of these nonwarring societies are also nonfeuding. In this volume, the Mardu, Paliyan, Semai, and Nubians are nonfeuding and nonwarring. Other examples of nonwarring societies include the Cayapa, Panare, Pemon, and Piaroa of South America; the Polar Eskimo and other Inuit societies of Greenland; the Hanunóo and Subanun Agta of the Philippines; the Badaga, Birhor, Irula, Kota, Lepcha, Toda, and Yanadi of South Asia; the Punan of Borneo; the Semang of Malaysia; and the Columbia, Copper Inuit, Kaibab Paiute, Karok, and Wenatchi of North

America, among many others (Fry 2001, forthcoming; see Bonta and Fry forthcoming). Thus, the problem becomes one of dismissing, at a minimum, some sixty societies ethnographically described as nonwarring and usually as nonfeuding as well.

Turning to internally peaceful societies—those cultural cases with very low levels of physical aggression and nonviolent core values—the case studies in this volume are only the tip of the iceberg. To mention but one example, anthropologists Edwin Burrows (1952), Catherine Lutz (1982, 1983, 1988), and Melford Spiro (1952) concur that life in Ifaluk society in Micronesia is nonviolent. Burrows elaborates:

> What is striking about Ifaluk...is the fact that there is no discrepancy between its cultural values (the ideal culture) and its actual behavior patterns (the real culture). Not one individual could remember a single case of murder, rape, robbery, or fighting; nor did the ethnographer witness such behavior in his seven-month study. It was almost impossible to convey to the people the concept of murder, the thought of wantonly killing another person is so completely alien to their thinking. (Burrows 1952:25)

Some of the nonwarring and nonfeuding societies are also internally peaceful; however, some societies—and past Hopi culture is a good example—practice warfare while maintaining a largely nonaggressive internal social order. More than eighty internally peaceful societies have been documented, again after several months of searching ethnographic reports (Fry forthcoming; Bonta and Fry forthcoming). In addition to the case studies in this volume, clearly documented examples of societies wherein nonviolence reigns include the Buid (Gibson 1989), Chewong (Howell 1989), Ifaluk (Burrows 1952; Lutz 1988; Spiro 1952), Ladakh (Mann 1986; Norberg-Hodge 1991), Lepcha (Gorer 1967), Sami (Anderson and Beach 1992; Holsti 1913; Montagu 1976), Saulteaux (Hallowell 1974), and Sherpa (Paul 1977, 1992; von Fürer-Haimendorf 1984), among numerous others (see Bonta 1993, 1996, 1997; Bonta and Fry forthcoming; Boulding 2000, esp. ch. 4; Fry 1999, 2001, forthcoming; Howell and Willis 1989; Levinson 1994; Montagu 1978; Sponsel and Gregor 1994). So, the problem of getting rid of peaceful societies is substantial.

Fortunately, there are ways to deny, debunk, and dismiss peaceful societies. Here, to be helpful, I will briefly suggest seven techniques and provide illustrations of their use. To most effectively eliminate peaceful societies, combining several methods is advisable. Readers should be warned, however, that sometimes these techniques can backfire; therefore, they should be used with caution.

1. *Stridently emphasize violence and simply ignore all evidence to the contrary.* Michael Ghiglieri (1999) makes a big fuss about violence and ignores

peaceful societies altogether. He asserts that "*murder is encoded into the human psyche*" (1999:133, italics in original); "robbery, like murder, is universal" (1999:147); "both jealousy itself and jealousy murder are *common*" (1999:149, italics added); "because rape is so widespread and rampant around the planet, by males both human and nonhuman, it is clearly a male biological adaptation" (1999:103); and, "are men born to be lethally violent? The answer is yes. Aggression is programmed by our DNA" (1999:30). Ghiglieri simply does not discuss the data on peaceful societies that might call such statements into question.

To take another example, Richard Wrangham and Dale Peterson propose that human males are violent by temperament and that modern humans are "the dazed survivors of a continuous, 5-million-year habit of lethal aggression" (1996:63). Obviously, the existence of peaceful societies poses a major contradiction to Wrangham and Peterson's assertion about the "ubiquity of warfare and violence across time and space" (1996:84). In attempting to make peaceful societies disappear, Wrangham and Peterson, like Ghiglieri, simply sidestep the bulk of relevant information about peaceful societies. They mention and then dismiss the nonviolent Semai in one short paragraph, although, as we have seen, Semai peacefulness is soundly documented (Dentan this volume). More generally, Wrangham and Peterson ignore nearly all of the sources on peaceful societies published prior to their book, including such major works as Ashley Montagu's *Learning Non-Aggression* (1978), Signe Howell and Roy Willis's *Societies at Peace* (1989), Bruce Bonta's *Peaceful Peoples* (1993), and Leslie Sponsel and Thomas Gregor's *Anthropology of Peace and Nonviolence* (1994), not to mention dozens of other sources (see Fry forthcoming).

2. *Set an impossible standard, such as requiring a peaceful society to be absolutely and totally free of all forms of aggression across time, find a few real or apparent exceptions to the impossible standard, and then dismiss the society in question as clearly NOT peaceful.* The Ju/'hoansi hunter-gatherers of the African Kalahari, for example, have been the subject of this approach. To first provide a little background, several researchers have concluded that the Ju/'hoansi (formerly called the Kung or !Kung) strongly devalue aggression and are for the most part very peaceful (Draper 1978:33; Kent 1989:704; Konner 1982:204; Lee 1993:93; Marshall 1961; Thomas 1994:71, 75). Ju/'hoansi social relationships seldom involve physical aggression. Ju/'hoansi manage the overwhelming majority of their conflicts through talk, humor, short- and long-term avoidance, friendly peacemaking by third parties, and—recently—by appealing to non-Ju/'hoansi mediators (Draper 1978; Lee 1979:ch. 13, 1993:ch. 7; Marshall 1961; Thomas 1994). Both Richard Lee (1979:367) and Susan Kent (1989) point out that, traditionally, the nomadic Ju/'hoansi could easily "vote with their feet." The

Ju/'hoansi not only prevent many conflicts from escalating to violence, but they also know how to reconcile following a dispute (Fry 2000:339, 348).

Based largely on his work among a *different* Kalahari society, the !Ko San (see also technique number six below), ethologist Irenäus Eibl-Eibesfeldt (1974, 1979) argues that verbal aggression—such as mockery and insults—sorcery, sibling rivalry among children, and children's aggression refute Ju/'hoansi peacefulness. He points out that !Ko San, and by extension the Ju/'hoansi, are not aggression free.

Melvin Konner (1982:204) makes an important point that is relevant to Eibl-Eibesfeldt's writings: From a culturally comparative view, the Ju/'hoansi are *relatively* peaceful, not *absolutely* nonviolent. Using terms like *aggression-free* implies some sort of black-or-white dichotomy—that is, either having aggression or being aggression-free. By contrast, notice that Richard Lee (1993:93, italics added) uses the word "relative" in his assessment: "The Ju/'hoansi managed to live in *relative* harmony with a few overt disruptions." Likewise, Elizabeth Thomas (1959:24, 186), who titled her book about the Ju/'hoansi *The Harmless People,* describes aggressive incidents. Although Thomas is impressed with the relative tranquility of Ju/'hoansi daily life, she is clearly not proposing that the Ju/'hoansi are aggression free. Neither is Lee (1979, 1993), who reports twenty-two homicide cases between 1920 and 1955, nor is Patricia Draper (1978:33), who concludes that physical aggression among the Ju/'hoansi is extremely rare, but nonetheless obviously does occur.

3. *Count any type of conflict as if it were aggression.* The following example illustrates this technique. Laura Betzig and Santus Wichimai (1991) argue that Ifaluk society in Micronesia is not peaceful, even though they acknowledge that "Betzig, Turke, Rodseth and Harrigan, in six months of combined observation, never saw any physical violence among adults, and saw adults punish children physically only twice." Betzig and Wichimai argue against Ifaluk peacefulness by moving beyond physical aggression to a more general discussion of social inequality and conflicts of interest within the society (for instance, the paying of tribute to chiefs). The key to using this technique is to muddle the distinction between conflict and physical aggression.

Conflict would be expected on Ifaluk, as it is expected and observable in any society. Betzig and Wichimai (1991) point out that Ifaluk chiefs take tribute from the commoners, Ifaluk traditionally paid tribute to Yap, legends of ancient wars exist on Ifaluk, people on Ifaluk sometimes have land disputes, and people fear sorcery; in short, they propose that "there is no question that *conflicts of interest* exist on Ifaluk" (Betzig and Wichimai 1991:245, italics added). But this does *not* imply that conflicts regularly take a violent form—as when Betzig and Wichimai argue that "individual differences were not infrequently resolved by *violence*" (1991:249, italics added). This assertion about violence widely overstates the facts and is contradicted not only by the observations of Burrows (1952), quoted earlier in the chapter, Spiro (1952), and Lutz (1982, 1983, 1988), but interestingly also by Betzig's own first-hand observations (Betzig and Wichimai 1991:240). In short, Ifaluk does not lack all forms of conflict; people do get angry and have disputes. However, an assessment of the various reports from Ifaluk shows that physical aggression is exceedingly rare and that violence, manifested in such acts as rape and murder, is practically nonexistent. Thus, in summary, the heart of this technique is to muddle the concepts and pass-off instances of conflict, which can be found in any society, as violence.

4. *Cite an inflated homicide rate to exaggerate violence.* The problem with this technique is finding inflated homicide rates. I know of only one case, but since it pertains to the extremely peaceful Semai, the exaggerated homicide rate could prove useful to anyone attempting to debunk Semai peacefulness. Anthropologists Clayton Robarchek and Carole Robarchek (1998: 124n2) explain how someone used a population figure for the Semai of 300, instead of 15,000, thus calculating a homicide rate that is about 50 times too high. When Robert Dentan (1988:626) recalculated the Semai homicide rate based on the correct population figures, he got .56 per 100,000—a very low rate compared to most other societies (see also Dentan 1995:230n2; and Fry forthcoming, for additional discussion).

One of the advantages of citing this erroneous homicide rate is that, despite attempts to correct the mistake, the fifty-times-too-high calculation error persists. This is illustrated, for example, when Raymond Kelly (2000:20) relies on the incorrect homicide rate in his intriguing book *Warless Societies and the Origin of War,* as does archaeologist Lawrence Keeley when he writes in *War before Civilization* that the Semai "homicide rate was numerically significant" (1996: 31). In actuality, of course, Robert Dentan's corrections show the Semai homicide rate to be extremely low—not even remotely close to the figure published earlier. Hopefully, however, Robert Dentan's correction will not become commonly known, and the erroneous homicide rate will continue to cast doubt on Semai peacefulness.

5. *Regarding warfare in particular, make clever use of terminology to exaggerate the number of societies that engage in war.* One way to do this is to devise a scheme that uses the word "war" for all possible categories of societies. If this sounds difficult to accomplish, there is no need for concern, because an excellent classification system already exists. In his landmark treatise, *A Study of War,* Quincy Wright (1942, 1964:40) acknowledged that some societies lack war, but included no corresponding label within his society-classifying scheme. Wright assumed that all societies, even those that do not engage in warfare, would fight back if attacked, so he put nonwarring societies in a category called *defensive war.* In fact, the ethnographic record shows many

instances of nonwarring and other societies fleeing or moving away from aggressive neighbors rather than automatically fighting back (Dentan this volume; Ferguson 1989:196; Fry forthcoming; Gardner this volume). But for our purposes, the beauty of Wright's system is that all societies are placed in the categories: *political war, economic war, social war,* or *defensive war.* There are simply no alternatives in the classification scheme such as *peaceful* or *nonwarring.* This is analogous to classifying everybody within illness categories, for instance, *critically ill, chronically ill, intermediately ill,* or *undiagnosed,* with no category for *healthy* or *not ill.* Such labels subtly imply that illness is the natural state of affairs. Similarly, Wright's labeling scheme gives the impression that all societies engage in war, even those that do not. This is a subtle technique that packs a weighty message: War is everywhere.

A second terminological approach for exaggerating war is to muddle the concepts. A section of Lawrence Keeley's *War before Civilization,* titled "Prehistoric War," includes instances of homicide and "violent death" (note the ambiguity of this term) along with evidence for warfare. In other words, many of the examples Keeley (1996:36–39) mentions under the label of *prehistoric war* do not actually involve war at all. By muddling the concepts, Keeley creates an inflated picture of prehistoric war. A problem with this technique, however, is that it is hard to hide the muddling. Anthropologist Keith Otterbein (1997:271) saw right away what Keeley was doing, "I object to sliding from 'violent death' in the Paleolithic to 'warfare' in the Late Paleolithic without comment upon his changing use of terminology." Similarly, anthropologist Raymond Kelly (2000:157) also questioned Lawrence Keeley's assertion that certain European mass burials can be presented as evidence of war:

> Communicable disease and starvation provide highly plausible alternative explanations for multiple burials and even mass graves. In winter there is no inducement to prompt burial, especially during a time of general illness and famine (and the first may conspire to produce the second). Multiple burials should not be interpreted as evidence of war unless skeletal indications of trauma or proximate projectile points support this. (Kelly 2000:157)

Thus, Lawrence Keeley intermingles archaeological examples of individual homicides, sometimes ambiguous cases of violent death, and perhaps even nonviolent deaths due to starvation or disease with the archaeological examples of warfare, calling all of these prehistoric war. Obviously, this can give an impression that there is more evidence for warfare, and older evidence for warfare, than actually exists. Although Keeley mixes and muddles within an archaeological context, the same technique could be used to inflate aggression within peaceful societies, by counting a mixed bag of phenomena as violence. For instance, accidents, cases of abandonment of the sick or dying, group sanctioned capital punishment, ostracism resulting in death, or the ambiguous "violent death" in any form, could be lumped together with homicides. A downside to this mixing and muddling approach, however, is that, as in the Keeley example, other people may rather easily realize what you have done.

6. *Apply cases of violence or war from a certain place or time to a totally different place or time.* Although situated only about an hour's walk from each other, the San Andrés Zapotec have a homicide rate more than five times that of the neighboring La Paz (Fry this volume). In illustration of this technique, I could try to cast doubt on the peacefulness of La Paz by simply ignoring its own homicide rate and instead mentioning the San Andrés rate as if it were in some way relevant to La Paz. !Ko and Ju/'hoansi are neighboring societies in Africa's Kalahari. Similarities *and* differences might be expected between them. As mentioned under technique number two, above, Eibl-Eibesfeldt (1979) sets up an impossible, absolute standard for the Ju/'hoansi to be aggression free. He also uses the current technique when he draws on data primarily from !Ko society to argue that the Ju/'hoansi are not aggression free.

The application of data from one time and place to another has also been used to exaggerate warfare. An examination of Margaret Mead's writings on Samoa shows that as a matter of practice she provides explicit time and place specifications for her work. In making a scathing attack on Mead's work, Derek Freeman (1983) routinely disregards Mead's time and place specifications (see Ember 1985; Fry forthcoming; Holmes 1987:148–51). For example, in her classic work *Coming of Age in Samoa,* Mead establishes that the book is set in the 1920s: "The reader must not mistake the conditions which have been described for the aboriginal ones, nor for typical primitive ones." (1928:199). Nonetheless, Wrangham and Peterson (1996), following the lead of Freeman, attempt to discredit Mead by citing historical examples of Samoan warfare from the eighteenth and nineteenth centuries—a time period prior to Mead's work. These examples of war actually pose no contradiction to Mead's writings, for Mead never states or implies that war did not exist in the past (for example, see Mead 1928:146). The historical accounts of Samoan warfare enumerated by Freeman and reiterated by Wrangham and Peterson do not contradict Mead's simple and accurate observation that warfare had been abolished in Samoa prior to her fieldwork.

7. *Create a bogus peaceful society, then destroy your creation.* Samoa also leads us to the most creative approach in this list of suggestions for making peaceful societies disappear. In using this technique, the first step is to create a myth that a given society is peaceful when in fact it is not particularly peaceful. The second step is to present evidence that demolishes the idea that the society is peaceful. This is relatively easy to do since the society in question

is not in actuality particularly peaceful. The third step is to extrapolate from the single case to a broader conclusion that peaceful societies in general do not exist.

Here is an amazing example of this technique. Derek Freeman (1983) asserts that Margaret Mead thought Samoa was a peaceful society. He ignores all of Mead's descriptions of Samoan aggression—that is, information that contradicts his argument—uses the time-and-place–switching technique (number six), and quotes Mead totally out of context. Having set Mead up for the fall, Freemen proceeds to dismantle the idea that Samoa is a peaceful place. He recounts a litany of martial events in Samoan history, presents statistics on violent crime, and reviews ethnographic accounts to thoroughly destroy the idea that Samoa is peaceful. Wrangham and Peterson (1996) adopt Freeman's stance and take it even further; they use Samoa as their showcase example that peaceful societies are nothing more than "paradise imagined." This unusual story is examined further in Fry (forthcoming).

Having now presented facetious suggestions for how to debunk peaceful societies, it is time to change styles and raise a serious question. Why bother to criticize arguments that dismiss peaceful societies and overemphasize the human capacity for violence? One answer is that the representation of such views as scientific fact may contribute to their becoming self-fulfilling prophecies in the real world of human interaction and politics. Images of humanity that exaggerate human belligerence and blood lust may actually promote violence by providing a rationalization that it is normal and natural. Psychologist David Barash points out:

> If war is considered inevitable, and societies therefore prepare to fight—for example, by drafting an army, procuring weapons that threaten their neighbors, following bellicose foreign policy—war may well result. And that fact will then be cited as proof that the war was inevitable from the start; moreover, it will be used to justify similar behavior in the future. (Barash 1991:22)

Peaceful societies demonstrate the human capacity to prevent, limit, and deal with conflicts nonviolently, and this offers hope for diminishing the violence in the world. I will next highlight conflict management themes apparent in this book and subsequently consider several examples of what peaceful societies might teach us about enhancing peace.

The Case Studies: Patterns of Nonviolent Conflict Management

Several themes in nonviolent conflict management emerge from this collection of case studies. First, societies with low levels of aggression tend to have *core values that promote nonviolent behavior*. For example, Schlegel (this volume) points out how the Hopi value harmony, humility, and good thoughts; correspondingly, "anger and violence have no part in the life of a humble person who respects the autonomy of others." Gardner (this volume) highlights the Paliyan core value of respect, and conversely, the importance of avoiding disrespect. Fry (this volume) makes a similar point regarding the La Paz Zapotec. Although cultural conceptions of respect differ from one setting to the next, in both Paliyan and La Paz Zapotec belief systems, aggression is antithetical to conceptions of respect. Fernea (this volume) explains that Nubians "value a peaceful life very highly." The fact that peace is a core value among Norwegians comes out in various ways: for example, in the public outcry over even a modest rise in violent crime, the implementation of numerous violence-prevention programs, and active participation of Norwegians in international conflict resolution initiatives (Dobinson this volume). Dentan (this volume) calls Semai nonviolence "a continuing choice." Thus, the case studies in this book reinforce Bonta's (1996:404) assessment: "As the examination of conflict resolution in these small-scale societies proceeds, one fundamental fact emerges: the peacefulness of their conflict resolution is based, primarily, on their world-views of peacefulness—a complete rejection of violence."

A second common theme is that many peaceful societies emphasize *avoidance* as a favored approach for dealing with conflict generally, and especially with the threat of violence. Avoidance entails curtailing or ceasing interaction with someone. "A typical way of dealing with individuals with whom one has quarreled is to avoid them," writes Howard (this volume) of Rotumans. The La Paz Zapotec not only use avoidance in response to conflict, but they also use it to prevent problems, for example, by keeping a distance from inebriated persons. The Sama Dilaut sea nomads sail away from conflict, literally, and also symbolically if they enter into the non-speaking *magbanta* relationship (Sather this volume). The avoidance theme is also illustrated in the chapters on the Norwegians and Semai (Dobinson this volume; Dentan this volume). For instance, at the interpersonal level, Semai withdraw contact when they are angry at someone; and "when they can't avoid the offenders entirely, angry people will simply not speak to them and will avoid meeting their eyes." At the group level, the primary Semai response to slave raiding, suggests Dentan, was "flight, not confrontation."

A third commonality regarding conflict management in peaceful societies involves responding to conflict with *self-restraint* and *self-control* rather than with aggression or threatening displays. Schlegel (this volume) refers to a nonviolent yet bitter village split as "self-control on a massive scale." Of Rotuma Islanders, an emphasis on self-control is evident: people say they are sad or disappointed, not angry, because anger "implies being out of control, hence prone to violence" (Howard this volume). The fact that Gardner (this volume) titles a subsection of his chapter "Self-Restraint" indicates its importance in Paliyan conflict management. In relation to Norwegian self-control, Dobinson (this volume) observers that "explosions are rare."

Keeping the peace in these societies, however, is not a matter of simply expecting each person to exercise self-restraint. A fourth common theme is that *third parties* readily become involved in conflict management in many peaceful societies, adopting the roles of friendly peacemakers, mediators, arbitrators, and adjudicators (see Black 1993). *Friendly peacemakers* simply separate and distract disputants, perhaps using humor to facilitate the cooling of tempers. Gardner (this volume), who calls such persons among the Paliyan *conciliators,* explains that "their subtle, self-appointed task is to soothe or distract without violating the rights of the people in conflict."

Mediators more actively help disputants find mutually agreeable solutions to their problems, as in the type of village hearing the Sama Dilaut call *magsalassai* (Sather this volume). Fernea (this volume) emphasizes how Nubians feel a sense of responsibility to help others resolve their conflicts. Fernea relates two versions of a parable, "Putting a Stone in the Middle," to illustrate the importance of third parties in Nubian conflict management. The Paliyan *kuTTam* and the Semai *bicaraa'* are further examples of culturally specific dispute resolution assemblies that involve mediation (Gardner this volume; Dentan this volume).

Arbitrators and *adjudicators* (judges) differ from mediators in that they render decisions in conflict cases. Judges have the authority and power to enforce their rulings, whereas arbitrators rely on the pressure of public opinion or the voluntary compliance of the disputants with the terms of the ruling. In this book, we have seen an example of arbitration among the Nubians as a council of kinfolk, presided over by the elders, gathered to decide "who was right and who was wrong and how the matter might best be rectified" (Fernea this volume). Among the Hopi and Rotumans, chiefs sometimes pass judgment about land disputes—a process that, given the cultural particulars, seems to rest in a gray area between arbitration and adjudication (Schlegel this volume; Howard this volume). The La Paz authorities have the power to judge cases, fine defendants, or jail them, but in practice they deal with many matters brought before them as mediators or even therapists rather than judges (Fry this volume). Tonkinson (this volume) describes the type of group-focused adjudication that occurs at Mardu big meetings: "Everyone present with a case to answer must come forward and face their accusers, then take whatever punishment is meted out, with the assembly acting as judge and jury."

A fifth recurring theme sometimes relates to conflict-resolution procedures and sometimes applies more generally to decision-making processes. This theme involves *reaching consensus and minimizing hard feelings.* Schlegel (this volume) notes how Hopi village council decisions strive for consensus and at least reflect the most widely held opinions. For the La Paz Zapotec, the phrase Laura Nader (1969, 1990) has made famous applies, as community authorities attempt to "make the balance" and restore normal relationships between disputants rather than declare one the winner and the other the loser (Fry this volume). Sather (this volume) points out that in Sama Dilaut conflict resolution hearings, a goal is to "reestablish amicable relations," and settlements typically call for "mutual concessions on both sides." Tonkinson (this volume) also explains how the Mardu make every attempt to obtain a consensus, although this is not always possible in practice. Recall how the adjudication at Mardu big meetings involves group decisions. Dobinson (this volume) highlights consensus-based decision making in Norway. Dentan (this volume) writes that the role of the Semai headman is to voice the group consensus at the conclusion of a *bicaraa'* (see also Robarchek 1979, 1997). The overall goal is to close the rifts that have opened during a dispute between persons.

Sixth, it is interesting that several of the peaceful societies discussed in this volume—for example, the Hopi, Paliyan, Nubians, and Mardu—*discourage or shun the consumption of alcohol.* One reason for this is that alcohol makes self-restraint more difficult. Based on life experience, the Paliyans, for example, believe that "alcohol begets violence" (Gardner this volume). Shifting to the laboratory, an interesting line of biochemical and genetic research is beginning to pin down some of the complicated relationships between alcohol use and aggression (see Virkkunen 2001).

Seventh, the members of peaceful societies use a number of *social control mechanisms* to prevent and discourage physical aggression. The chapters in this book contain examples of both formal and informal social control mechanisms (see Black 1993; Fry 1999). *Formal* mechanisms include, for example, when the La Paz authorities punish fighting by jailing the participants in a drunken exchange. Criticism, harangues, ridicule, shaming, gossip, and fear of supernatural sanction, witchcraft accusations, or loss of social support illustrate the diverse array of *informal* social control mechanisms used to prevent acts of violence and other deviant behaviors in peaceful societies. The Hopi make use of rituals to put social pressure on deviants (Schlegel this volume). Rotumans believe in immanent justice (Howard this volume). Conflict and aggression are kept in check among the La Paz Zapotec in part due to concern over becoming the target of witchcraft, fear of being accused of witchcraft, and beliefs about the causation of certain types of illness (Fry this volume). Sama Dilaut reconcile and pressure others to reconcile in part due to beliefs that prolonged enmity leads to illness and other misfortunes (Sather this volume). The *-lees,* or harangue, used by Semai is also an informal social control mechanism (Dentan this volume). The Mardu ridicule nonconformists and punish serious wrongdoers by wounding them during expiatory encounters (Tonkinson this volume). The idea is to pressure a person into behaving correctly, in accordance with Mardu Law which generally discourages aggression. In peaceful societies, the occasional acts of aggression—whether minor or not—are taken seriously. Strong reactions to occasional violations send clear messages to the perpetrators that such behavior is unacceptable and also reaffirm for everyone in the society the importance of nonviolence. This phenomenon is illustrated by the active reactions of Norwegians against violence "both in popular discourse and in action, exemplified most visibly by the torch-lit peace marches" (Dobinson this volume).

Finally, in their discussion of conflict management, several contributors mention *socialization* as a process through which children *internalize* core values, beliefs, and expected codes of behavior (see Schlegel this volume; Howard this volume; Fry this volume; Tonkinson this volume). Children growing up in a peaceful society not only witness few acts of physical aggression, but are also taught nonviolent values, attitudes, and beliefs. For instance, if avoidance as a response to conflict is favored in the society, children learn this. Another pattern also emerges across most of the case studies: children do not receive much physical punishment in peaceful societies. This generalization holds, for instance, for the Paliyan, Rotuma Islanders, La Paz Zapotec, Mardu, Norwegians, and Semai. Physical punishment is illegal in Norway (Dobinson this volume), as in the Nordic countries overall (Fry 1993). Outlawing corporal punishment helps to reinforce nonviolent core values in Norwegian society by reaffirming the belief that striking another person is unacceptable.

Learning from Peaceful Societies

> [P]unishments and armed conflicts are NOT essential for keeping the peace. The answer is for us to build, in our societies, world-views of peacefulness that are as strong as those of the peaceful peoples. This is the first step. (Bonta 1996:416)

If we want to reduce acts of aggression in the world, does a study of conflict management in peaceful societies lead to any suggestions? At the very least, the case studies presented in this book raise some possibilities. First, I will make some points related to warfare, and second, mention a couple of possible lessons for enhancing intrasocietal peace.

Reducing the Threat of War

The belief that humanity is naturally warlike is embedded in Western culture, and resignation to war as a social institution is widespread. For instance, nearly half of the U.S. university students surveyed believe that "war is an intrinsic part of human nature" and that "human beings have an instinct for war" (Adams and Bosch 1987). United Nations Secretary-General Kofi Annan (1998:6) does not reject the notion that war may be part and parcel of human nature: "No one ever promised that it would be easy to rid the world of the scourge of war, which is so deeply rooted in human history— perhaps, even in human nature." Widely held beliefs that war is inevitable can hinder the search for alternatives, and thus the prophecy that war is inevitable becomes self-fulfilling. However, the existence of cultures that do not engage in war, although they are a minority, nonetheless shows that humans are capable of living without war. The existence of nonwarring societies such as the Mardu (Tonkinson this volume), the Semai (Dentan this volume), the Sama Dilaut (Sather this volume), and many others carries an important message: War does not stem inevitably from human nature.

The case studies in this book have underscored that nonviolent beliefs and values help to promote peaceful behavior. Other types of beliefs and values can facilitate aggressive and warlike actions. Many world leaders and citizens alike see the institution of warfare as permissible, at times necessary, and perhaps inevitable (see, for example, "Letters" 2002:8–11). Such pervasive beliefs facilitate both the waging of war and the continuing acceptance of the institution of war. Survey research demonstrates that persons who believe war to be part of human nature tend not to participate in peace-promoting activities (Adams and Bosch 1987). War as a social institution continues, in part, because large numbers of people, believing that war is inevitable or believing that war is acceptable, take no action to abolish the institution. Two hundred years ago, a similar situation existed regarding the institution of slavery; the first abolitionists were lone voices crying in the wilderness.

Albert Einstein (see Krieger 1994:319), in an often-quoted passage, expresses that in the nuclear age, "everything has changed, save our modes of thinking." Changes in attitude can facilitate the replacement of war with other approaches to intergroup conflict. The tremendous variation in cultural belief systems apparent in the ethnographic record, including those in peaceful societies, suggests that shifting to beliefs that favor nonviolent forms of conflict management instead of war are certainly possible. Thus, one important lesson stemming from the mere existence of peaceful societies is that views portraying humans as inevitably warlike are simply false.

But propagating nonviolent beliefs and values alone will not do the trick. If two Mardu bands are unable work out their differences, they do not fight it out; instead, they wait until the next big meeting and anticipate the help of third parties (Tonkinson this volume). Nations could also learn to institutionalize variations of the big meeting approach as an alternative to war. Some institutions already exist—such as the United Nations and the

European Union—and others could be created (Fry and Fry 1997; see also Boehm 2003). Nations could also make greater use of the International Court of Justice for dealing with disputes.

Another lesson for preventing intergroup violence comes from the Nubians. Fernea (this volume) attributes the lack of feuding to cross-cutting ties in Nubian society that interlink the members of society in a web of relationships. This network of ties helps to prevent the development of hostile factions (see also Glazer 1997; Rubin, Pruitt, and Kim 1994:138–39).

There is a parallel in today's world. In terms of a multitude of security, environmental, and economic issues, the nations and peoples of the world have never been so interdependent. Interdependencies theoretically should make warfare less likely. However, awareness of interdependence seems to be lagging behind this new reality. Recognizing interdependence and forging mutually beneficial cooperative ventures could help prevent war, while simultaneously addressing urgent common challenges. After all, military options cannot effectively address threats to the security and survival of every person on the planet that stem from global warming, environmental degradation, overpopulation, and so forth. The nonwarring, nonfeuding Mardu long ago figured out that they need each other and that reciprocity works better than hostile competition. Tonkinson (this volume) explains that:

> to permit intergroup conflict or feuding to harden social and territorial boundaries would be literally suicidal, since no group can expect the existing water and food resources of its territory to tide it over until the next rains; peaceful intergroup relations are imperative for long-term survival.

Is there an insight here, from this peaceful society, for the other members of the global village?

Lessons for Promoting Peace within Societies

The goal of this section is to explore a couple of lessons that peaceful societies might offer for reducing violence in other cultural settings, for example, in the United States. I will return to two of the conflict management themes discussed above—first, core values and beliefs that promote nonviolent behavior, and second, the favoring of nonphysical modes of child rearing over corporal punishment—to illustrate how lessons for promoting peace can be gleaned from studies of peaceful societies. No doubt, readers will see many other lessons besides the ones discussed here.

The case studies in this book suggest that shared cultural beliefs that counter the expression of violence contribute to social tranquility. In any society, through a number of interrelated psychosocial processes involving the socialization of the young, the regular reiteration of important values and beliefs by the members of the culture, the reinforcement and punishment of certain behaviors, and the internalization by individuals of shared beliefs and societal expectations, most individual conduct comes to conform with valued group standards. Within peaceful cultures, as several case studies suggest, nonviolent beliefs are internalized during an individual's social development. For instance, striking another person becomes almost unthinkable to members of a Semai band. Overall, the behavior of individuals in peaceful societies tends to correspond with the nonviolent ideals (see Bonta and Fry forthcoming).

The ideals differ, but similar processes apply in cultures with moderate to high levels of aggression. For example, beliefs that one must vigorously defend one's honor contribute to fights and homicides in response to insults and other affronts among Montenegrins, Italian Peasants, and various other groups (cf. Boehm 1987; Brögger 1968). But even in such cases, cultural rules still limit the extent of the aggression (cf. Boehm 1987).

Gelles and Straus (1988:194) propose that one way to reduce aggression involves the elimination of "cultural norms and values that accept violence as a means of resolving conflict and problems in families." How might beliefs and values within a society be shifted from aggression accepting to aggression nonaccepting to promote peace?

The United States provides an example of a society with various beliefs and values that are aggression accepting. In contrast to most European nations, for instance, capital punishment continues to be practiced in some U.S. states and is favored by many citizens. Laws allow sniper rifles to be purchased at gun shows. An acceptance of aggression pervades the media. Television programming is saturated with beatings, stabbings, shootings, rapes, and atrocities of all kinds. Gerbner (1991:6) reports that the *Teenage Mutant Ninja Turtle* children's movies have 133 acts of mayhem in one hour. *GI Joe* and other war toys are extremely popular, as are violent video games. Domestic violence is sometimes not treated seriously by authorities. Even a U.S. senator was reported as saying, "If you outlaw wife beating, you take all the fun out of marriage" (Gelles and Straus 1988:199). A final example of the acceptance of physical aggression is the reliance of parents on spanking and on more severe forms of corporal punishment (Ellison and Bartkowski 1997; Straus 2001; Walters 1977). In short, this list of phenomena suggests that cultural attitudes and beliefs that favor or accept violence within the family and society are pervasive.

The presence of aggression-accepting beliefs and attitudes may seem so natural to cultural insiders that alternative ways of thinking and acting may not even come to mind. However, consider the way that cultural outsiders, the nonviolent people of Ifaluk, react to portrayals of violence in U.S. films.

> The horror that the idea of violence evokes for the Ifaluk was evident in their discussions of the rumored aggressive tendencies of Americans and some other groups. Several people checked with me to see if the stories they had heard about

> the existence of murder in the United States were in fact true. . . . One of the most riveting and stressful experiences for people in the postwar period has been their exposure to violence in Western movies that have been brought to the island by U.S. Navy vessels stopping on "goodwill" tours. People frequently talk about their panic on seeing people shot and beaten in those movies and relate how some individuals were terrified for days afterwards. (Lutz 1988:199)

Numerous steps could be taken to chink away at a culture's acceptance of violence. In the United States, for example, some steps might include: (1) abandoning the use of corporal punishment in schools nationwide; (2) outlawing spanking and other forms of physical punishment by parents under any circumstances, as has been done in Norway and some other countries; (3) abolishing capital punishment; (4) presenting ongoing media campaigns against wife beating, corporal punishment, elder battering, or any form of interpersonal aggression; (5) encouraging TV and movie producers to reduce explicit, severe portrayals of violence or adopting other means to achieve this end; (6) banning TV commercials for violence-related toys (paralleling the ban on cigarette commercials); (7) outlawing handguns, sniper rifles, and so on. These suggestions are not intended to constitute an all-inclusive list; they simply represent several possibilities (Fry 1993). Obviously, many of these ideas are controversial, a point that further highlights the anthropological observation that U.S. culture includes a variety of aggression-accepting beliefs and values. However, if such initiatives were seriously undertaken, studies of peaceful societies suggest that beliefs and values could be shifted over time away from an aggression-accepting constellation toward much less violent orientations.

Turning to child rearing, in peaceful societies, such as the Paliyan, Rotuma, La Paz Zapotec, Mardu, Semai, and Norway, children are rarely punished physically. The rarity of physical punishment in peaceful societies suggests a specific recommendation for reducing aggression in such contexts as the United States, for as Straus (2001) points out on the basis of empirical findings, both witnessing and receiving corporal punishment as a child increases the probability of engaging in physical aggression as an adult. La Paz parents prefer verbal alternatives to corporal punishment; they discuss, explain, and teach (Fry this volume). Children in La Paz turn out obedient and respectful. This observation argues against the validity of the aggression-accepting adage still expressed in the United States, "Spare the rod and spoil the child." Data from La Paz and other peaceful societies converge with the findings on family violence to suggest that if parents employ nonphysical child-training techniques, then children will be less likely to behave aggressively. While many factors are involved in the etiology of aggression, it is reasonable to conclude that the learning of aggression in childhood, which may carry over into adulthood (Huesmann, Eron, Lefkowitz, and Walder 1984; Straus 2001), could be reduced through less reliance on corporal punishment and greater use of discussion, explanation, and the positive reinforcement of desired behaviors.

Conclusion: Balancing the View

Humans are clearly capable of engaging in violence and war; however, as the cases in this volume illustrate, humans also have a capacity for living in peace and solving disputes without violence. Viewing humans as having a universal warlike nature is simply not in accord with the facts. It is high time to stop using a supposed bellicose human nature as a justification for using violent force—or as a solvent for the collective guilt we might feel after pursuing lethal military policies. By contrast, focusing more attention on the human capacity for conflict prevention, management, and reconciliation—as illustrated by the case studies in this book—may expand our perceptions to encompass various nonviolent alternatives to war and other forms of violence.

Study Questions

1. The use of corporal punishment, whether by parents or in schools, provokes debate in some societies. How do data from peaceful societies contribute to this debate?
2. Do most or all of the peaceful societies discussed in this book share similar core values? If so, what are they? How are these core values similar to or different from core values in your own society?
3. How do the members of peaceful societies deal with social transgressions such as acts of physical aggression? What insights might we draw for maintaining peace from a consideration of how peaceful societies respond to occasional acts of aggression?
4. A number of the chapters on peaceful societies refer to problems associated with alcohol consumption. How do some peaceful societies deal with this problem? Do you see any lessons for your own society for dealing with antisocial behavior stemming from alcohol or other types of drug abuse?
5. Avoidance is a common theme in peaceful societies. How effective is avoidance at preventing physical aggression? How effective is avoidance for resolving disputes? Is avoidance also used in your own society?
6. Based especially on the book's first and last chapters, do you think that politics and philosophical considerations affect the study of peaceful societies? Explain your thinking on this topic.

7. Based on the material in the book, what do you think should be the next steps to bring about a more peaceful world, to work toward achieving the United Nations' goal of replacing a culture of war and violence with a "Culture of Peace"?
8. In your opinion, what are the most valuable lessons to be learned from peaceful societies?

References

Foreword

Boulding, E. (2000) *Cultures of peace: the hidden side of history,* Syracuse: Syracuse University Press.

European Platform for Conflict Prevention and Transformation (1999) *Searching for peace in Africa: an overview of conflict prevention and management activities,* Utrecht: European Center for Conflict Prevention.

Malan, J. (1998) *Conflict resolution wisdom from Africa,* Durban, South Africa: African Center for the Constructive Resolution of Disputes (ACCORD), University of Durban.

Ross, R. (1996) *Returning to the teachings: exploring aboriginal justice,* New York: Penguin Books.

Chapter 1

Björkqvist, K. (1994) "Sex differences in physical, verbal, and indirect aggression: a review of recent research," *Sex Roles* 30:177–88.

Björkqvist, K., Österman, K., and Kaukiainen, A. (1992) "The development of direct and indirect aggressive strategies in males and females," in Björkqvist, K. and Niemelä, P. (eds) *Of mice and women: aspects of female aggression,* San Diego: Academic Press.

Boland, J. (1995) "American Indian influences on the America of the Founding Fathers, US political thought, Lecture 6." Online. Available: http://www.uoregon.edu/~jboland/lect-6.html (Accessed: 2003, May 12).

Bonta, B. (1996) "Conflict resolution among peaceful societies: the culture of peacefulness," *Journal of Peace Research* 33:403–20.

Bookin-Weiner, H. and Horowitz, R. (1983) "The end of youth gang, fad or fact?" *Criminology* 21:585–602.

Chagnon, N. (1968) *Yanomamö: the fierce people,* New York: Holt, Rinehart and Winston.

―――― (1992) *Yanomamö: the last days of Eden,* London: Harcourt, Brace, Jovanovich.

Dentan, R. K. (1968) *The Semai: a non-violent people of Malaya,* New York: Holt, Rinehart and Winston.

Eckhardt, W. (1972) "Cross-cultural theories of war and aggression," *International Journal of Group Tensions* 2:34–51.

Ehrlich, P. (2000) *Human natures: genes, cultures and the human prospect,* Washington, D.C.: Shearwater Books/Island Press.

Eibl-Eibesfeldt, I. (1971) *Love and hate;* trans. G. Strachan, London: Methuen.

―――― (1975) *Ethology: the biology of behavior,* 2nd ed; trans. E. Klinghammer, New York: Holt, Rinehart and Winston.

Fabbro, D. (1976) "A qualitative analysis of some peaceful societies," unpublished presentation to the Programme of Peace and Conflict Research, Lancaster University.

―――― (1978) "Peaceful societies: an introduction," in *Journal of Peace Research* 15:67–83.

Fox, G. (1975) *The journal of George Fox*, J. L. Nickalls (ed.) London: London Yearly Meeting.

Furnham, A. and Henderson, M. (1983) "Lay theories of delinquency," *European Journal of Social Psychology* 13:107–20.

Galtung, J. (1965) "A structural theory of aggression" *Journal of Peace Research* 2:95–119.

Grossman, Lt. Col. D. (1995) *On killing*, London: Bay Books.

HRH The Prince of Wales (1990) *Extracts from the rainforest lecture*, 6 February, London: Survival International.

Hobbes, T. (1651) *Leviathan*, Plamenatz, J. (ed.) 1962, London: Fontana.

Kemp, G. (1987) "The biology of nonviolence" *Medicine and War* 3:181–90.

―――― (1988) "People kill to be sociable: a culture perversion of human altruism," paper presented at the 12th General Conference of the International Peace Research Association, Rio de Janeiro.

―――― (1997) "Cultural implicit conflict: a re-examination of Sorokin's socio-cultural dynamics," *Journal of Conflict Processes* 3:15–25.

Johansen, B. E. (1982) *Forgotten founders*, Ipswich, Mass.: Gambit Incorporated.

Lagerspetz, K., Björkqvist, K., and Peltonen, T. (1988) "Is indirect aggression typical of females? Gender differences in aggressiveness in 11-to-12-year-old children," *Aggressive Behavior* 14:403–14.

Lee, R. B. (1979) *The !Kung San: men, women and work in a foraging society*, Cambridge: Cambridge University Press.

Lentz, T. (1972) *Towards a technology of peace*, St. Louis: Peace Research Laboratory.

Lorenz, K. (1965) *Evolution and modification of behaviour*, London: Methuen.

McLuhan, T. C. (1973) *Touch the Earth: a self portrait of Indian existence*, London: Abacus.

Marshall, S. L. A. (1978) *Men against fire*, Gloucester, Mass.: Peter Smith.

Martin, H. (1997) "How Indians helped to create the US Constitution." Online. Available: http://www.freeamerica.com/RelAndHist/relhist2.html (Accessed: 2003, May 12).

Oldfield, S. (1989) *Women against the iron fist: alternatives to militarism 1900–1989*, Oxford: Blackwell.

Purves, D., Lotto, R. B., and Nundy, S. (2002) "Why we see what we do," *American Scientist* 90:236–43.

Rifaat, A. M. (1979) *International aggression*, Stockholm: Almquist and Wiksell International.

Rousseau, J. J. (1755) *Discourse on the origin of inequality*, trans. F. Phillip; P. Coleman (ed.) 1999, Oxford: Oxford Paperbacks.

Schuster, R. (1978) The ethological theories of aggression and violence, in Kutash, I. L., Kutash, S. B., and Schlesinger, L. B. (eds) *Violence: perspectives on murder and aggression*, San Francisco: Jossey-Bass.

Sorokin, P. (1962) *Socio-cultural dynamics, vols. 1–4*, New York: Bedminster Press.

Survival International (1990) *Yanomami: survival campaign*, London: Warners Printers.

Tinbergen, N. (1973a) Ethology 1969, in Tinbergen, N. (ed.) *The animal in its world (explorations of an ethologist 1932–1975) vol. 2*, London: George Allen and Unwin.

―――― (1973b) The animal roots of human behaviour, in Tinbergen, N. (ed.) *The animal in its world (explorations of an ethologist 1932–1975) vol. 2*, London: George Allen and Unwin.

Williams R. (1981) Legitimate and illegitimate uses of violence: a review of ideas and evidence, in Gaylin, W. and Mackin, R. (eds) *Violence and the politics of research*, London: Plenum Press.

Chapter 2

Botero, D. (1998) "El cículo dantesco de la violencia" ["The dantesque circle of violence"], *Revista de la Facultad de Derecho, Ciencias Políticas y Sociales de la Universidad Nacional de Colombia*, Politeria, Bogotá, D.C.: Unibiblos.

Comisión Interamericana de Derechos Humanos [Inter-American Human Rights Commission] (1999) *Tercer Reporte de la situación de Derechos Humanos en Colombia* [*Third Report on the Human Rights Situation in Colombia*], OEA/Ser. L/V/II 102, Doc 9 revised February 26, 1999, Bogotá, D.C.: Comisión Colombiana de Juristas.

Conroy, H. (1971) Man's natural desire for peace, in Hoover Institution (ed.) *Peaceful Change in Modern Society*, Stanford: Stanford University Press.

Galtung, J. (1975) *Essays in Peace Research, Volume 1*. Copenhagen: Christian Ejlers.
—— (1985) "Twenty-five years of peace research: ten challenges and some responses," *Journal of Peace Research* 22:141–158.
—— (1998) *Peace by peaceful means: peace, conflict, development and civilization*, Oslo: International Peace Research Association.
Lentz, T. (1955) *Towards a science of peace: turning point in human destiny*, 2nd ed, 1965, New York: Bookman Associates.
Richardson, L. (1960) *Statistics of Deadly Quarrels*, London: Stevens and Sons.
Wiberg, H. (1981) "1964–1980: what have we learnt about peace? *Journal of Peace Research* 18:111–148.
Wright, Q. (1942) *A Study of War*, 2nd ed, 1965, Chicago: University of Chicago Press.

Chapter 3

Benedict, R. (1934) *Patterns of culture*, Boston: Houghton Mifflin.
Brandt, R. (1954) *Hopi ethics: a theoretical analysis*, Chicago: University of Chicago Press.
Clemmer, R. (1995) *Roads in the sky: the Hopi Indians in a century of change*, Boulder: Westview Press.
Cox, B. A. (1970) "What is Hopi gossip about? Information management and Hopi factions," *Man* 5: 88–98.
Geertz, A. W. (1994) *The invention of prophecy: continuity and meaning in Hopi Indian religion*. Berkeley: University of California Press.
Levy, J. E. (1992) *Orayvi revisited: social stratification in an "egalitarian" society*, Santa Fe: School of American Research Press.
Malotki, E. and Gary, K. (1999) "Hopisosont—'human cravers': echoes of anthropophagy in Hopi oral traditions," *European Review of Native American Studies* 13:9–15.
Parsons, E. C. (ed.) (1936) *Hopi journal of Alexander M. Stephen, vols. 1 and 2*, New York: Columbia University Contributions to Anthropology.
Schlegel, A. (1979) "Sexual antagonism among the sexually egalitarian Hopi," *Ethos* 7:124–41.
—— (1988) Hopi widowhood, in Scadron, A. (ed.) *On their own: widows and widowhood in the American Southwest, 1848–1939*, Urbana: University of Illinois Press.
—— (1991) "African political models in the American Southwest: Hopi as an internal frontier society," *American Anthropologist* 94:376–97.
Simmons, L. W. (ed.) (1942) *Sun Chief: the autobiography of a Hopi Indian*, New Haven: Yale University Press.
Titiev, M. (1944) Old Oraibi, *Papers of the Peabody Museum of American Archaeology and Ethnology*, Harvard University, vol. 22, no. 1.
Waters, F. (1963) *Book of the Hopi*, 2nd ed, 1969, New York: Ballentine Books.
Whitely, P. M. (1988) *Deliberate acts: changing Hopi culture through the Oraibi split*, Tucson: University of Arizona Press.

Chapter 4

This chapter is a revised and shortened version of a paper entitled "Dispute management in Rotuma," which appeared in 1990 in the *Journal of Anthropological Research* 46:263–92.

Churchward, C. M. (1940) *Rotuman grammar and dictionary*, Sydney: Australasian Medical Publishing Company Limited for the Methodist Church of Australasia, Department of Overseas Missions.
Eason, W. J. E. (1951) *A short history of Rotuma*, Suva, Fiji: Government Printing Department.
Gardiner, J. S. (1898) "Natives of Rotuma," *Journal of the Royal Anthropological Institute* 27:396–435, 457–524.
Honolulu Star-Bulletin (1988) "'King' of Fiji isle vows to secede," May 11.
Howard, A. (1963) "Land, activity systems and decision-making models in Rotuma," *Ethnology* 2:407–40.
—— (1964) "Land tenure and social change in Rotuma," *Journal of the Polynesian Society* 73:26–52.

———— and Kjellgren, E. (1994) "Martyrs, progress and political ambition: reexamining Rotuma's 'religious wars'," *Journal of Pacific History* 29:131–52.

Inia, E. K. (2001) *Kato'aga: Rotuman ceremonies*, Suva, Fiji: Institute of Pacific Studies, University of the South Pacific.

Lesson, R. (1838–39) *Voyage Autour du Monde... sur... 'La Coquille,'* Paris: Pourrat Fréres.

Titifanua, M. and Churchward, C. M. (1995) *Tales of a lonely island*, Suva, Fiji: Institute of Pacific Studies, University of the South Pacific.

Watson-Gegeo, K. and White, G. M. (1990) *Disentangling: conflict discourse in Pacific societies*, Stanford: Stanford University Press.

Chapter 5

Bender, B. (1978) "Gatherer-hunter to farmer: a social perspective," *World Archaeology* 10:204–22.

Firth, R. (1951) *Elements of social organization*, Boston: Beacon.

Gardner, P. M. (1991) "Pragmatic meanings of possession in Paliyan shamanism," *Anthropos* 86: 367–84.

———— (2000a) "Respect and nonviolence among recently sedentary foragers," *Journal of the Royal Anthropological Institute* 6:215–36.

———— (2000b) *Bicultural versatility as a frontier adaptation among Paliyan foragers of South India*, Lewiston, N.Y.: Edwin Mellen Press.

Ghiglieri, M. P. (1999) *The dark side of man*. Cambridge, Mass.: Perseus Publishing.

Kent, S. (1989) "And justice for all: the development of political centralization among newly sedentary foragers," *American Anthropologist* 91:703–12.

Rafferty, J. E. (1985) The archaeological record on sedentariness: recognition, development, and implications, in Schiffer, M. B. (ed.). *Advances in archaeological method and theory, vol. 8*, Orlando: Academic Press.

Turnbull, C. M. (1972) *The mountain people*, New York: Simon and Schuster.

Wilson, E. O. (1978) *On human nature*. Cambridge: Harvard University Press.

Wrangham, R. and Peterson, D. (1996) *Demonic males: apes and the origins of human violence*, Boston: Houghton Mifflin.

Chapter 6

This research was funded by the National Science Foundation (81-17478), the Wenner-Gren Foundation for Anthropological Research (4117), and the Department of Anthropology at Indiana University (Skomp fellowship), and I appreciate this financial support. I am also very grateful to the citizens of La Paz and to field assistants Crescenciano, Gregorio, Bartolo G., and Bartolo J., without whose kindness and cooperation the field research would not have been possible. Kathy M. Fry, Paul L. Jamison, Carl W. O'Nell, and John Paddock facilitated the research in various ways, and I thank each of them for their cooperation and generosity. I also thank Sirpa Fry for encouraging me to prepare this chapter in the first place and for feedback on its readability. Bruce Bonta, Alan Howard, and Graham Kemp were also kind enough to read the chapter and offer suggestions. Of course, any remaining deficiencies are my sole responsibility.

Black, D. (1993) *The social structure of right and wrong*, San Diego, Cal.: Academic Press.

Flannery, K., Kirkby, A., Kirkby, M., and Williams, A. (1967) "Farming systems and political growth in ancient Oaxaca," *Science* 158: 445–54.

Fry, D. P. (1988) "Intercommunity differences in aggression among Zapotec children," *Child Development* 59: 1008–19.

———— (1990) "Play aggression among Zapotec children: Implications for the practice hypothesis," *Aggressive Behavior* 16:321–40.

———— (1992a) "'Respect for the rights of others is peace': learning aggression versus non-aggression among the Zapotec," *American Anthropologist* 94:621–39.

———— (1992b) Female aggression among the Zapotec of Oaxaca, Mexico, in Björkqvist, K. and Niemalä, P. (eds) *Of mice and women: aspects of female aggression*, Orlando, Fla.: Academic Press.

———— (1993) "Intergenerational transmission of disciplinary practices and approaches to conflict," *Human Organization* 52:176–85.

——— (1994) Maintaining social tranquility: internal and external loci of aggression control, in Sponsel, L. E. and Gregor, T. (eds) *The anthropology of peace and nonviolence,* Boulder, Colo.: Lynne Reinner.

——— (Forthcoming) *The human potential for peace: challenging the war assumption.*

Guerra, N. G., Eron, L. D., Huesmann, L. R., Tolan, P. H., and van Acker, R. (1997) A cognitive/ ecological approach to the prevention and mitigation of violence and aggression in inner-city youth, in Fry, D. P. and Björkqvist, K. (eds) *Cultural variation in conflict resolution: alternatives to violence,* Mahwah, N.J., Lawrence Erlbaum.

Nader, L. (1964) "An analysis of Zapotec law cases," *Ethnology* 3: 404–19.

——— (1969) Styles of court procedure: to make the balance, in Nader, L. (ed.) *Law and culture in society,* Chicago: Aldine.

——— (1990) *Harmony ideology: justice and control in a Zapotec mountain village,* Stanford: Stanford University Press.

O'Nell, C. W. (1969) "Human development in a Zapotec community with an emphasis on aggression control and its study in dreams," unpublished doctoral dissertation, University of Chicago.

——— (1972) "Aging in a Zapotec community," *Human Development* 15:294–309.

——— (1978) "Antiviolent behavior and some hypothetical personality correlates: a paradox within an enigma," paper presented at the meetings of the International Society for Research on Aggression, Washington D.C., September.

——— (1979) "Nonviolence and personality dispositions among the Zapotec," *Journal of Psychological Anthropology* 2:301–22.

——— (1981) "Hostility management and the control of aggression in a Zapotec community," *Aggressive Behavior* 7:351–66.

——— (1989) The non-violent Zapotec, in Howell, S. and Willis, R. (eds) *Societies at peace: anthropological perspectives,* London: Routledge.

Paddock, J. (1978) "The face of human nature," paper presented at the meetings of the International Society for Research on Aggression, Washington D.C., September.

——— (1982) "Anti-violence in Oaxaca, Mexico: archive research," paper presented at the meetings of the American Society for Ethnohistory, Nashville, Tenn., October.

——— (1986) Personal communication.

Ross, M. H. (1993) *The culture of conflict,* New Haven: Yale University Press.

Selby, H. (1974) *Zapotec deviance,* Austin: University of Texas Press.

Chapter 7

Berndt, R. M. and Berndt, C. H. (1988) *The world of the first Australians,* revised ed, Canberra: Aboriginal Studies Press.

Chase, A. (1984) "Belonging to country: territory, identity and environment in Cape York Peninsula, Northern Australia," *Oceania Monograph* 27:104–22.

Edgerton, R. B. (1992) *Sick societies: challenging the myth of primitive harmony,* New York: Free Press.

——— (1999) Maladaptation: a challenge to relativism, in Cerroni-Long, E. L., (ed.) *Anthropological theory in North America,* Westport, Conn.: Bergin and Garvey.

Malinowski, B. (1913) *The family among the Australian Aborigines,* New York: Schocken.

Sahlins, M. (1972) *Stone age economics,* Chicago: Aldine Atherton.

Sutton, P. (2001) "The politics of suffering: indigenous policy in Australia since the 1970s," *Anthropological Forum* 11:125–73.

Tonkinson, R. (1974) *The Jigalong mob: victors of the desert crusade,* Menlo Park: Cummings.

——— (1978) *The Mardu Aborigines: living the dream in Australia's desert,* 2nd ed, 1991, Fort Worth: Holt, Rinehart and Winston.

——— (1987) Mardujarra kinship, in Mulvaney, D. and White, J. (eds) *Australians to 1788, vol. 1, Australians: a historical library,* Sydney: Fairfax, Syme and Weldon.

——— (1988a) One community, two laws: aspects of conflict and convergence in a Western Australian Aboriginal settlement, in Morse, B. and Woodman, G. (eds), *Indigenous law and the state,* Dordrecht: Foris.

——— (1988b) "Egalitarianism and inequality in a Western Desert culture," *Anthropological Forum* 5:545–58.

———— (1988c) "Ideology and domination" in Aboriginal Australia: a Western Desert test case, in Ingold, T., Riches, D., and Woodburn, J. (eds) *Hunters and gatherers, vol. 1: property, power and ideology*, Oxford: Berg.

Warner, W. L. (1937) *Black civilization: a study of an Australian tribe*, New York: Harper and Row.

Woodburn, J. (1982) "Egalitarian societies," *Man* 17:431–51.

Chapter 8

This chapter is based on research carried out as part of the Ethnographic Survey of Egyptian Nubia, which I directed and participated in during 1963 and 1964 while I was a professor at the American University in Cairo. It is based on work published in Fernea and Fernea with Rouchdy (1991). I am indebted to Bahiga Hailkal El Ghamry, who first brought the nog to my attention. Along with Abdel Hamid El Zein and myself, she was a member of the Ethnography Survey staff.

El Zein, A. H. (1966) Socio-economic implications of the waterwheel in Adendan, Nubia, in Fernea, R. (ed.) *Contemporary Egyptian Nubia, vol. II*, New Haven, Conn.: Human Relations Area Files Press.

Fernea, E. W. and Fernea, R. A. with Rouchdy, A. (1991) *Nubian ethnographies*, Prospect Heights, Ill: Waveland Press.

Chapter 9

The fieldwork on which this paper is based was carried out in the Semporna district of Sabah, Malaysia, initially in 1964–65, with the support of a predoctoral fellowship and grant from the U.S. National Institute of Mental Health (MH 10159-01), and for shorter periods in May 1974, July and August 1979, and July 1995. During my initial fieldwork in 1964–65, I lived as a member of Panglima Tiring's house group. I wish to acknowledge, with deep appreciation, the hospitality of Panglima Haji Tiring bin Hawani, then the headman of Bangau-Bangau, and his wife, Amjatul, who welcomed me into their home. In addition to enjoying the generosity and good humor of my hosts and the patient instruction of the headman, living as part of this house group at the physical and social center of the village proved an ideal situation; most matters of contention in the community were brought, or eventually found their way, to the headman's house for discussion, debate, and sometimes litigation. In addition to the headman and other villagers, I wish to thank Mohamad Said Hinayat, an inexhaustible source of insight into all matters relating to the Sama, for stimulating my thinking about Sama Dilaut ways of keeping the peace and for providing me with some fine examples of formulaic speech. Finally, I thank my wife, Louise. The present chapter has profited greatly from her comments, and without her encouragement, it might never have been written.

Kiefer, T. (1969) *Tausug armed conflict: the social organization of military activity in a Philippine Moslem society*, Philippine Studies Program Research Series, no. 7, Chicago: University of Chicago.

———— (1972a) *The Tausug: violence and law in a Philippine Moslem society*, New York: Holt, Rinehart and Winston.

———— (1972b) "The Tausug polity and Sultanate of Sulu: a segmentary state in the southern Philippines," *Sulu Studies* 1:19–64.

Nimmo, H. A. (2001) *Magosaha: an ethnography of the Tawi-Tawi Sama Dilaut*, Quezon City: Ateneo de Manila University Press.

Sather, C. (1993) Bajau, in Levinson, D. (ed.) *Encyclopedia of world cultures, vol. 5, East and Southeast Asia*, Boston: G. K. Hall and Company.

———— (1997) *The Bajau Laut: adaptation, history, and fate in a maritime fishing society of South-Eastern Sabah*, Kuala Lumpur: Oxford University Press.

———— (2000) "Bajau Laut boat-building in Semporna," *Techniques and Culture* 35–36:177–98.

———— (2002) "Commodity trade, gift exchange, and the history of maritime nomadism in southeastern Sabah," *Nomadic Peoples* 6: 23–47.

———— (in press) Sulu and the Sulu Archipelago, in Ooi, K. G. (ed.) *Encyclopedia of Southeast Asian history*, Santa Barbara: ABC-Clio.

———— (forthcoming) "Sama Dilaut locality and ways of being at sea," in Sather, C. and Kaartinen, T. (eds) *Maritime Worlds*, Southeast Asian Studies Monographs, New Haven: Yale University Press.

Scott, J. C. (1998) *Seeing like a state: how certain schemes to improve the human condition have failed*, New Haven: Yale University Press.

Shärer, H. (1963) *Ngaju religion: the conception of God among a south Borneo people*, trans R. Needham, The Hague: Martinus Nijhoff.

Chapter 10

Archer, C. (1996) "The Nordic area as a 'zone of peace'," *Journal of Peace Research* 33:451–67.

Archetti, E. (1984) Om maktens ideologi—en krysskulturell analyse, in Klausen, A. M. (ed.) *Den Norske Væremåten: antropologisk søkelys på norsk kultur*, Oslo: J. W. Cappelens forlag.

Barclay, G. C. and Tavares, C. (2000) *International comparisons of criminal justice statistics 1998*, Research development and statistics directorate (RDS) bulletin, issue 04/00, February, U.K. The Home Office.

Bondevik, K. M. (2002) "Prime Minister Bondevik's New Year speech 2000." Available (in Norwegian): *http://odin.dep.no/odinarkiv/norsk/dep/smk/2000/taler/099005-994220/index-dok000-b-n-a.html* (Accessed: October 2002).

Boulding, E. (1996) Peace behaviors in various societies, in UNESCO peace and conflict issues series, *From a culture of violence to a culture of peace*, Paris: UNESCO.

Burgess, P. M. (1968) *Elite images and foreign policy outcomes: a study of Norway*, Columbus: Ohio State University Press.

Campbell, D. (1993) *Politics without principle: sovereignty, ethics, and the narratives of the Gulf War*, Boulder: Lynne Rienner.

Center for Conflict Management-Norway (2002). Available: *www.ccm.no* (Accessed: October 2002).

Curle, A. (1971) *Making peace*, London: Tavistock.

Dahl, H. F. (1986) Those equal folk, in Graubard, S. R. (ed.) *Norden: the passion for equality*, Oslo: Norwegian University Press.

Dobinson, K. (2000) *Waging peace: international mediation and Norwegian society*, PhD dissertation, University of Kent at Canterbury, U.K.

Eckstein, H. (1966) *Division and cohesion in democracy: a study of Norway*, Princeton: Princeton University Press.

Egeland, J. (1988) *Impotent superpower—potent small state: potentials and limitations of human rights objectives in the foreign policies of the United States and Norway*, Oslo: Norwegian University Press.

Elder, N., Thomas, A., and Arter, K. (1982) *The consensual democracies? the government and politics of the Scandinavian states*, 2nd ed, 1988, London, Basil Blackwell.

Eriksen, N. M. (1998) "Drapstrusler—en del av jobben," *Aftenposten*, June 30.

Eriksen, T. H. (1993a) *Typisk Norsk: essays om kulturen i Norge*, Oslo: Huitfeldt forlag.

—— (1993b) Being Norwegian in a shrinking world, in Kiel, A. C. (ed.) *Continuity and change: aspects of contemporary Norway*, Oslo: Scandinavian University Press.

Galtung, J. (1969) "Violence, peace and peace research," *Journal of Peace Research* 6:167–91.

—— (1974) Norway in the world community in Rogoff Ramsøy, N. (ed.) *Norwegian society*, trans. S. Høivik in cooperation with N. Rogoff Ramsøy, Oslo: Universitetsforlaget.

—— and Ikeda, D. (1995) *Choose peace: a dialogue between Johan Galtung and Daisaku Ikeda*, London: Pluto Press.

Giddens, A. (1984) *The constitution of society: outline of the theory of structuration*, 2nd ed, 1997, Cambridge: Polity Press.

Gullestad, M. (1992) *The art of social relations: essays on culture, social action and everyday life in modern Norway*, Oslo: Universitetsforlaget.

—— (1996) *Everyday life philosophers: modernity, morality, and autobiography in Norway*, Oslo: Scandinavian University Press.

Habermas, J. (1987) *The theory of communicative action: a critique of functionalist reason*, vol. 2, Cambridge: Polity Press.

Hafstad, A. and Leander, S. (1999) "Ny rapport viser gamle holdninger: Sjokkerende hverdag for homofile," *Aftenposten*, February 26.

Holbek, J. A. (1995) "Er fem eller 93 prosent av nordmenn kristne?" *Vårt Land*, December 1.

Hollos, M. (1974) *Growing up in Flathill*, Oslo: Universitetsforlaget.

International Labor Office (1984) *The trade union situation and industrial relations in Norway: report of an ILO mission*, Geneva: International Labor Office.

Jakobsen, S. E. (2001) "Gir mot til de motløse," *Forskning 5.*

Johnsen, N. (2001) "Oslos elever biter, sparker og truer stadig flere lærere," *Aftenposten aftenutgave,* December 18:14.

Knudsen, O. (1990) "Norway: domestically driven foreign policy," *The Annals of the American Academy of Political and Social Sciences* 512:101–15.

Knutsen, T. L. (1995) Norsk utenrikspolitikk som forskningsfelt, in Knutsen, T. L., Sørbø, G. M., and Gjerdåker, S. (eds) *Norges Utenrikspolitikk,* Chr. Michelsen Institute, Bergen and Oslo: Cappelen Akademisk Forlag.

Monsen, N. K. (1998) "Kampen alle kan vinne. Likhetssamfunnet: hvis det særegne og personlige defineres bort, blir det øde rundt oss," *Aftenposten, I dag,* July 13.

Nergård, T. B. (1993) "Solving conflicts outside the court system—experiences with the conflict resolution boards in Norway," *British Journal of Criminology* 33:81–94.

Norsk Senter for Barneforskning (1998) Report number 50/98 (School mediation), Oslo: Norwegian Center for Research on Children.

Norvik, (1997) "Nordisk rasehygiene i Auschwitz' skygge," *Aftenposten,* August 30.

Norwegian Peace Center (2002). Available: *www.fredssenter.no* (Accessed: October 2002).

Norwegian Red Cross (2002) *Stopp Volden* (Stop Violence). Available: *www.redcross.no/stopp-volden/ dette_er_/index.html* (Accessed October 2002).

Nygaard, O. (2002) "Voldsbruk blir importert," *Aftenposten,* April 20:3.

Østerud, Ø. (1986) "Nasjonalstaten Norge—en karakteriserende skisse," in Alldén, L., Rogoff Ramsøy, N., and Vaa, M. (eds) *Det Norske Samfunn,* 3rd ed, Oslo: Gyldendal Norsk Forlag.

Pharo, H. (1993) "Norway and the world since 1945," in Kiel, A. C. (ed.) *Continuity and change: aspects of contemporary Norway,* Oslo: Scandinavian University Press.

Ross, M. H. (1993a) *The management of conflict: interpretations and interests in comparative perspective,* New Haven: Yale University Press.

——— (1993b) *The culture of conflict: interpretations and interests in comparative perspective,* New Haven: Yale University Press.

Sætran, F. (2002) "Familier rømmer fra rå voldsgjeng," *Aftenposten aftenutgave,* April 19:6.

Schutz, A. (1966) *Collected papers III, studies in phenomenological philosophy,* I. Schutz, (ed.) The Hague: Martinus Nijhoff.

Shaughnessy, E. J. (1992) *Conflict management in Norway: practical dispute resolution,* Lanham: University Press of America.

Statistics Norway (2002). Available: *www.ssb.no* (Accessed: October 2002).

Tjersland, O. A. (1995) "Extended mediation in Norway," *Mediation Quarterly* 12:339–51.

Tvedt, T. (1995) "Norsk utenrikspolitikk og de frivillige organisasjonene," in T. L. Knutsen, G. M. Sørbø, and S. Gjerdåker (eds.) Norges Utenrikspolitikk, Chr. Michelsens Institutt/Cappelen Akademisk Forlag A.S.

Ugelvik Larsen, S. and Ugelvik, I. L. (1997) Scandinavia, in Eatwell, R. (ed.) *European political cultures: conflict or convergence?* London: Routledge.

Vormeland, O. (1993) Education in Norway, in Kiel, A. C. (ed.) *Continuity and change: aspects of contemporary Norway,* Oslo: Scandinavian University Press.

Weldes, J. (1996) "Constructing national interests," *European Journal of International Relations* 2:275–318.

——— (1999) *Constructing national interests: the US and the Cuban missile crisis,* Minneapolis: University of Minnesota Press.

Wiberg, H. (1990) "De nordiske lande: et særligt system?" in Gleditsch, N. P., Møller, B., Wiberg, H., and Wæver, O. (eds) *Svaner på Vildveje?* Copenhagen: Vindrose.

Woon, L. L. (1993) Recent immigration to Norway, in Kiel, A. C. (ed.) *Continuity and change: aspects of contemporary Norway,* Oslo: Scandinavian University Press.

Yearbook of Nordic statistics (1994) Copenhagen: Nordic Council of Ministers.

Chapter 11

Adas, M. (1992) From avoidance to confrontation: peasant protest in pre-colonial and colonial Southeast Asia, in Dirks, N. B. (ed.) *Colonialism and culture,* Ann Arbor: University of Michigan Press.

Anderson, B. (1990) *Language and power: exploring political cultures in Indonesia,* Ithaca: Cornell University Press.

Aronowitz, S. (2001) "Test time vs. dreamtime: towards a totally administered adolescence," *First of the Month: a Newspaper of the Radical Imagination* 6 (1 July):12.

Bateson, G. (1958) *Naven,* Stanford: Stanford University Press.

Bingham, P. A. (2000) "Human evolution and human history: a complete theory," *Evolutionary Anthropology* 9:248–57.

Bird, I. L. (1883) *The Golden Chersonese and the way thither,* London: John Murray.

Boehm, C. (2000) "Conflict and the evolution of social control," *Journal of Consciousness Studies* 7:79–101, 149–83.

Brison, K. J. (1989) "All talk and no action? Saying and doing in Kwanga meetings," *Ethnology* 28:97–116.

Cady, J. F.(1964) *Southeast Asia: its historical development,* New York: McGraw-Hill.

Card, C. (1996) "Rape as a weapon of war," *Hypatia* 11:5–18.

Clastres, P. (2000) *Chronicle of the Guayaki Indians,* New York: Zone Books.

Coedes, G. (1968) *The Indianized states of Southeast Asia,* Kuala Lumpur: University of Malaya Press.

Cohen, L. (1997) *The future,* New York: Sony Music Entertainment.

Colinvaux, P. (1978) *Why big fierce animals are rare: an ecologist's perspective,* Princeton: Princeton University Press.

Colvard, K. (1997) "Crime is down? don't confuse us with the facts," *The HFG Review* 2:19–26.

Dentan, R. (1976) "Identity and ethnic contact: Perak, Malaysia, 1963," *Journal of Asian Affairs* 1:79–86.

——— (1978) Notes on childhood in a nonviolent context: the Semai case, in Montagu, A. (ed.) *Learning non-aggression,* New York: Oxford University Press.

——— (1979) *The Semai: a nonviolent people of Malaya,* New York: Holt, Rinehart and Winston.

——— (1992) The rise, maintenance and destruction of peaceable polity in Silverberg, J. and Gray, J. P. (eds), *Aggression and peacefulness in humans and other primates,* New York: Oxford University Press.

——— (1994) Surrendered men: peaceable enclaves in the post-enlightenment West, in Sponsel, L. E. and Gregor, T. (eds) *The anthropology of peace and nonviolence,* Boulder: Lynne Rienner.

——— (1995) "Bad day at Bukit Pekan," *American Anthropologist* 97:225–50.

——— (1997) The persistence of received truth: how the Malaysian ruling class constructs Orang Asli, in Winzeler, R. (ed.) *Indigenous peoples and the state: politics, land, and ethnicity in the Malaysian peninsula and Borneo, monograph 46, Southeast Asia Studies,* New Haven: Yale University Press.

——— (1999) "Spotted doves at war: the Praak Sangkiil," *Asian Folklore Studies* 58:397–434.

——— (2000a) The Semai of Malaysia, in Sponsel, L. (ed.) *Endangered peoples of East and Southeast Asia,* Westport, Conn.: Greenwood Publishing Group.

——— (2000b) "Ceremonies of innocence and the lineaments of ungratified desire," *Bijdragen tot de Taal-, Land- en Volkenkunde* 156:193–232.

——— (2000c) "This is passion and where it goes: despair and suicide among Semai, a non-violent people of West Malaysia," *Moussons* 2:31–56.

——— (2001a) "Ambivalence in child training by the Semai of Peninsular Malaysia and other peoples," *Crossroads: An Interdisciplinary Journal of Southeast Asian Studies* 15:89–129.

——— (2001b). "Big pun: corporal punishment in American schools," *First of the Month: a Newspaper of the Radical Imagination* 6 (1 July):12.

——— (2001c) "A vision of modernization: an article on a drawing by Bah Rmpent, a child of the Sengoi Semai, a traditionally nonviolent people of the Malaysian Peninsula," *Anthropology and Humanism* 26:3–15.

——— (2001d) Peace and nonviolence: anthropological aspects, in Hannerz, U. (ed.) *Encyclopedia of the social and behavioral sciences, vol. 3, anthropology,* London: Elsevier Science.

——— (2002a) "Hawks, doves and birds in the bush: a response to Keith Otterbein, Neil Whitehead, and Leslie Sponsel," *American Anthropologist* 104:278–80

——— (2002b) " 'Disreputable magicians,' the dark destroyer, and the trickster lord: reflections on Semai religion and a possible common religious base in South and Southeast Asia," *Asian Anthropology* 1:153–94.

Dentan, R. and Otterbein, K. F. (1996) "Sterile quarrels," *These Times* 11:5.

Dentan, R. and Williams-Hunt, B. T. A. (1999) "Untransfiguring death: a case study of rape, drunkenness, development and homicide in an apprehensive void," *RIMA: Review of Indonesian and Malaysian Affairs* 33:17–65.

Devine, J. (1997) "Violence: the latest curricular specialty," *The HFG Review* 2:27–31.

Endicott, K. M. (1983) The effects of slave raiding on the aborigines of the Malay Peninsula, in Reid, A. (ed.) *Slavery, bondage and dependency in Southeast Asia*, Brisbane: University of Queensland Press.

———(1997) "Review of Leary's *Violence and the dream people*," *Journal of Asian Studies* 56:262–63.

Endicott, K. L. and Endicott, K. M. (n.d.) *The Batek: sexually egalitarian foragers of Peninsular Malaysia*, Book length MS in the possession of the author.

Fisher-Nguyen, K. (1994) Khmer proverbs: images and rules, in Ebihara, M., Mortland, C. A., and Ledgerwood, J. (eds) *Cambodian culture since 1975: homeland and exile*, Ithaca: Cornell University Press.

Freud, A. (1966) *The ego and the mechanisms of defense*, New York: International Universities Press.

Fry, D. P. (in preparation) *The human potential for peace: challenging the war assumption*.

Gomes, A. (1988) The Semai: the making of an ethnic group in Malaysia, in Rambo, A. T. Gillogly, K., and Hutterer, K. L. (eds) *Ethnic diversity and the control of natural resources in Southeast Asia*, Ann Arbor: University of Michigan Center for South and Southeast Asian Studies.

——— (1990) Confrontation and continuity: simple commodity production among the Orang Asli, in Lim, T. G. and Gomes, A. (eds) *Tribal peoples and development in Southeast Asia*, Kuala Lumpur: Jabatan Antropologi dan Sosiologi, Universiti Malaya.

——— (1999) "Modernity and indigenous minorities in Malaysia and Indonesia," *RIMA: Review of Indonesian and Malaysian Affairs* 33:1–13.

Heelas, P. (1989) Identifying peaceful societies, in Howell, S. and Willis, R. (eds) *Societies at peace*, London: Routledge.

Hoskins, J. (1996) Introduction, in Hoskins, J. (ed.) *Headhunting and the social imagination in Southeast Asia*, Stanford: Stanford University Press.

Hrdy, S. B. (2001) "Mothers and others," *Natural History* 110:50–62.

Kappeler, S. (1995) *The will to violence*, New York: Teachers College Press.

Katz, J. (1988) *Seductions of crime*, New York: Basic Books.

Kemper, T. D. (1990) *Social structure and testosterone*, New Brunswick: Rutgers University Press.

Kroes, G. (2002) *Same hair, different hearts: Semai identity in a Malay context: a systematic analysis of ideas and practices about health and illness*, Leiden.: CNWS [Research School of Asian, African, and Amerindian Studies], Universiteit Leiden.

Leary, J. D. (1995) *Violence and the dream people: the Orang Asli in the Malayan emergency, 1948–1960, Center for International Studies monographs in international studies, Southeast Asia series, no. 95*, Athens: Ohio University.

Le Guin, U. K. (1998) *Lao Tzu: Tao Te Ching: A new English version*, New York: Shambhala.

Leyton, E. (1997) *Men of blood: murder in modern England*, Harmondsworth: Penguin Books.

Maggioncalda, A. N. and Sapolsky, R. M. (2002) "Disturbing behavior of the orangutan," *Scientific American* June:60–65.

Maxwell, A. R. (1996) Headtaking and the consolidation of political power in the early Brunei State, in Hoskins, J. (ed.) *Headhunting and the social imagination in Southeast Asia*, Stanford: Stanford University Press.

McDade, T. W. (2001) "Lifestyle incongruity, social integration, and immune function among Samoan adolescents, *Social Science and Medicine* 53:1351–62.

McGarrell, E. F., Giacomazzi, A. L., and Thurman, Q. C. (1997) "Neighborhood disorder, integration, and the fear of crime," *Justice Quarterly* 14:479–500.

McWilliam, A. (1996) Severed heads that germinate the state, in Hoskins, J. (ed.) *Headhunting and the social imagination in Southeast Asia*, Stanford: Stanford University Press.

Nicholas, C. (1990) In the name of the Semai? The state and Semai society in Peninsular Malaysia, in Lim, T. G. and Gomes, A. (eds) *Tribal peoples and development in Southeast Asia*, Kuala Lumpur: Jabatan Antropologi dan Sosiologi, Universiti Malaya.

——— (1994) *Pathway to dependence: commodity relations and the dissolution of Semai society, Monash papers on Southeast Asia, no. 33*, Clayton, Victoria: Centre of Southeast Asian Studies, Monash University.

——— (2000) *The Orang Asli and the contest for resources: indigenous politics, development and identity in peninsular Malaysia*, IWGIA document no. 95, Copenhagen: International Work Group for Indigenous Affairs.

——— (2001) "SUHAKAM and the indigenous peoples' question," *Aliran Monthly* 21:14–17.

Nordstrom, C. (1997) *A different kind of war story*, Philadelphia: University of Pennsylvania Press.

Obeyesekere, G. (1985) Depression, Buddhism, and the work of culture in Sri Lanka, in Kleinman, A. and Good, B. (eds)*Culture and depression*, Berkeley: University of California Press.

Peterson, C., Maier, S. F., and Seligman, M. P. (1993) *Learned helplessness: a theory for the age of personal control*, New York: Oxford University Press.

Peterson, N. (1993) "Demand sharing: reciprocity and the pressure for generosity among foragers," *American Anthropologist* 95:860–74.

Pollack, W. (1999) *Real boys: rescuing our sons from the myths of boyhood*, New York: Henry Holt.

Prosser, M. (2000) "'It's only someone who's been through it that understands': social constructions and personal realities of domestic violence," M.A. thesis, State University of New York, Buffalo.

Robarchek, C. A. (1977) "Frustration, aggression and the nonviolent Semai," *American Ethnologist* 4:762–79.

—— (1979) "Conflict, emotion and abreaction: resolution of conflict among the Semai Senoi," *Ethos* 7:104–23.

—— (1980) "The image of nonviolence: world view of the Semai Senoi," *Federation Museums Journal* 25:103–17.

—— (1986) "Helplessness, fearfulness and peacefulness: the emotional and motivational context of Semai social relations," *Anthropological Quarterly* 58:117–83.

—— (1988) "Ghosts and witches: the psychocultural dynamics of Semai peacefulness," paper presented at the 87th Annual Meeting of the American Anthropological Association, Phoenix, Ariz., November.

—— (1990) Motivations and material causes: on the explanation of conflict and war, in Haas, J. (ed.) *The anthropology of war*, Cambridge: Cambridge University Press.

—— (1997) A community of interests: Semai conflict resolution, in Fry, D. P. and Björkqvist, K. (eds) *Cultural variation in conflict resolution: alternatives to violence*, Mahwah, N.J.: Lawrence Erlbaum Associates.

Robarchek, C. A. and Dentan, R. K. (1987) "'Blood drunkenness' and the bloodthirsty Semai: unmaking another anthropological myth," *American Anthropologist* 89:356–65.

Sampson, R. J., Raudenbush, S. W., and Earls, F. (1997) "Neighborhoods and violent crime: a multilevel study of collective efficacy," *Science* 227:918–24.

Skeat, W. W. and Blagden, C. O. (1906) *Pagan races of the Malay Peninsula*, London: Frank Cass.

Sommer, V., Denham, A., and Little, K. (2002) "Postconflict behaviour of wild Indian langur monkeys: avoidance of opponents but rarely affinity," *Animal Behaviour* 63:637–48.

Sponsel, L. E. (1996) Peace and nonviolence, in Levinson, D. and Ember, M. (eds) *Encyclopedia of cultural anthropology*, New York: Henry Holt.

Taylor, R. B., Gottfredson, S. D., and Brower, S. (1984) "Block crime and fear: defensible space, local social ties, and territorial functioning," *Journal of Research in Crime and Delinquency* 21:301–31.

Taylor, S. (2002) *The tending instinct: how nurturing is essential to who we are and how we live*, New York: Times Books.

Thambiah, S. (1999) "Orang Asli women and men in transition," in Jomo, K. S. (ed.) *Rethinking Malaysia*, Hong Kong: Malaysian Social Science Association.

Tijah knoon Yok Chopil, Thambiah, S., and Leong Yoke Lian, R. (forthcoming) The ungendered god: an investigation into gender relations in Semai religion and cosmology, in Martinez, P. (ed.) *Gender, culture and religion in Malaysia*.

Trankell, I.-B. and Ovesen, J. (1998) Introduction, in Trankell, I.-B. and Summers, L. (eds) *Facets of power and its limitations: political culture in Southeast Asia, Acta Universitatis Upsaliensis, Upsala Studies in Cultural Anthropology 24*, Uppsala, Sweden: Uppsala University.

Walker, L. E. (1979) *The battered woman*, New York: Harper and Row.

Watson, L. (1995) *Dark nature: a natural history of evil*, New York: HarperCollins.

Wilson, P. L. (1998) *Escape from the nineteenth century and other essays*, New York: Autonomedia.

Chapter 12

This chapter is dedicated to Bruce Bonta, an insightful scholar of peaceful societies. I gratefully thank Roger Archer for sharing his thoughts on certain topics related to peaceful societies. Sirpa Fry deserves thanks for encouraging me to tell it like I see it in the section of the chapter penned in somewhat unconventional tongue-in-cheek style. The chapter has also benefited substantially from the comments of Robert Knox Dentan and Graham Kemp. Some of the material presented in this chapter was collected in the course of working on a project funded by the United States Institute of Peace (USIP 023 99F), and I am very grateful to the USIP for this support. Any errors of fact or expression are my sole responsibility.

Adams, D. and Bosch, S. (1987) The myth that war is intrinsic to human nature discourages action for peace by young people, in Ramírez, J. M., Hinde, R. A., and Groeble, J. (eds) *Essays on violence,* Sevilla: Publicaciones de la Universidad de Sevilla.

Anderson, M. and Beach, H. (1992) Saami, in Bennett, L. A. (ed.) *Encyclopedia of world cultures,* vol. 4, Europe, Boston: G. K. Hall.

Annan, K. (1998) "Secretary-General Kofi Annan's closing plenary address," *World Federalist: The Quarterly Newsletter of the World Federalist Association,* July.

Barash, D. P. (1991) *Introduction to peace studies,* Belmont, Calif.: Wadsworth.

Betzig, L. and Wichimai, S. (1991) "A not so perfect peace: a history of conflict on Ifaluk," *Oceania* 61:240–56.

Black, D. (1993) *The social structure of right and wrong,* San Diego: Academic Press.

Boehm, C. (1987) *Blood revenge: the enactment and management of conflict in Montenegro and other tribal societies,* Philadelphia: University of Pennsylvania Press.

—— (2003) An ethological perspective on world order, in Dess, N. K. and Bloom, R.W. (eds) *Evolutionary perspectives on aggression and its antidotes: research and policy implications,* New York: Praeger.

Bonta, B. D. (1993) *Peaceful peoples: an annotated bibliography,* Metuchen, N.J.: The Scarecrow Press.

—— (1996) "Conflict resolution among peaceful societies: the culture of peacefulness," *Journal of Peace Research* 33:403–20.

—— (1997) "Cooperation and competition in peaceful societies," *Psychological Bulletin* 121:299–320.

Bonta, B. D. and Fry, D. P. (forthcoming) Cultures of peace already exist: the peaceful societies, in de Rivera, J. (ed.) *Cultures of peace* (working title).

Boulding, E. (2000) *Cultures of peace: the hidden side of history,* Syracuse: Syracuse University Press.

Brögger, J. (1968) "Conflict resolution and the role of the bandit in peasant society," *Anthropological Quarterly* 41:228–40.

Burrows, E. G. (1952) "From value to ethos on Ifaluk Atoll," *Southwestern Journal of Anthropology* 8:13–35.

Dennen, J. M. G. van der (1995) *The origin of war, vol. 1 and 2,* Groningen, Netherlands: Origin Press.

Dentan, R. K. (1988) "On reconsidering violence in simple human societies," *Current Anthropology* 29:625–29.

—— (1992) The rise, maintenance, and destruction of peaceable polity, in Silverberg, J. and Gray, J. P. (eds) *Aggression and peacefulness in humans and other primates,* New York: Oxford University Press.

—— (1995) "Bad day at Bukit Pekan," *American Anthropologist* 97:225–31.

—— (2001) Peace and nonviolence: anthropological aspects, in Hannerz, U. (ed.) *Encyclopedia of the social and behavioral sciences, vol. 3, anthropology,* London: Elsevier.

—— (2002) Personal Communication, October 5, 2002.

Draper, P. (1978) The learning environment for aggression and anti-social behavior among the !Kung, in Montagu, A. (ed.) *Learning non-aggression: the experience of non-literate societies,* New York: Oxford University Press.

Eibl-Eibesfeldt, I. (1974) The myth of the aggression-free hunter and gatherer society, in Holloway, R. (ed.) *Primate aggression, territoriality, and xenophobia: a comparative perspective,* New York: Academic Press.

—— (1979) *The biology of peace and war: men, animals, and aggression,* trans. E. Mosbacher, New York: Viking Press.

Ellison, C. G. and Bartkowski, J. P. (1997) Religion and the legitimization of violence: conservative Protestantism and corporal punishment, in Turpin, J. and Kurtz, L. R. (eds) *The web of violence: from interpersonal to global,* Urbana: University of Illinois Press.

Ember, M. (1985) "Evidence and science in ethnography: reflections on the Freeman-Mead controversy," *American Anthropologist* 87:906–10.

Ferguson, R. B. (1989) "Game wars? ecology and conflict in Amazonia," *Journal of Anthropological Research* 45:179–206.

Freeman, D. (1983) *Margaret Mead and Samoa: the making and unmaking of an anthropological myth*, Cambridge: Harvard University Press.

Fry, D. P. (1993) "The intergenerational transmission of disciplinary practices and approaches to conflict," *Human Organization* 52:176–85.

—— (1999) Peaceful societies, in Kurtz, L. R. (ed.)*Encyclopedia of violence, peace, and conflict*, San Diego: Academic Press.

—— (2000) Conflict management in cross-cultural perspective, in Aureli, F. and de Waal, F. B. M. (eds) *Natural conflict resolution*, Berkeley: University of California Press.

—— (2001) Is violence getting too much attention? cross-cultural findings on the ways people deal with conflict, in Ramirez, J. M. and Richardson, D. S. (eds)*Cross-cultural approaches to research on aggression and reconciliation*, Huntington, N.Y.: Nova Science.

—— (forthcoming) *The human potential for peace: challenging the war assumption.*

Fry, D. P. and Fry, C. B. (1997) Culture and conflict resolution models: exploring alternatives to violence, in Fry, D. P. and Björkqvist, K. (eds) *Cultural variation in conflict resolution: alternatives to violence*, Mahwah, N.J.: Lawrence Erlbaum.

Fürer-Haimendorf, C. von (1984) *The Sherpas transformed: social change in a Buddhist society of Nepal*, New Delhi: Sterling.

Gelles, R. J. and Straus, M. (1988) *Intimate violence*, New York: Simon and Schuster.

Gerbner, G. (1991) "The turtles ooze again," *Peace Paper: Tampa Bay peace education project* 11:6.

Ghiglieri, M. P. (1999) *The dark side of man: tracing the origins of male violence*, Reading, Mass.: Perseus.

Gibson, T. (1989) Symbolic representations of tranquility and aggression among the Buid, in Howell, S. and Willis, R. (eds) *Societies at peace: anthropological perspectives*, London: Routledge.

Glazer, I. M. (1997) Beyond the competition of tears: Black-Jewish conflict containment in a New York neighborhood, in Fry, D. P. and Björkqvist, K. (eds) *Cultural variation in conflict resolution: alternatives to violence*, Mahwah, N.J.: Lawrence Erlbaum.

Gorer, G. (1967) *Himalayan village: an account of the Lepchas of Sikkim*, New York: Basic Books.

Hallowell, A. I. (1974) Aggression in Saulteaux society, in Hallowell, A. I. (ed.) *Culture and experience*, Philadelphia: University of Pennsylvania Press.

Holmes, L. D. (1987) *Quest for the real Samoa: the Mead/Freeman controversy and beyond*, South Hadley, Mass.: Bergin and Garvey.

Holsti, R. (1913) *The relation of war to the origin of the state*, Helsinki: Annales, Academiae Scientiarum Fennicae.

Howell, S. (1989) "To be angry is not to be human, but to be fearful is": Chewong concepts of human nature, in Howell, S. and Willis, R. (eds)*Societies at peace: anthropological perspectives*, London: Routledge.

Howell, S. and Willis, R. (eds) (1989) *Societies at peace: anthropological perspectives*, London: Routledge.

Huesmann, L. R., Eron, L., Lefkowitz, M., and Walder, L. (1984) "Stability of aggression over time and generations," *Developmental Psychology* 20:1120–34.

Keeley, L. H. (1996) *War before civilization: the myth of the peaceful savage*, New York: Oxford University Press.

Kelly, R. C. (2000) *Warless societies and the origin of war*, Ann Arbor: University of Michigan Press.

Kent, S. (1989) "And justice for all: the development of political centralization among newly sedentary foragers," *American Anthropologist* 91:703–12.

Konner, M. (1982) *The tangled wing: biological constraints on the human spirit*, New York: Henry Holt.

Krieger, D. (1994) Ending the scourge of war, in Elias, R. and Turpin, J. (eds) *Rethinking peace*, Boulder: Lynne Rienner.

Lee, R. B. (1979) *The !Kung San: men, women, and work in a foraging society*, Cambridge: Cambridge University Press.

—— (1993) *The Dobe Ju/'hoansi*, 2nd ed, Fort Worth: Harcourt Brace College Publishers.

"Letters" (2002) *Time*, European ed, 14 Oct. 160:8–11.

Levinson, D. (1994) *Aggression and conflict: a cross-cultural encyclopedia*, Santa Barbara, Calif: ABC-CLIO.

Lutz, C. (1982) "The domain of emotion words on Ifaluk," *American Ethnologist* 9:113–28.

—— (1983) "Parental goals, ethnopsychology, and the development of emotional meaning," *Ethos* 11:246–62.

—————— (1988) *Unnatural emotions: everyday sentiments on a Micronesian atoll and their challenge to Western theory,* Chicago: University of Chicago Press.

Mann, R. S. (1986) *The Ladakhi: a study in ethnography and change,* Calcutta: Anthropological Survey of India.

Marshall, L. (1961) "Sharing, talking, and giving: relief of social tensions among !Kung Bushmen," *Africa* 31:231–49.

Mead, M. (1928) *Coming of age in Samoa: a psychological study of primitive youth for western civilization,* Dell-Laurel (ed), 1973, New York: Dell-Laurel, William Morrow.

Montagu, A. (1976) *The nature of human aggression,* New York: Oxford University Press.

Montagu, A. (ed.) (1978) *Learning non-aggression: the experience of non-literate societies,* New York: Oxford University Press.

Nader, L. (1969) Styles of court procedure: to make the balance, in Nader, L. (ed.) *Law and culture in society,* Chicago: Aldine.

—————— (1990) *Harmony ideology: justice and control in a Zapotec mountain village,* Stanford: Stanford University Press.

Norberg-Hodge, H. (1991) *Ancient futures: learning from Ladakh,* San Francisco: Sierra Club Books.

Nordstrom, C. (1997a) *A different kind of war story,* Philadelphia: University of Pennsylvania Press.

—————— (1997b) The eye of the storm: from war to peace—examples from Sri Lanka and Mozambique, in Fry, D. P. and Björkqvist, K. (eds) *Cultural variation in conflict resolution: alternatives to violence,* Mahwah, N.J.: Lawrence Erlbaum.

Otterbein, K. F. (1968) "Internal war: a cross-cultural study," *American Anthropologist* 70:277–89.

—————— (1970) *The evolution of war: a cross-cultural study,* New Haven: HRAF Press.

—————— (1997) "The origins of war," *Critical Review* 11:251–77.

Otterbein, K. F. and Otterbein, C. S. (1965) "An eye for an eye, a tooth for a tooth: a cross-cultural study of feuding," *American Anthropologist* 67:1470–82.

Paul, R. A. (1977) "The place of truth in Sherpa law and religion," *Journal of Anthropological Research* 33:167–84.

—————— (1992) Sherpa, in Hockings, P. (ed.) *Encyclopedia of world cultures, vol. 3, South Asia,* Boston: G. K. Hall.

Robarchek, C. A. (1979) "Conflict, emotion, and abreaction: resolution of conflict among the Semai Senoi," *Ethos* 7:104–23.

—————— (1997) A community of interests: Semai conflict resolution, in Fry, D. P. and Björkqvist, K. (eds) *Cultural variation in conflict resolution: alternatives to violence,* Mahwah, N.J.: Lawrence Erlbaum.

Robarchek, C. A. and Robarchek, C. (1998) "Reciprocities and realities: world views, peacefulness, and violence among Semai and Waorani," *Aggressive Behavior* 24:123–33.

Rubin, J. Z., Pruitt, D. G., and Kim, S. H. (1994) Social conflict: escalation, stalemate, and settlement, 2nd ed, New York: McGraw-Hill.

Spiro, M. E. (1952) "Ghosts, Ifaluk, and teleological functionalism," *American Anthropologist* 54:497–503.

Sponsel, L. E. and Gregor, T. (eds) (1994) *The anthropology of peace and nonviolence,* Boulder: Lynne Rienner.

Straus, M. A. (2001) Physical aggression in the family: prevalence rates, links to non-family violence, and implications for primary prevention of societal violence, in Martinez, M. (ed.) *Prevention and control of aggression and the impact on its victims,* New York: Kluwar Academic/Plenum.

Thomas, E. M. (1959) *The harmless people,* New York: Knopf.

—————— (1994) Management of violence among the Ju/wasi of Nyae Nyae: the old way and a new way, in Reyna, S. P. and Downs, R. E. (eds) *Studying war: anthropological perspectives,* Langhorne, Pa.: Gordon and Breach.

Virkkunen, M. (2001) Biochemical and molecular genetic factors in habitual violence and antisocial alcoholism: control and preventive interventions, in Martinez, M. (ed.) *Prevention and control of aggression and the impact on its victims,* New York: Kluwar Academic/Plenum.

Walters, D. (1977) *Physical and sexual abuse of children: causes and treatment,* Bloomington: Indiana University Press.

Wrangham, R. and Peterson, D. (1996) *Demonic males: apes and the origins of human violence,* Boston: Houghton Mifflin.

Wright, Q. (1942) *A study of war,* Chicago: University of Chicago Press.

Wright, Q. (1964) *A study of war,* 2nd ed, abridged, Chicago: University of Chicago Press.

Glossary

Absentia belli   Absence of war.

Adaptation   Overall, the process through which organisms adjust to an environment. This term has biological and cultural meanings. Biological adaptation involves natural selection acting over many generations. Cultural adaptation can occur much more rapidly, even within a generation, as organisms make behavioral and social changes.

Adjudication   Third-party type of dispute resolution wherein the adjudicator (judge) makes a ruling and possesses the authority and power to enforce the decision. *See also* Arbitration, Mediation, and Friendly Peacemaking.

Aggression   Acts that inflict physical, psychological, and/or social harm (pain or injury) on an individual or individuals. Aggression can stem from emotional arousal (for example, anger, fear, frustration) or be instrumental (that is, engaged in for a reward or to avoid punishment). Aggression can be verbal or physical. *See also* Indirect Aggression.

Arbitration   Third-party type of dispute resolution wherein the arbitrator makes a ruling but lacks the power to enforce the decision. Disputants regularly adhere to arbitration rulings for any number of reasons such as social pressure to do so, assessment that the ruling is just, desire to avoid further disputing, and so on. *See also* Adjudication, Mediation, and Friendly Peacemaking.

Avoidance

A common approach to conflict in peaceful societies (and in many other societies also) that involves reducing or cutting off interaction with a disputant. Avoidance may be temporary or long-term.

Bicaraa'

A dispute-resolving assembly used by the Semai. The goal is the restoration of an amicable relationship between disputants and more widely a restoration of feelings of group harmony that are threatened by unresolved conflicts.

Bilateral Descent

A pattern of recognizing descent through both parental lines. The reckoning of descent can relate to a person's group membership, place of residence, inheritance rights, and so forth. *See also* Patrilineal and Matrilineal.

Boundary Permeability

Peaceable, open movement and communication among groups as practiced by the Mardu and certain other nomadic hunter-gatherer societies.

Chiefdom

A hierarchical form of sociopolitical organization, less complex than a state, with one or more chiefs possessing authority over persons lower in the social hierarchy.

Clan

A group of persons who claim descent from a common ancestor but without knowing the specific genealogical links to the ancestor.

Composite Society

See Pluralistic Society.

Conciliation

See Mediation.

Conflict

A perceived divergence of interests—where interests are broadly conceptualized to include values, goals, needs, and wishes—between two or more parties, often accompanied by feelings of anger or hostility.

Conflict Management

Actions and conventions for dealing with conflict that do not necessarily remove the conflict. Major strategies of conflict management include Avoidance, Toleration, Negotiation, Self-Redress, and third-party–assisted Settlement processes such as Mediation and Adjudication. Physical Aggression is most likely when a party resorts to self-redress.

Consensus
General agreement or unanimity in group sentiment or decision making.

Core Value
The values that are especially promoted and held dear within a particular culture. Typically, some conceptualization of nonviolence is a core value within peaceful societies.

Cultural Relativism
The idea that judgments about other culture's practices should be suspended and instead the practices should be understood on their own terms. In other words, under the tenet of cultural relativism, cultures and cultural practices are not thought of as better or worse, but simply as *different* from each other.

Direct Violence
Severe acts of physical aggression ranging from the interpersonal to the intergroup level that result in injury or death to the recipient(s), as occurs in feuding and war. *See also* Aggression and Structural Violence.

Egalitarianism
A social order and set of values based on a presumption of equality among the members; the opposite of a stratified or hierarchical social order. An egalitarian social order and values are typical of nomadic hunter-gatherer societies.

Endogamous Marriage
Marriage occurring within the social group or within some subgroup of persons.

Exogamous Marriage
Marriage occurring outside the social group, or in other words, marriage occurring between two social groups.

Expiatory Encounter
A form of justice in which a person atones for an inappropriate deed by allowing others to punish him or her, as occurs among the Mardu.

Feud	The cycle of violence that can arise from two, usually kinship-based, groups reciprocally seeking blood revenge following homicides.
Friendly Peacemaking	A third-party type of intervention wherein one or more persons attempt to prevent aggression or its escalation by distracting or separating disputants. *See also* Adjudication, Arbitration, and Mediation.
Hopi (*see also Kahopi*)	In Hopi language, a person who behaves properly.
Hunter-Gatherers (Nomadic)	Small-scale band societies that subsist primarily on hunting and collecting vegetable products. Such societies are typically small, mobile groups of related persons, with changing group composition over time, low population density, egalitarian values, and lack of warfare.
Indirect Aggression (or Indirect Violence)	When an individual uses social networks, third parties, elements of the social order, and/or other covert means to inflict harm (physical, psychological, or social) on another person or persons. The aggression, covertly delivered, may be verbal or physical. *See* Aggression.
Initiation Ritual	*See* Rite of Passage.
Internalization	The process wherein beliefs become so thoroughly ingrained that each individual takes on his or her own responsibility for acting in accordance with the beliefs.
Joking Relationship	When, according to cultural prescription, the interaction between particular classes of individuals (for example, between mothers-in-law and sons-in-law) should be characterized by joking.
Kahopi (*see also Hopi*)	In Hopi language, a person who does not behave properly.
Kiva	Special ceremonial buildings used both for religious purposes and secular gatherings among the Hopi.
Law (Mardu)	Among the Mardu, the rules for living that should be unquestionably obeyed.

-lees	Semai word for a lecture or harangue. This constitutes a form of informal social control.
Matrilineal	Refers to tracing descent relationships or group membership through the female parental line. *See also* Patrilineal and Bilateral Descent.
Matrilocal	A pattern of residence wherein a husband and wife live with or close to the relatives of the wife.
Mediation	A third-party type of intervention wherein one or more persons assist disputants to arrive at a mutually agreeable solution to their conflict. Mediation can also be viewed as negotiation assisted by one or more third parties. *See also* Adjudication, Arbitration, and Friendly Peacemaking.
Nature-Nurture	A longstanding and problematic polarization between biology and culture, genes and environment, heredity and learning.
Negative Peace	The absence of war or violence. *See also* Positive Peace.
Patrilineal	Refers to tracing descent relationships or group membership through the male parental line. *See also* Matrilineal and Bilateral Descent.
Patrilocal	A pattern of residence wherein a husband and wife live with or close to the relatives of the husband.
Peaceful Society	A society characterized by an extremely low level of physical aggression among its members as well as shared beliefs and core values that do not accept aggression and/or positively value nonviolent behavior. As in all societies, conflicts occur in peaceful societies; however, they are almost always handled in ways that do not involve aggression.
Play Aggression	A class of behavior (for example, punches and slaps) that superficially resembles aggression but which differs from aggression in that the participants display play signals (for example, smiles and laughs). Additionally, play aggression rarely results in harm or injury to the participants. Play aggression is sometimes called rough-and-tumble play.

Pluralistic Society	A society with a cultural diversity of sub-groups—a multicultural society.
Polygyny	A form of polygamy. A marriage pattern wherein a man can have two or more wives at once.
Positive Peace	A conceptualization of peace as more than the mere absence of war. On the one hand, positive peace has been equated with the absence of structural violence and with traits such as social justice, equality, freedom, and security. Another conceptualization of positive peace involves a commitment to life and life-enhancement. *See also* Negative Peace and Structural Violence.
Psychosocial Mechanisms	A class of social control mechanisms that reflect an interaction between psychological and social features (for example, denial, fear of supernatural sanctions, shared beliefs in folk illnesses, concern about reputation, and so on).
Rite of Passage	Rituals, usually of a religious nature, that signify important life transformations or stages such as birth, circumcision, first menstruation, marriage, and death.
Self-Redress	A conflict management strategy based on unilateral initiative. One party uses threats, coercion, or force against the other in an attempt to attain a desired goal. Self-redress can take the form of theft, vandalism, physical assault, murder, and so forth. Feuding can be seen as reciprocal acts of self-redress between two kin groups.
Self-Restraint	Self-control. When a person abstains from action (such as aggression) out of his or her own volition.
Slaamad	Semai variation on the Arabic word for peace (*salaam*): the content and tranquil way of life that allows people to cooperate.

Social Control	The multitude of ways in which persons in society exert pressure on their compatriots to behave in acceptable ways and in accordance with social norms. Social control is also achieved during socialization and the process of internalization. Thus social controls stem from others in the society and also from within the individual once societal beliefs and values have become internalized. *See also* Internalization and Socialization.
Socialization	The process through which children are taught the norms, beliefs, values, and expected patterns of behavior of the culture in which they are raised.
Structural Violence	Violence resulting from social, political, and economic institutions of a society that are, for instance, unjust or exploitative.
Toleration	A common approach to conflict in peaceful societies (and in many other societies also) that involves simply putting up with an unpleasant situation. Toleration occurs when a person ignores a grievance but continues a relationship.
War	Violent, armed fighting that takes place between different political communities.
Witchcraft	A class of culturally variable beliefs that share the feature of attributing misfortunes such as sickness and death to the supernatural or psychic powers of other individuals.
Worldview	Explicit and implicit conceptions about how the world works that are learned and shared to a large extent by the members of a society.

Contributors

Elise Boulding is Professor Emeritus of Sociology at Dartmouth College in New Hampshire. Her books include *Cultures of Peace: The Hidden Side of History*, *New Agendas for Peace Research*, and *Building a Global Civic Culture: Education for an Interdependent World*.

Ximena Davies-Vengoechea is a constitutional and human rights lawyer from Colombia currently working on concepts of peace at the Richardson Institute of Peace Studies at Lancaster University in the U.K.

Robert Knox Dentan is Professor of Anthropology at the State University of New York in Buffalo and author of *The Semai: A Nonviolent People of Malaya*, and coeditor of *Malaysia and the "Original People": A Case Study of the Impact of Development on Indigenous Peoples*.

Kristin Dobinson of the University of Oslo is a political scientist specializing in international conflict resolution initiatives. Her dissertation is titled *Waging Peace: International Mediation and Norwegian Society*.

Robert A. Fernea is Professor of Anthropology and Middle Eastern Studies at the University of Texas and coauthor of *Nubian Ethnographies* and author of *Nubians in Egypt: Peaceful People*.

Douglas P. Fry is an anthropologist at Åbo Akademi University in Finland and at the Bureau of Applied Research in Anthropology at the University of

Arizona. He is coeditor of *Cultural Variation in Conflict Resolution: Alternatives to Violence.*

Peter M. Gardner is Professor of Anthropology at the University of Missouri in Columbia and is the author of *Bicultural Versatility As a Frontier Adaptation Among the Paliyan Foragers of South India.*

Alan Howard is Professor of Anthropology at the University of Hawaii. A specialist on the Rotuma Islanders of Fiji, he has authored *Learning to Be Rotuman.*

Graham Kemp is a Peace Researcher and a Director of the Lentz Foundation in Lancaster, U.K. He is the coeditor-in-chief of the *Journal of Conflict Processes* and an active member of the International Peace Research Association.

Clifford Sather is a Visiting Professional Fellow in Southeast Asian Studies in the Anthropology Department at Helsinki University. He has written *The Bajau Laut: Adaptation, History, and Fate in a Maritime Fishing Society of South-Eastern Sabah.*

Alice Schlegel is Professor of Anthropology at the University of Arizona and has conducted fieldwork among the Hopi. She is author of *Male Dominance and Female Autonomy: Domestic Authority in Matrilineal Society* and coeditor of *Cross-Cultural Codes and Samples.*

Robert Tonkinson is Professor of Anthropology at the University of Western Australia. He is author of *The Jigalong Mob: Aboriginal Victors of the Desert Crusade* and *The Mardudjara Aborigines: Living the Dream in Australia's Desert.*

Index